# User Guide

D1308143

# *Legacy 7.0*®

## Family Tree

**For Microsoft® Windows®98 or higher**

**Millennia Corporation**

Document No. 08-012815
ISBN 978-1-878012-14-2
Printed and bound in the United States of America

# *Contents*

# Chapter 1

# *Introduction to Legacy*
### Installing Legacy and Learning the Basics

Welcome to Legacy, the premier program for working with your family history. In this introduction you will find the following information: How to install Legacy and what to do when it opens on your screen; what the options are on the menu bar and toolbars; what the different views (Family, Pedigree, Descendant, Chronology, and Index) show; and what you can do in the views.

## Installing and Starting Legacy

- Insert the Legacy CD-ROM into your CD-ROM drive. The Setup procedure begins automatically.
- Follow the prompts, being sure to enter your name and customer ID number when asked.

At the conclusion of the installation, Legacy will be located in its own folder on the C drive (or another drive, if you changed the default). You can start Legacy from the icon

 on the computer desktop, or choose:

**Start > Programs > Legacy 7 > Legacy 7**.

## When Legacy Begins

**Menu Bar**

The menu bar at the top of the form gives you access to all the major options of Legacy. To display a menu from the menu bar, click the desired menu name. When the menu is displayed, you can choose an option by clicking on it.

**Toolbar**

The Toolbar is located just below the menu bar. Each button represents a commonly used feature of Legacy. To choose a feature, click the tool with the left mouse button. Hovering over any button to see the popup tooltip indicating its purpose.

# Legacy Home

The new Legacy Home tab on the main screen of Legacy brings you important information about your family file and also gives you a global view into the world of genealogy.

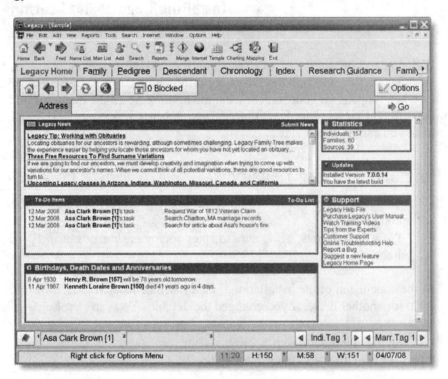

# Family View

The *Family View* window displays information about both a husband and a wife along with their marriage information, their children, and their parents. Navigation within this window is very easy and logical.

Click this tab to display the *Family View*.

Three generations are shown.

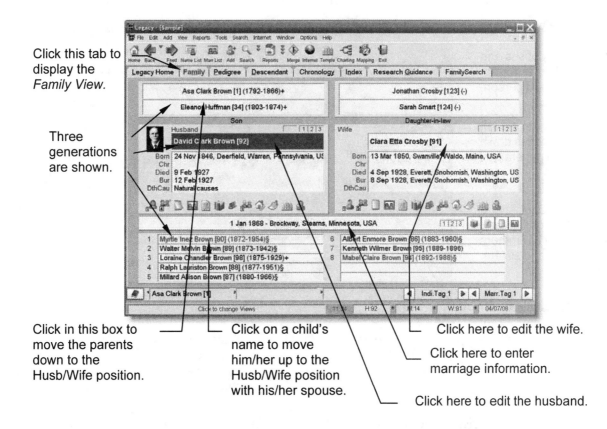

Click in this box to move the parents down to the Husb/Wife position.

Click on a child's name to move him/her up to the Husb/Wife position with his/her spouse.

Click here to edit the wife.

Click here to enter marriage information.

Click here to edit the husband.

Three generations are shown in this view. A single click on any parent's or child's name moves that person to the central *Husband/Wife* position, thus moving the display up or down one generation.

If pictures have been linked to the husband or wife, small thumbnail views are shown. Also note the icon buttons for spouses, siblings, notes, and pictures shown in the *Husband* and *Wife* boxes. These icons take on color if there is data in their respective windows.

# Pedigree View

The *Pedigree View* shows an individual with ancestral lines to the fourth or fifth generation.

Spouses and children for the current person.

Clicking on the left arrow moves down one generation.

Click on the Siblings tab for a list of brothers and sisters.

Vital statistics for the current person.

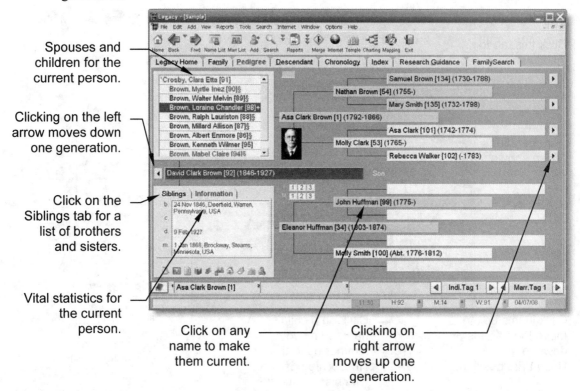

Click on any name to make them current.

Clicking on right arrow moves up one generation.

Also included are the *Spouses* and *Children; Siblings;* and *Information* tabs for the current individual. Clicking once on a name box makes that person the "current person," displaying that person's information in the *Spouses/Children, Siblings,* and *Information* boxes. Double-clicking on a name moves the individual to the primary position at the left of the screen. Double-clicking on a spouse, child, or sibling in either of the lists moves that person to the primary position. Clicking the left arrow on the left of the primary individual moves the display one generation younger (to the *preferred* child). Clicking on a right arrow next to the oldest generation along the right, moves the display back one ancestral generation.

# Descendant View

The *Descendant View* displays the current person and all his or her descendants in chart form for a given number of generations. Each name is color-coded to show gender and many columns of information can be selected to include in the table.

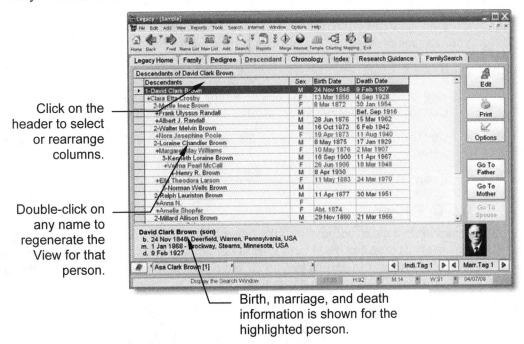

Click on the header to select or rearrange columns.

Double-click on any name to regenerate the View for that person.

Birth, marriage, and death information is shown for the highlighted person.

## Navigating the Descendant View

As each name is highlighted, the birth and death information is shown at the bottom of the window along with marriage details. If there is more than one spouse/partner, an **M+** button appears that can be used to show a list of all the spouses/partners.

By default, the *Descendant View* shows up to 10 generations of descendants for the starting person shown at the top of the chart.

If you double-click on any person in the list, that person becomes the main person and is moved to the top and the chart is regenerated to show the descendant of that person.

If you right-click on any person a menu pops up allowing you to **Edit** the person's individual or marriage information, **Add** surrounding relatives (siblings, parents, spouses, and children), **View** lists (parents, spouses, and siblings), and add Notes, Pictures, etc.

The following options are available along the right side of the window:

## Edit

Clicking the **Edit** button along the right side displays the current person's *Information* screen where you can view, edit, and add information.

## Print

Clicking the **Print** button takes you to the **Descendant Tab** on the *Report Menu* where you can then print a Descendant Chart for the main person.

## Options

Clicking on the **Options** button pops up a submenu where you can:

**Customize Display**--Select display options for the descendant chart.

**Customize Columns**--Choose the columns of information to display with each name.

**Zoom**--Choose the text size for the descendant chart.

## Go To Father

Jumps up in the descendant list to the father of the highlighted person. If the highlighted person is a spouse and his or her father is not in the current list, the list is regenerated with the father as the starting person. If the person does not have a father in the family file, a message is shown to indicate this.

## Go To Mother

Jumps up in the descendant list to the mother of the highlighted person. If the highlighted person is a spouse and his or her mother is not in the current list, the list is regenerated with the mother as the starting person. If the person does not have a mother in the family file, a message is shown to indicate this.

## Customize Descendant Display

The *Customize Descendant Display* screen is reached by choosing **Customize Display** from the **Options** button on the Descendant View.

**Generations to display** - Sets the number of generations to show in the chart and the maximum number of individuals (up to 5000 at a time).

**Indent each generation** - Spaces to indent each generation from the left column.

**Include RIN numbers** - shows the RIN number after each name.

**Include Years Lived** - shows the birth and death year range after each name.

**Don't Repeat Duplicate Lines** – suppresses the printing of descendant lines that have already been show previously on the report. This can happen when a person marries someone he or she is related to.

**Maximum Individuals to Show** – limits the report to a maximum number of individuals.

## Customize Descendant View Columns

You can select up to 15 pieces of information to be displayed on the *Descendant View* list. To add, remove, or rearrange the columns, either click on an existing column heading or click the **Options** button and choose **Customize Columns**.

### Selecting a Column

To change a column, click the ⬜ icon to the right of it. This pops up the *Field Names to Display* list where you can select the piece of information you want to show. Highlight the field you want to include and then click **Select**.

### Rearranging Columns

You can move a column to anywhere in the list by clicking it to highlight it and then

clicking the **up** or **down** ⬜ arrows to reposition it. You can also use drag and drop to move fields around.

### Deleting Columns

To remove a field from the list, highlight it and then click **Delete**. You don't have to worry about blank spaces in the list. When saved, the blanks are removed.

### Saving the Column Layout

If you find that you are reusing a particular column layout, you can save it to disk for use in the future. Up to ten different setups can be saved. To save a setup, click **Save**.... When the *Save Column Layout* window appears, select one of the ten save positions by clicking on it. Next, enter a name (up to 40 characters) in the **Name** field to describe the setup and then click **Save**.

### Loading a Saved Column Layout

If you have saved the setup from one or more column layouts, you can quickly load them back in by clicking **Load**.... When the *Load Column Layout* window appears, highlight the entry you want to load and then click **Load**. (Or just double-click on the entry.)

### Restoring the Defaults

To reset the column layout to just include name, sex, birth date and place, and death date and place, click **Default**.

When you are done, click **Close**. The new column layout is then displayed in the *Descendant View*.

# Chronology View (Deluxe Edition only)

The *Chronology View* shows the name of the current individual and all the surrounding events associated with that person. These events include the person's birth, christening, death, and burial information, his or her individual events, marriages and marriage events, the birth of children, parents, and the individual and marriage notes. All these events are arranged on the view in sorted order so you can see what affected this person throughout his or her life.

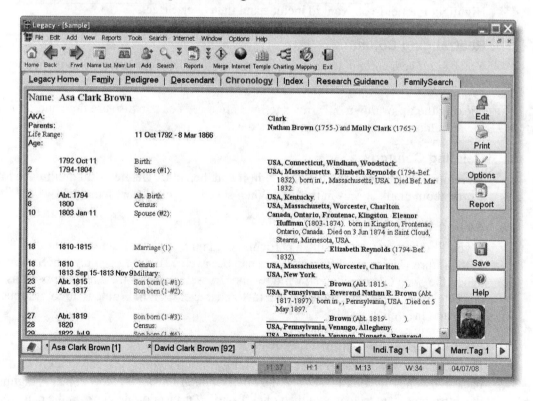

Along the right side of the screen are several buttons that are described next:

## Edit

Clicking the **Edit** button opens the Information screen for the current individual. Here you can add or edit information and individual events for this person. (See *Information Window* on page 29 for more information.)

## Print

The **Print** button sends the contents of the *Chronology View* to your printer pretty much as it is shown on the screen. (See **Report** below for producing a printed report with many options.)

## Options

Clicking the **Options** button displays the *Chronology View Options* screen. This screen lets you select and deselect the information that is shown on the view, change color highlighting, change column widths, and set report options. (See *Chronology View Options* on page 18 for more information.)

## Report

Clicking the **Report** button generates a print preview of the *Chronology Report* using the options set in the *Chronology View Options*. This report can include a timeline chart and an ages column as well as other color and formatting options. (See Chronology Report on page 128 for more information.)

## Save

You can save the current chronology display as an RTF (Rich Text Format) file by clicking the **Save** button, specifying a location and filename, and clicking **Save**. This can then be loaded into your favorite word processor for editing, printing, or inclusion in other reports.

## Navigating

You can use all the standard navigation features available in Legacy while viewing the Chronology. These include **Bookmarks** and **Quick Bookmarks**, **Individual** and **Marriage tags**, the **Back** and **Fwrd buttons**, and the **History List**. You can also change to other individuals by using the **Name List** and **Marriage List**, as well as by using the **Search** features and the **Go To ID Number** feature.

## Rotating Through Tagged Records

When you have more than one individual tagged with the same tag number, you can click the right and left arrows on the tag level button at the bottom of the screen
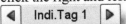, to rotate forward and backward through all the individuals tagged.

To display the *Chronology View*, click on the **Chronology** tab on the main window.

# Chronology View Options

This options screen lets you select and deselect the information that is shown on the view, change color highlighting, change column widths, and set report options. The options are arranged on four tabs, each of which is described below. All the options on all the tabs apply to both the *Chronology View* and the *Chronology Report*.

## Include Tab

**Individual Events**   includes the person's individual events. You can then choose whether or not to include the notes, private events, event addresses, phone numbers, e-mail addresses, or home page URLs.

**Marriages**   includes the marriage events. You can then choose from the options below it, which include the same choices as the Individual Events with the addition of whether or not to include children and spouse's life range information.

**Parents**   includes the current individual's parent's names. You can also choose to include the death information of the parents.

**LDS Information**   includes the LDS ordinance information for the current person.

**Notes**   Select the note types you would like to include on the view or report.

**Background Timelines**   You can include background timeline events in the chronology to give historical perspective to your ancestor's life. Legacy installs several general timelines to choose from, or you can create your own. You can select one or more timelines and limit your selection to one or more events from each timeline. To select one or more timelines, click the **Select Background Timelines** button.

(Help index: *Selecting Timelines*)

## Formatting Tab

**Color Coding**   more easily identifies certain elements of the report by showing or printing them in color. These include the color of the main person's name, children's names, marriage information, and spouse names. You can choose between four standard colors: blue, red, green, and purple.

**Other Formatting**   options are to print all names in bold, print event names in bold, remove one or more leading commas on locations, and remove two or more leading commas from locations.

**Analysis Formatting**   The *Chronology View* and *Chronology Report* are very useful when trying to see where people traveled during their lifetimes. Legacy offers two options that make this information much more noticeable on the report. The first is the reversal of the date column so that the year comes first. This makes it easier to glance down the column to see what years the events occurred. The second is to reverse the order of the location field and place it at the beginning of the descriptive column in optional bold type. You can then quickly see the locations encountered during the person's life.

**Birth and Death Information**   You have the choice of including the years only, or the full dates and locations of the birth and death on individual names within the report.

## Column Widths Tab

You can set the width of the Date and Event columns by entering the desired width measurements in the fields. The Descriptive column (on the right) will take up the remaining width on the page (with a minimum of about 2 inches [5 cm]).

## Report Options Tab

Report options apply to the creation of a *Chronology Report*. (See *Chronology Report* on page 128 for more information.)

**Timeline Column**   is a graphical representation of the timespan of each event represented on the report. It allows you to easily see how events overlapped and shows everything that was happening at any particular time. The bars in the timeline are colored according to the settings on the **Formatting** tab.

**Shading the Life Range**   extends the life range of the main person down the entire timeline behind all other events. This way you can easily see where the events occurred within the life of the individual.

**Age Column**   shows how old the main person was when each event happened.

**Printing in Color**   The *Chronology Report* normally prints in color, but if you have only a black-and-white printer you can change the color to only black and white.

**Lines**   This option allows you to print horizontal lines between each event.

**Average Life Span**   specifies the average lifespan you want to use for child and spouse bars when the death dates are not available.

**Print Individual's Picture**   includes the picture of the individual.

**Print Private Individuals**   includes the names of individuals that are marked as Private on their Information screens.

**Report Title**   You can change the title of the report as desired.

## Page Setup

- **Page Numbering**—Each page can include the page number in various locations and can optionally be preceded by the word "Page". You can also specify the starting page number. This is useful if you are going to insert the album into another report, such as an Ahnentafel Book report.
- **Margins**—You can set the top, bottom, left and right margins of the pages being printed.
- **Orientation**—The pages can be printed in portrait or landscape modes.

## Printer Setup

Lets you change the page size and orientation before generating the report. You can also change the target printer and its specific settings.

## Change Fonts

You can specify the font name, size, and style to be used in each section of the photo album. See Report Fonts for more information.

# Sources Tab

Here you can choose to include source citations when printing the Chronology report, and specify the formatting and contents of the citations.

# Index View

The *Index View* displays all the individuals in your family file. The information displayed by default includes the record identification number (RIN), full name, gender, and the birth and death date and place.

Click **RIN** to sort the list in record number order.

Enter a RIN here to jump to that record in the list.

Click **Given** to sort the list in order of given name(s).

Click **Surname** to sort the list in surname order.

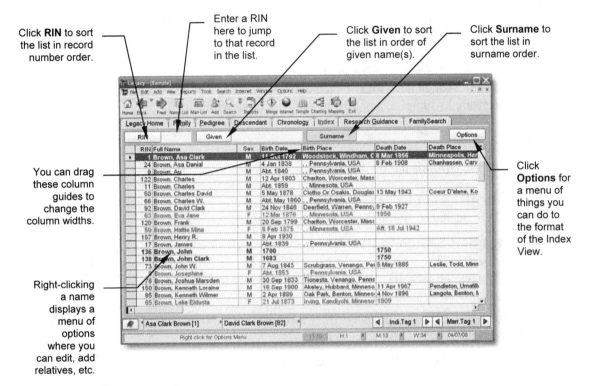

You can drag these column guides to change the column widths.

Click **Options** for a menu of things you can do to the format of the Index View.

Right-clicking a name displays a menu of options where you can edit, add relatives, etc.

## Sorting the List

The *Index View* can be displayed in either surname, given name order, or RIN number. Click the **Surname, Given** or **RIN** button at the top of the window, or click in the **Surname**, **Given** or **RIN** box. The list is then redisplayed in that order.

## Finding an Individual

If the list is long, you can search for an individual in the list by RIN, given name or surname. To search by surname, click in the **Surname** box and type the name you want to find. Enter the surname first, followed by a comma and then the given name(s). To search by given name, click in the **Given** box and type the given names, followed by a comma and then the surname if known. To search by RIN, click in the **RIN #** field and type the number you want to locate.

### Changing the Columns

▶ **To customize the columns:**

1. Click on any of the column headings. This displays the *Customize Index View Columns* screen.
2. Add or change the pieces of information you want to display in each column.

(Help index: **Customize Index View columns**)

3. Click **Close**.

▶ **To change the width of the columns:**

You can change the width of each column by dragging the right header boundary to the desired width. Legacy then remembers these widths.

### Options

Clicking the **Options** button displays a shortcut menu:

**Include AKAs in List** inserts the alternate names for each individual into the name list. Alternate names are displayed with a leading tilde character (~).

**Change Sort/Search to User ID** changes the RIN # search field to User #. When you use this field to search, the closest matching User ID number is located in the list. (If you are using the User ID # for searching you should include the User ID # as one of the columns in the Index View.)

**Customize Columns** displays the Customize Index View Columns screen where you can select the columns you want to include.

**Zoom** lets you select the font size for the Index View list.

### Edit

You can edit any individual in the list by right-clicking his or her name and choosing **Edit** from the shortcut menu. (You can also double-click the name.) The *Information* screen for that person is displayed.

# Research Guidance View

The *Research Guidance* tab on the main screen of Legacy is your starting point for getting help finding more information about your ancestors. This fantastic resource points you to specific suggested sources from the tens of thousands contained in the research guidance system. And more are being added all the time. For complete information about the Research Guidance process, see Chapter 8.

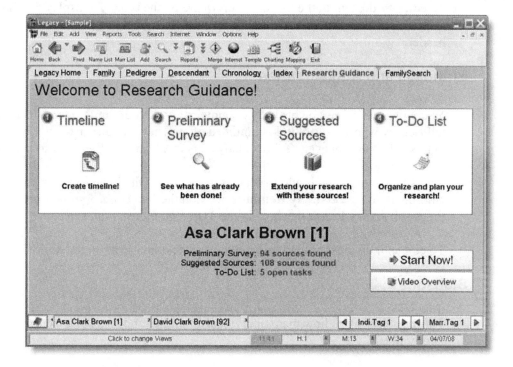

## Legacy News

The Legacy News box brings you articles and announcments about genealogy-related subjects. The contents of this box are changed often so be sure to check back on a regular basis to see what is new. Most of the articles and announcments contain only a summary of their content but each title is a link to complete information about the subject.

If you have an article or announcement that you would like to submit for inclusion in the newsletter, click the **Submit** link to the right side of the *Legacy News* box header.

## To-Do Items

You can select the to-do tasks that you would like to be reminded of. These reminders are displayed on the day you specify in the to-do item itself and remain visible until you either reschedule or cancel the reminder.

To edit a to-do item in the list, click anywhere on the task. To display the full list of to-do items, click the **To-Do List** link to the right side of the *To-Do Items* box header.

## Birthdays and Anniversaries

You will never forget the birthday or anniversary of your family members again. Just tell Legacy who you want to be reminded of and they will automatically be displayed in this list. You can even set how many days in advance of the event to include them.

Selecting the individuals and marriages to include in the list is done by putting a checkmark in the **Birthday Reminder** box on the *Individual Information* screen and the **Anniversary Reminder** box on the *Marriage Information* screen.

To edit an individual or marriage in the list, click anywhere on the desired entry.

## Statistics

This box shows you how many individuals, families and sources are currently in your family file.

## Updates

The current Legacy version is displayed. If a newer version is available, it is also shown along with a **Download Now!** link that you can use to download the newest update.

## Support

The *Support* box gives you easy access to a variety of technical support options as well as training material, bug reporting and submitting suggestions to make Legacy even better. Just click on the desire option. (All of the options here, except for the **Legacy Help File** link, require you to be connected to the Internet.)

## Navigation

The Legacy Home tab has a built-in browser that lets you view Internet content without ever leaving Legacy. As you click the various links in the boxes, the navigation buttons in the upper-left corner can be used move **Back** and **Forward**, **Refresh** the current page, **Stop** the loading of a new page, or return to the original **Legacy Home** tab contents.

## Options

Clicking the **Options** button in the upper-right corner of the *Legacy Home* tab displays a popup menu with the following options:

**Reminders** – Displays the *Legacy Home Options* screen where you can specify how many days in advance you want to be reminded of To-Do items, birthdays, and anniversaries.

**Zoom** – Lets you specify the font size to use in the browser window.

# Chapter 2

# *Using Online Help*
### Looking for Assistance When You Need It

## Getting Help

### The Online Help System

Legacy includes an extensive online Help system to provide you with easily accessible information about program features and techniques. The help system contains all the information in the Legacy User Guide, optimized for use online. In addition, the help system includes a description of new features.

To open the Help system, choose **Contents** from the **Help** menu. The *Contents* screen opens where you can select the type of help you need.

You can also get immediate help about any window or dialog box in Legacy by clicking **Help** on that window.

For a complete description on how to use the online Help system, choose **How to Use Help** from the **Help** menu.

## General Information

Choosing **General Information** from the **Help** menu brings up the *Family File Information* window:

This window shows the licensed user name and registration number, program version, build date (date of the program or last update), along with the location of your family file. In addition, the window displays the number of individuals and families in the current file, plus the number of unique surnames and Master Source entries.

# About Legacy

The **About Legacy** menu option displays the splash screen giving the Legacy copyright. Clicking **Company** displays a screen showing the different ways you can contact Millennia. Clicking **General** displays the *General Information* screen. (See *General Information* on page 27.)

# Order Form

Selecting this function from the **Help** menu brings up a window with three tabs allowing you to enter information to order Legacy. **Order Information**, **Pricing**, and **User Profile** tabs are available to customize the needed information. This information, when complete, can then be printed and sent to Millennia.

# Order on the Internet

This option takes you to the Legacy web site order form where you can quickly order the latest version of the program as well as other genealogy-related products.

# Chapter 3

# *The Information Screens*
### Recording All the Facts and Events for an Individual

## Individual's Information Window

The *Individual's Information* window is where you enter all the individual information for the current person. This includes his or her name; birth and death dates and locations; gender; reference numbers; and extra event data. The name and location fields use type-o-matic (auto completion) fields.

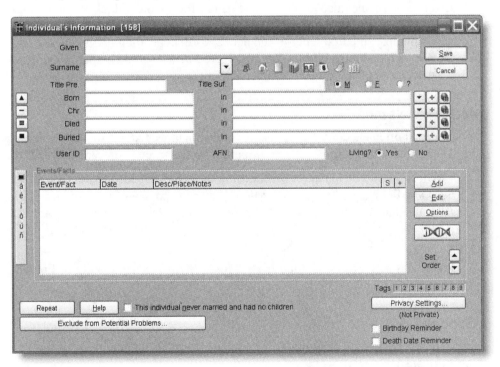

When data is initially entered, it is placed into a master database registry. An example of such an entry is the city, county, and state information for an individual. When this entry is repeated, whether in the current information screen or an information screen for a different individual, the user need only enter the first few characters and then the entire entry appears. The *Information* screen also contains an unlimited **Events** section where separate items can be entered relative to that individual's life.

Also from this window, the user can access the *Notes* section, the *Picture Gallery*, the *To-Do List*, and the *Address* screen, as well as the *Calendar* and *Date Calculator*. The access buttons change color to indicate when data has been entered. The detailed identification of the different functions on this screen follow:

## Given Names

Enter all the given names for the individual. This includes the first name and all middle names. Don't include nicknames or alternate names, which should be entered in the *Alternate Names* window (see below). Given names can be up to 120 characters long.

## Surname

Enter the surname (also known as last name) for the individual. When you leave the field, Legacy applies the formatting specified in the *Customize* section (see page 236) and capitalizes the first letter or the entire word, depending on the format selected. Do not include things like Jr., Sr., II, III, etc., which should be put in the title fields. Surnames can be up to 120 characters in length.

## Alternate Names

You will often encounter given names and surnames that are spelled differently. Many times, the spellings differ within the same source. You can record all these variations as alternate names by choosing the **AKA** icon to the right of the *Surname* field. (See *Entering Alternate Names* on page 43 for more information.) Alternate names can be up to 120 characters in both the given and surname fields.

## Title

Prefix and suffix titles, include Jr., Sr., Rev., Major, General, King of England, etc. These fields can hold up to 50 characters.

## Gender

Choose either **Male** or **Female**. If you don't know the gender of the individual, click **?** (means unknown).

## Dates

Enter the date for each event, such as birth, death, burial, etc., that you know. You can enter the dates in any format desired and Legacy changes them to the current date format set in the *Customize* section (see page 236). (See *Enter > Dates in date fields* in Legacy Help for more information.) Dates can be up to 45 characters long.

## Calendar

Whenever you are filling in a date field, you can use the pop-up calendar for help by clicking the **Calendar** 📆 icon. Selecting a date from the calendar automatically fills in the current date field.

## Locations

Locations for events should be entered in a consistent format. It is suggested that you use the format of city; county; state or province; country. When entering place names in the United States, you may think that it is sufficient to just include the state abbreviation and leave off the country; however, for completeness, it is suggested that you always include the country. You never know who might be using your family file in the future and in what country they might be living. Locations can be up to 255 characters long. You should use all the intermediate commas to show where information is missing and to clarify what each piece means. **Bergen, New Jersey** could mean Bergen County or the city of Bergen. **Bergen, , New Jersey, USA** makes it all perfectly clear that Bergen is the city and that the county name is missing.

## US County Verifier  (Deluxe Edition Only)

When you exit a location field, Legacy checks the validity of county names for location in the United States (if the **Verify US Counties in Place Names** option is turned on in the *Customize* section).   An error is reported if:

- No county by that name was ever found in that state.  (This could be also be the result of a misspelling.)
- The county was not in existence in this state at the date specified.
- The County had been dissolved in this state before the date specified.

When an error is reported, you can choose to view a list of all the counties in that state to see when they were founded and their term of existence.

You can turn off **US County Verification** while viewing any error message.  (To turn it back on, you must do so on the **Data Entry** tab of the *Customize* section.)

## User ID Number

The **User ID#** field is for any reference number you want to record for this individual. You can use any combination of letters, numbers, and punctuation marks.

### Ancestral File Number

The **AFN** field is for the identifying number assigned by the Church of Jesus Christ of Latter-day Saints when the individual has been submitted to the Ancestral File. Each person is assigned a unique number. The Ancestral File Number can be up to 20 characters.

### Using the Source Clipboard

The *Source Clipboard* is a feature in Legacy that can tremendously increase the efficiency with which you document the sources of the information you enter into your family file. (See *Source Clipboard* on page 69 for information on how and why to use this feature.)

# Events

You can add unlimited additional events to any individual. These can include things like occupation, graduation, immigration, engagements, awards, ordinations, etc. Legacy comes with many predefined event names like those previously mentioned. You can use these and also add any new events you need.

An event consists of a name, description, date, place, and comment. Only the event name is required, but it may seem meaningless without a date, place, or comment. If you have the **Deluxe Edition** of Legacy, your events are automatically formed into sentences when printed on reports. (If you don't have the **Deluxe Edition**, see page 315 for many, many reasons why you *should* have it.)

### Adding a New Event

▶ **To add a new event to an individual:**

1. Click **Add** to the right of the *Events* box to display the *Add Event* window.

2. To select an event from the *Master Event Definition List*, either type the name of the event in the **Event** field, or click the ▼ button to the right of the **Event** field to scroll through the list and select an event by clicking on it. (If you

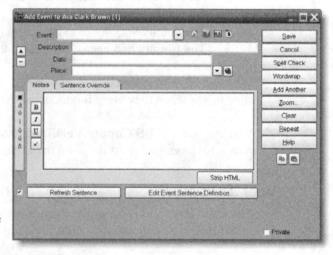

want to define a new event that is not already in the *Master Event Definition List*, see *Editing The Master Event Definition List* on page 34.)

3. In the **Description** field, enter the event description.
4. In the **Date** field, enter the date the event occurred.
5. In the **Place** field, enter the location where the event took place.
6. In the **Notes** tab, enter any information you want to record, concerning this event.
7. If you are using the ***Deluxe Edition*** of Legacy, you will see the event sentence being built as you enter your information. You can override the sentence definition for this particular event by entering a new sentence on the **Sentence Override** tab.
8. Click the **Source**  icon to record the source of this information if you have it. (See *Citing Your Sources* on page 53 for more information.)
9. Click the **Picture** icon to add pictures, sounds, and video clips to the event.
10. Click the **Address** icon to record an address associated with this event.

(Help index: ***Add or edit an event***)

## Editing an Event

▶ **To change the name, description, date, location, or comments of an existing event:**

1. Highlight the event line you want to edit in the *Event* Box.
2. Click **Edit** to the right of the list to display the *Edit Event* window.
3. Make the desired changes and click **OK** to save them.

(Help index: ***Add or edit an event***)

## Changing the Order of the Events

▶ **To change the display order of the events:**

1. Highlight the event line you want to move.

2. Click the **Up** or **Down** arrow at the lower-right corner of the *Events* box (labeled "Set Order") in the direction you want to move the line.

## Other Options in the Events Box

The following options are available by pressing the **Options** button.

**Swap with Birth Information**  lets you swap alternate birth (Alt. Birth) information with the main Birth information.

**Swap with Christening Information**  lets you swap alternate christening (Alt. Christening) information with the main Christening information.

**Swap with Death Information**  lets you swap alternate death (Alt. Death) information with the main Death information.

**Swap with Buried Information**  lets you swap alternate burial (Alt. Buried) information with the main Buried information.

**Sort Events by Name**  lets you automatically sort your list of events by the event name. When sorting, any events that do not have a name or date are moved to the top of the list.

**Sort Events by Date**  lets you automatically sort your list of events by date.

**Delete Event**  lets you delete the highlighted event in the *Information* window.

**Zoom**  lets you vary the font size of the *Events List*.

## DNA Marker Test Information

There are many companies that offer DNA Analysis so that you can explore your ancestry, lineage, and geographic origins.  These tests result in marker values that can be recorded in Legacy.  Many of these companies offer comparison searches to find other individuals that have also been tested and found to be related to you.  Clicking the DNA ⬛ button opens the DNA Records screen where you can enter the test results of one or more tests.

## Editing the Master Event Definition List

▶ **To display the *Master Event Definition List*:**

Click the **Down** arrow ▾ to the right of the **Event** field. The *Master Event Definition List* is displayed.

## Adding or Editing an Event Definition

Use the *Add/Edit Event Definition* screen to add a new event definition or to edit an existing event definition that you want to include on an individual or marriage record.

The *Add/Edit Event Definition* screen is reached by clicking the **Add** button on the *Master Event Definition List* screen. (The *Master Event Definition List* screen can be reached by clicking the **down arrow** at the right side of any event name field or by choosing **Master Lists / Event Name** from the **View** menu.)

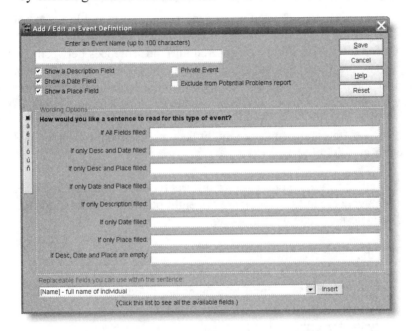

Defining an event includes giving it a name, indicating which information fields you want to go with it, and defining how to create a sentence from the event information when printing a report. Legacy comes with many predefined events that all include sentence definitions if you would like to see examples.

▶ **To define a new event definition:**
1. Enter the name of the event. This name will appear on the *Master Event Definition List* and on the event screens and reports.
2. Indicate the additional fields you want to include with the event. Choose from a **Description** field, a **Date** field and a **Place** field. Most events will include all three fields. The **Description** field, for example, might hold the name of the occupation for an Occupation or Employment event or the name

of a school for an Education event. The **Date** field records the date or date range of the event. The **Place** field records where the event happened.

3.  Fill in the eight sentence possibilities in the **Wording Options** box (if you are using the *Deluxe Edition* of Legacy).

4.  Click **Save**.

(Help index: ***Add or edit event definition***)

## Defining the Event Sentences (*Deluxe Edition* only)

The sentence definitions are used when generating reports and indicate how the pieces fit together. The definitions can include one or more fields to show where each piece of information fits. Fields are entered into the sentences between opening and closing square brackets, such as [Desc], [Date], and [Place]. When the sentence is put together for a report, the fields are replaced with the actual contents of those fields from each event. For example, let's say you are defining a School event. The sentence might look like this: He went to school at [Desc] in [Place] in [Date]. When the report is generated, the sentence might become: He went to school at Harvard College in Cambridge, MA in 1979.

Because a sentence will be put together differently depending on the pieces of information available at the time, there are eight possible combinations that need to be handled. These include the following:

*   All the fields are filled in.
*   Only the Description and Date fields are filled in.
*   Only the Description and Place fields are filled in.
*   Only the Date and Place fields are filled in.
*   Only the Description field is filled in.
*   Only the Date field is filled in.
*   Only the Place field is filled in.
*   None of the fields are filled in.

### Fields Available

There are [fields] associated with the pieces of information from the event:
**[EventName]** – The name of the event.
**[Desc]** – The contents of the Description field.
**[Date]** – The event date.
**[Place]** – The event place.
**[Notes]** – The event notes.
**[Address]** – The event address.

**[Desc/Notes]** – The event description if it is filled in, otherwise the Notes are used. This is to accommodate previous users who put the descriptive words in the Notes field before Legacy had a Description field.

There are [fields] that pull information from the current individual or couple:
**[Name]** – The full name of the current person.
**[FirstName]** – The first given name of the current person.
**[HeShe]** – He or She, depending on gender.
**[HisHer]** – His or Her, depending on gender.
**[FirstHeShe]** – First given name, then He (or She). Alternates back and forth on successive events. This makes it read more like a book.

There is one [field] for putting in source citations:
**[Sources]** – The source citation reference that prints as small superscript numbers.

And one [field] that lets you insert a carriage return:
**[CR]** – Inserts a carriage return, moving to the next line.

There are also some modifiers available for some of the fields:
Putting a hyphen (-) at the beginning causes the first letter of that piece of information to be lowercased when used. For example, an Occupation sentence might be: [HeShe] was a [-Desc]. If you had entered "Lawyer" into the occupation field, the sentence would be built with a lowercase 'l', thus ending up with: She was a lawyer. This is available in the following fields:
**[-EventName]**
**[-Desc]**
**[-Notes]**
**[-Desc/Notes]**

Putting a tilde (~) at the beginning of the [Place] field causes the short location name to be used instead of the long name. For example, [~Place] might use Seattle, WA instead of Seattle, King, Washington, USA.

Although the fields are shown as mixed case, the case doesn't matter. [EventName] is the same as [eventname] and [EVENTNAME] and [EvEnTnAmE]:

## Inserting the [Fields]

You can either type the [fields] into the sentences as you define them, or you can select the desired field name from the drop-down combo box at the bottom of the form. To insert a field from the list, click the down arrow, highlight the desired field, and then click **Insert** to the right. The field will be inserted at the current cursor position.

(Help index: ***Add or edit event definition***)

## Other Master Event Definition Options

Clicking **Options** on the *Master Event Definition List* brings up a shortcut menu where you can choose the following:

**Delete** removes the name of the highlighted event if the event is not being used in any individual's or marriage event list. If the event is currently being referenced, a message displays and the event is not removed. You must remove all references to a particular event before it can be removed from the *Master Event Definition List*.

**Tag and Untag** all master events or just the currently highlighted names.

**Combine Duplicates** combines any event names that are identical in every way.

**Purge Unused Sources** removes any event names that are not being cited from anywhere in the entire family file.

**Import Lists** allows you to import various lists from other family files. These include *Locations, Surnames, Event Definitions, Temples, Marriage Status, Source Types, Child Status, Picture Locations,* and other *Master Source Lists*.

**Print** lets you print a report of all the event names on the list.

**Zoom** allows you to vary the font size of the *Master Event Definition List*.

**Remove Name-Only Events** If you have events that only have an event name and no other information, you may want to remove them from your family file.

> **Warning**: This could incorrectly remove events attached to individuals or marriages where an event name is the only known information, for example, you might have and "Immigration" event. You know the person immigrated but you don't know when or where.

**Jump with Edit Sorting** The Master Event Definition List is sorted by Event Name. If you edit an event name, changing it so that it will now sort to a different location in the list, you can choose to jump to the new location in the list when you Save the change, or you can choose to remain where you were after the edited event is moved to its new sort position.

**Set Bookmark** lets you "mark your place" in the list so that you can jump back to it at any time in the future using the Go To Bookmark option.

**Go To Bookmark** allows you to jump back to a previously placed bookmark.

## Combining Event Names

If you find that you have two event names that you want to combine (for example, if you misspell a name), this can easily be done:

▶ **To combine event names:**
1. Highlight the event name you want to change.
2. Click **Combine the Highlighted Event Name with Another one in the List** at the bottom of the window.
3. Highlight the event name you want to change it to.
4. Click the same button again, which now reads, **Highlight the Destination, then Click this Button**.

# LDS Ordinance Information

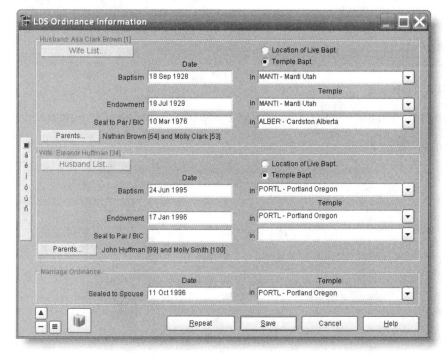

From the *Individual's Information* window, you can display the *LDS Ordinance*

*Information* window by clicking the **Temple**  icon, provided you have LDS fields turned **On** in the *Options* section. This dialog box lets you record the date and the temple name for baptism, endowment, sealing to parents, and sealing to spouse.

(Help index: ***LDS ordinance information***)

# Notes

You can add or edit the *General*, *Research*, and *Medical* notes belonging to the individual by clicking the **Note**  icon or by clicking the **F5** function key.

(Help index: ***Notes***)

# Adding Pictures, Sound, and Video

You can attach pictures, sounds, and video to an individual by clicking the **Picture** icon. (See *Adding Pictures* on page 275 or *Adding and Recording Sounds* on page 282 for more information.)

(Help index: ***Picture gallery***)

# Adding an Address

You can enter a mailing name, address, up to two phone numbers, an e-mail address, and a home page address for each individual in your family file.

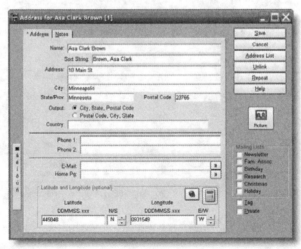

▶ **To add an address:**

1.  Click the **Address** icon. If you are entering an address for the first time, Legacy builds a standard name and puts it in the name field. You can leave it as is or change it as desired.

2. Fill in the Sort String field if you want to print labels in a different sorted order than what is in the Name field. For example, you might want to enter Surname, Given Name so that labels will print in surname order.

3. Continue filling in the address, phone number(s), e-mail address, and home page address.

4. Click the  button at the right of **E-mail** and **Home Pg** fields to send a message or connect to the Internet without leaving Legacy.

5. You can include the latitude and longitude for the location.

6. You can associate the person with various mailing lists. The choices are Newsletter, Family Association, Birthday, Research, Christmas, and Holiday.

7. Click the **Tag** box in the bottom right corner to select or deselect this address for future reporting purposes.

8. Click the **Private** box to select or deselect whether or not you want this address printed on reports or exported to other files.

9. Click the **Notes** tab to enter additional comments about this address.

(Help index: ***New address***)

**Save**   saves the address and closes the window.

**Cancel**   closes the window without saving any entries or changes.

**Address List**   opens the *Master Mailing Address List.*

**Delete**   clears all the existing fields and closes the Address window.

**Repeat**   duplicates the entry made in the same field of the last address you entered during the current session. If the current field already contains an entry that would be overwritten by the Repeat option, Legacy asks for permission before replacing it. You can also use **F8** to repeat a field. Clicking the line labels also repeats the entries. Clicking the "Address" label repeats both address lines. Clicking any other, repeats just that line (including the "Name" field label). To repeat the entire address, right-click the **Repeat** button.

**Help**   opens Legacy Help.

**Picture**   opens the *Picture Gallery* where pictures, sounds, and video can be added.

# Repeating Fields (Ditto)

Legacy has a *Repeat* feature, commonly known as Ditto. This feature lets you quickly enter recurring information. In all the input fields on the *Information* screen, except the **User Reference Number** and **Ancestral File Number**, you can click **Repeat** at the bottom of the screen to repeat the same information from the same field from the last record saved. If the current field already has an entry that would be overwritten, Legacy asks permission before replacing it. **F8** or **Alt-R** work the same way, as does clicking the label to the left of each field, such as "born" or "died" or "in."

# Special Characters

When entering information, Legacy offers a feature to help you quickly enter international characters. You can choose up to eight characters to be displayed in a ribbon on all input screens. (This ribbon can be turned off if not needed. See **Customize – Data Defaults** in the Help system.) Whenever you need one of these letters within a field, simply click on one and that character automatically fills in where you are typing. To select characters for the ribbon, click the small blue button at the top of the ribbon and then double-click on up to eight characters from the *Character Map*. You can also press **F6** whenever you are in a text input field to display the *Character Map* where you can then select any character needed.

# Memorizing Locations (Deluxe Edition Only)

As you enter places into location fields in Legacy, the ten most recent place names are remembered and can be quickly displayed in a popup list and selected. To display the list of the last ten place names, right-click on the field label to the left of any location field.

From the resulting popup list of place names you can select one to fill into the location field by clicking on it. To clear the location list and start over, click **(Clear all memorized locations)** at the bottom of the list.

You can also memorize and play back the contents of location fields. If you are in a *location* field (found on *Information*, *Event*, and *Marriage* screens), there are three sets of keys you can use for this. For example, you can press **Shift-F9** to have Legacy memorize the current place name. Thereafter, pressing **F9**,

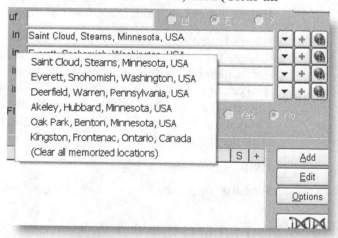

while in a *location* field, automatically enters the place name. This also applies to **Shift-F11** and **F11**, and **Shift-F12** and **F12**. These are very useful when entering records where everything happened in the same place.

# Dates Memorized (Deluxe Edition Only)

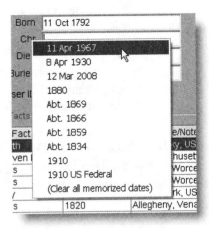

As you enter dates into date fields in Legacy, the ten most recent dates are remembered and can be quickly displayed in a popup list and selected. To display the list of the last ten dates, right-click on the field label to the left of any date field. From the resulting popup list of dates you can select one to fill into the date field by clicking on it. To clear the date list and start over, click **(Clear all memorized dates)** at the bottom of the list.

# Saving the Record

When you have filled in the *Information* screen with all the available information, click **Save** to record the entries to disk and return to the previous screen.

# Additional Details

The following topics give additional information on topics already discussed in this chapter.

# Entering Alternate Names

Many times you will find that a person's name is represented in more than one way. Either the spelling of the name will differ in various sources or the name will be completely different. Sometimes names were changed when a person immigrated to a new country. Sometimes names were recorded wrong because of misunderstandings or bad transcription. Many people go by different names as they grow up, going from nickname to nickname. All of these names should be recorded because you never know when a variation will be used in a new source.

▶ **To display the *Alternate Name List:***

Click 🐾 to the right of the **Surname** field.

## Adding New Alternate Names

▶ **To add a new name to the *Alternate Names List:***

Click **Add**. An input window appears where you can type in the new name.

(Help index: *Alternate names*)

## Editing an Existing Alternate Name

▶ **To edit an existing alternate name:**
Highlight the name and click **Edit**. An input window, filled with the current spelling, appears where you can make the desired changes.

## Deleting an Alternate Name

▶ **To delete an existing alternate name from the list:**
Highlight the name and click **Delete**.

## Sources

▶ **To add a source:**
Click **Source** to add a citation to the highlighted name.

(Help index: *Citing your sources*)

## Swapping an Alternate Name With the Main Name

▶ **To replace the primary name with one of the alternate names:**
Highlight the name and click **Swap Name with Main Name on Record**.

# The Marriage Information Screen

The *Marriage Information* screen records the date, place, status, and sources of information for the current marriage.

## General Tab

### Marriage Date

If the date is known, enter it in any recognized format.

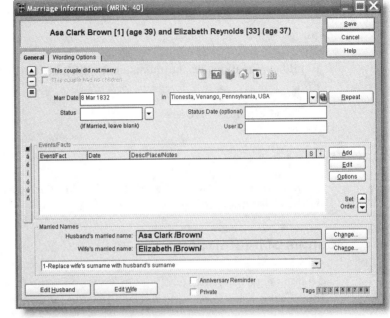

### Marriage Place

If you know where the marriage took place, enter the location here.

### Marriage Status

This field records the final disposition of the marriage. The default is blank and should be left blank if the couple was actually married and never separated before one or the other died. The other standard choices for the **Ending Status** field are: Divorced, Unmarried, Annulled, Common Law, and Other. If you choose Other, an explanatory note in the **Notes** field of the marriage is advisable. You can also add additional status words to the list. If you have recorded an ending status and there is a date associated with it, enter the date in the **Status Date** field.

### Did Not Marry

If the two people of the relationship did not get married, put a checkmark in the **This couple did not marry** box to show this. Doing this alters the wording used when describing this relationship on reports and web pages. The wording for narrative paragraphs is shown on the **Wording Options** tab. You can override this wording if you want to. See **Wording Options** below.

## Had Children

If you know that this couple had no children you can click the **This Couple Had No Children** checkbox to indicate this. When this is done, the message, "Had No Children" appears in the *Child List* on the *Family View*.

## Button Bar

The following buttons are found on the toolbar:

## Notes

To add explanations or comments about the marriage, click the **Notes** icon.

(Help index: ***Notes***)

## Pictures

To add a picture to the marriage, click the **Picture** icon. (See *Adding Pictures* on page 275 for more information.)

## Sources of Information

To document where the marriage information came from, click the **Sources** icon. (See *Citing Your Sources* on page 53 for more information.)

(Help index: ***Source citations***)

## Address

To enter the address of the marriage place, click the **Address** icon.

## Dates From the Calendar

You can use the built-in pop-up calendar to help you with the Marriage Date field.

Just click the **Calendar** icon.

(Help index: ***Calendar***)

## LDS Information

If you are recording LDS ordinance information, click the **LDS Ordinance**  icon to display the *LDS Ordinance Information* screen where you can fill in the *Sealed to Spouse* date and *Temple* name, if known.

(Help index: ***LDS ordinance information***)

## Source Clipboard

The *Source Clipboard* is a feature in Legacy that can tremendously increase the efficiency with which you document the sources of the information you enter into your family file. (See *Source Clipboard* on page 69 for information on how and why to use this feature.)

(Help index: ***Source clipboard***)

## Events

You can add unlimited additional facts and events to a marriage. These can include things like engagements, residences, etc. Legacy comes with many pre-defined events like those previously mentioned. You can use these and also add any new events you need.

An event consists of an Event Name, Event Date, Event Place and an Event Comment. Only the Event Name is required, but it may seem meaningless without a date, place or comment.

## Adding a New Event

**To add a new event to a marriage:**

1.  Click **Add** to the right of the *Events* box to display the *Add A New Event* window.
2.  To select an event from the *Master Event Definition List*, either type the name of the event in the *Event* field or click the **DOWN ARROW** to the right of the field to scroll through the list and select an event by clicking on it. (If you want to define a new event that is not already in the *Master Event Definition List*, see **Editing The Master Event Definition List** below.)
3.  In the *Date* field, enter the date the event occurred.
4.  In the *Place* field, enter the location where the event took place.

5. In the *Comments* field, enter any information you want to record concerning this event.

6. Click the **Source** icon to record the source of this information if you have it.

## Editing an Event

**To change the name, date, location or comments of an existing event:**

1. Highlight the event line you want to edit in the event list.
2. Click **Edit** to the right of the list to display the *Edit An Event* window.
3. Make the desired changes and click **OK** to save them.

## Editing the Master Event Definition List

If you would like to add or edit an event name definition in the *Master Event Definition List* or remove an existing event from the list, click the ▼ icon to the right of the **Event** field on the *Add Event* window to display the *Master Event Definition List*.

**To add a new event to the list:**

1. Click **Add** to the right of the event list. The **Add/Edit Event Definition** window is displayed.
2. Enter the name and sentence definition of the new event and click **Save**.
3. Click **Close** to return to the *Edit An Event* window.

**To remove an event from the list:**

1. Highlight the name of the event you want to erase.
2. Click **Options** and choose **Delete** from the shortcut menu. If the event is not being used in any individual's event list, the event is removed from the list. If the event is currently being referenced, a message displays and the event is not removed. You must remove all references to a particular event before it can be removed from the *Master Event Definition List*.

**To remove the reference of an event from the current marriage:**

1. On the *Information* window, highlight the name of the event you want to delete.
2. Click **Delete** to the right of the event box.

**Sorting the Event List**

You can have Legacy automatically sort your list of events by the event name or date by clicking **Sort** to the right of the event list. When sorting, any events that don't have a name or date are moved to the top of the list.

**To change the display order of the events:**

1. Highlight the event line you want to move.
2. Click on the **UP** or **DOWN** arrow in the lower right corner of the *Facts and Events* box (labeled "Set Order") in the direction you want to move the line.

## Combining Event Names

If you find that you have two event names that you want to combine, (for example, if you misspell a name), this can easily be done:

1. Highlight the event name you want to change.
2. Click **Map Highlighted Event Name to Another Event Name in List** at the bottom of the window.
3. Highlight the Event name you want to change it to.
4. Click the same button again, which will now read, **Highlight Destination Event Name, Then Press This Button**.

## Privacy Settings for Marriages

If you would like to be able to exclude this marriage from being included on reports, exports, and web pages, put a checkmark on the **Private** setting near the lower-right corner of the window. All reports, exports, and web pages have an option to include or exclude **Private** marriages.

## Anniversary Reminder

If you would like to be reminded of the anniversary of this couple a few days before it happens, put a checkmark in the **Anniversary Reminder** option in the lower-right corner of the window. The reminder will be displayed on the **Legacy Home** tab.

## Tags

You can tag individuals and marriages to mark them for various reasons.

## Wording Options Tab

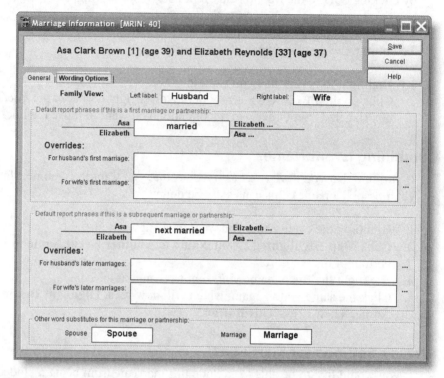

### Family View Labels

Choose the labels you would like to use when displaying this marriage couple. The default labels are **Husband** and **Wife**.

### Default Report Phrases for a First Marriage

The traditional (and default) phrase used when printing reports is **"married"**. **John married Sarah**..., or **Sarah married John**.... If the **This couple did not marry** option has been selected, the default changes to **"had a relationship with"**. **John had a relationship with Sarah**..., or **Sarah had a relationship with John**.... (The defaults for these two phrases can be changed globally in the **Options > Customize > View > Default Family View Labels and Report Wording** box.) If you want to change the phrase for this marriage/partnership only, you can type a new phrase into the box. Keep in mind that this phrase is used to build the beginning of a sentence. The sentence will then have the date and place added to it. **John married Sarah on 12 Dec 1888 in London, England**...

## Overriding the Report Phrases

If you would like to completely change the narrative wording that Legacy normally uses to construct a sentence for a report, you can change it to anything you want to. Whereas the default wording above automatically inserts the first name of each of the spouses/partners, these new override phrases does not. You must include the names in the phrase. This gives you the option to modify the names and to change the order of the parts. **Johnny took Sarah as his wife** ... or **Johnny and Sarah got married** ... or **John married his high school sweetheart Sarah** .... Again, this is the beginning portion of a sentence that will have the date and location added to it, so keep this in mind.

You must construct two versions of the sentence, one describing the husband's first marriage (or partnership) and the other describing the wife's first marriage.

## Default Report Phrases for a Subsequent Marriage

Similar to the wording for a first marriage, the default phrase used for a second or later marriage is "**next married**" or "**next had a relationship with**". **John next married Sarah**..., or **Sarah next had a relationship with John**.... If you want to change the phrase for this subsequent marriage/partnership only, you can type a new phrase into the box.

## Overriding the Report Phrases

Just as with the first marriage, you can enter your own wording for later marriages. **Later in his life Johnny got remarried to Ruth** ... or **Several years after her divorce, Sarah met a man named Alfred and they were married** .... Again, this is the beginning portion of a sentence that will have the date and location added to it, so don't put a period at the end.

Again, as with the first marriage, you must construct two versions of the sentence.

## Other word substitutes

You can also change the terms **Spouse** and **Marriage** to other words that will be used in various reporting situations.

## Special Characters

When entering information, Legacy offers a feature to help you quickly enter international characters.

The *Marriage Information* screen is reached by clicking the **Marriage Bar** just below the **Husb** and **Wife** boxes on the Family View. It can also be reached by choosing **Marriage** from the **Edit** menu or **Edit Marriage** from the right-click menu of the husband or wife.

(To use the tagging feature in Legacy you must have the tagging option turned on. This is done on the **General** tab of the **Options > Customize** screen.

# Chapter 4

# *SourceWriter*

Creating Perfect Source Citations

## Citing Your Sources

When you do family history research, you should keep track of each piece of information you collect and also where you found it. Your records should be detailed enough so that any other person in the future could find the same information.

As you add individuals and families to the family file, you can either document the sources of the information as you go, or you can return later and add the documentation. Of course, by putting things off, you tend to forget about them, so it is strongly suggested that you resist the urge to save time and go ahead with documenting your sources as you initially enter the names.

A particular source of information may be cited hundreds of times within a family file. You might find a book or census that contains scores of family members. The location of each piece of information for each individual should be recorded. Rather than record the entire source description dozens (or hundreds) of times, taking up huge amounts of storage space, it is much more efficient to enter a general source description once, point to it in a master list, and record just the unique information for each piece's place within that source.

# Assigned Sources Window

Displaying the *Assigned Sources* screen can be done by clicking the

**Source**  icon on either the *Individual* or *Marriage Information* window, or with one of the **Source** buttons on the *Family View* or *Pedigree View* screen.

The *Assigned Sources* window contains three columns: Events, Name of Source, and Detail.

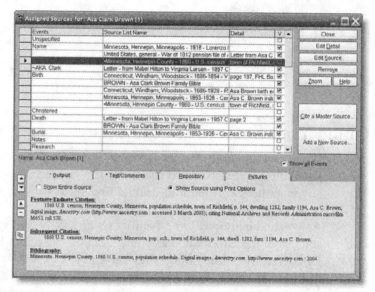

**Events**   Event names in the left column are taken from the data headings on the individual or marriage information sheets. As sources are added, they are assigned to a particular event name. Multiple sources can be assigned to the same event title.

**Source List Name**   When a source is assigned to a specific event, the field then shows the name of the source or sources that have been assigned. There is also a category named **Unspecified**. This is a catch-all category where data can be assigned when specific sources are not available.

**Detail**   Data in the *Detail* field shows the information entered in the *Source Detail* window shown below.

(For much more information on this topic, look in the Legacy Help index for: **assigning sources to your information**)

## *SourceWriter* Template System

Version 7 of Legacy heralds the introduction of ***SourceWriter***. *SourceWriter* is a template driven sourcing system that makes it easy for you to select the correct input screen so that you enter all the pieces needed to correctly cite any source of information in the thousands of formats that exist for them. The information you enter is correctly and precisely formatted to match the genealogy industry standards for source citations.

Prior to version 7, Legacy's citation methods were rudimentary and straight forward but didn't offer the expert help needed in order to automatically produce correct citations. Actually, in version 7, you can use either of the citation methods, the new or the old. We will call the new system *SourceWriter* and the previous system the "Basic System." If you always want to use the old system, go to **Options** > **Customize** > **Sources** and select the **Basic Source System**. To use the new *SourceWriter* system, make sure the option is set to **SourceWriter System**.

# Adding a New Source Using *SourceWriter*

There are several ways to reach the *Add a New Master Source* screen:

- From the **Assigned Sources List** from an **Individual**, **Marriage**, or **To-Do** screen, click **Add a New Source**.
- From **View** > **Master Lists** > **Source**, click the **Add** button.

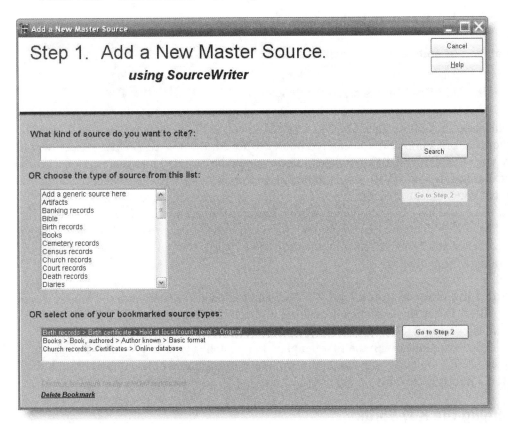

# Choosing a Source Template

The first step is to select the proper source template that matches the source you are documenting. A source template is made up of all the potential pieces of information that you should record about the source. These include both the fields for the master source and the fields for the details of the citation. Some sources require only a few bits of information and others require many.

There are two different ways to find the source template that you want to use. The first is by entering keywords to display the *Source Template Index* showing you all the templates that match your query. From there, you select the template that matches the source you are entering. The second method is to select the template by first selecting the general type of source and then choosing subcategories that refine the choice down further and further until you have the desired template that matches the source. These two methods are described in detail below.

## Selecting by Keyword(s)

**What kind of source do you want to cite?:**

| book authored| | Search |

Begin by entering one or more keywords into the field and then click the **Search** button. This then displays the *Source Template Index* showing you all the templates that match your keywords. For example, if you entered **book authored**, the *Source Template Index* would show you a list of about 100 templates. These would be grouped into four sections; **Audio book, Book, CD,** and **DVD**. It would be fairly straightforward to then select the actual book type that you are dealing with. If you knew that you were citing a source from a basic printed book, you could have entered the keywords, **book authored basic**, the resulting index list would have only contained 12 templates. As you use the *Source Index* more and more, you will get better and better at selecting the desired keywords that will make the template selection go more quickly.

**Filtering the Source Index List** – There is an option at the bottom of the *Source Template Index* called, **Filter the list when searching**. Selecting this option cause the list to only show the templates that match all of your keywords. With the option unchecked, the list will include the entire index with the first template that matches your keywords highlighted. You can then use **F3** to jump from matching template to matching template down through the list. (**Shift-F3** jumps backwards up the list.)

## Changing the Keywords

You can add or remove keywords from the search field at the top and then click the **Search** button to create a new list of matches.

## Choosing the Template from the List

When you find the correct template, click on it to highlight it and then click the **Go** button. (Or you can simply double-click the template line.)  You are then taken to the screen where you actually enter your source information into the template fields.  See **Filling in the Source Template** below for more information.

## Selecting a Template by Type

Selecting a template by type is a multi-step process.  Begin by selecting the desired type from the list box on the left.  When you have clicked on the type you want to select, you may be prompted for subcategory types to narrow the choice for the final template you should use.  Some types require up to four subcategories, others don't require any.  For example, it you selected the **Books** type of source, the next prompt would be:

**1) Was the book authored or edited?**

Click on the down arrow 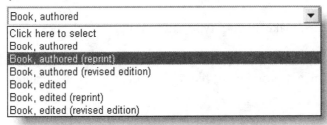 to display the possible choices:

**1) Was the book authored or edited?**

| Book, authored |
|---|
| Click here to select |
| Book, authored |
| Book, authored (reprint) |
| Book, authored (revised edition) |
| Book, edited |
| Book, edited (reprint) |
| Book, edited (revised edition) |

Choose the appropriate subcategory.  For example, **Book, authored**.  The next prompt would be:

**2) Select the type of author:**

| Click here to select |
|---|
| Click here to select |
| Author known |
| Author unidentified, but known |
| Authored by an agency |
| Two authors |

Selecting **Author known** would then bring up the final prompt:

**3) Select the medium:**

As soon as you have answered the last prompt in the series, the [Go to Step 2] button is enabled so that you can click it to continue on to the actual source template. See **Filling in the Source Template** below for more information.

# Bookmarks

After you have cited many sources in your family file you may find that you are using one or more of the same templates on a regular basis. For example many people cite a basic format authored book many times. A certain type of cemetery record or federal census found online may also be a popular choice. When you find a particular template that you are using over and over again, you can save a bookmark for it so that you can easily and quickly select it again in the future.

To save a bookmark, first make all your type and subcategory selections until the

[Go to Step 2] is enabled. But before you click it, click on the **Create a bookmark for the selected source** link at the bottom of the screen. Legacy saves the template in the *Bookmark List*:

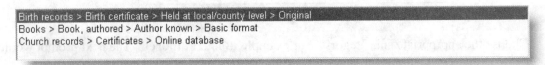

***Create a bookmark for the selected source***
***Delete Bookmark***

To select and use one of your bookmarks, click on the desired bookmark to highlight it and then click the [ Go to Step 2 ] button to the right of the *Bookmark List* to continue on to the actual source template. See **Filling in the Source Template** below for more information.

To delete a bookmark, highlight it and then click the **Delete Bookmark** link.

# Filling in the Source Template

The second step to adding a new source using *SourceWriter* is to fill in the actual fields of the template for the master source. Here is a typical master source template for an online census record:

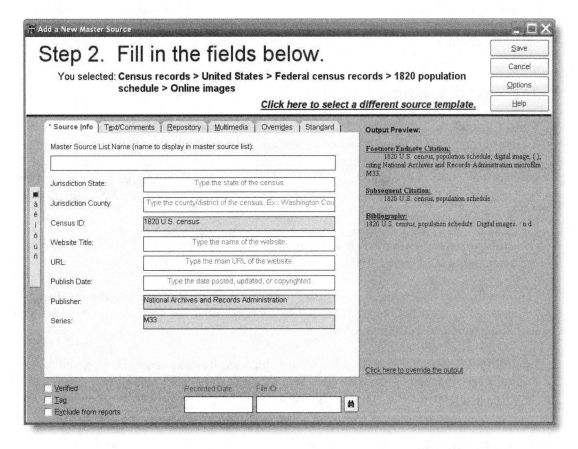

The name of the source template that you have selected is shown in the header. In this example it is: **Census records > United States > Federal census records > 1820 population schedule > Online images**. It is a long name but it precisely identifies the template type and subcategories. Many names are shorter, some are longer.

Below the header is the actual template. The first tab, **Source Info**, contains the fields that you will be filling in. The other four tabs, **Text**, **Repository**, **Multimedia**, and **Overrides** are included so that you can add additional information about the source as well as pictures and other items of interest.

To the right of the input section is the **Output Preview**. As you enter the information about the source, it is instantly processed and displayed in three different formats so that you can see how it will look when included on a report or book. The **Footnote/Endnote Citation** output is used for the first occurrence of a footnote (at the bottom of each page where a source is cited) or endnote (at the end of each generation, chapter, or book) on a report. The **Subsequent Citation** is used in the same places as the footnotes and endnotes but uses a condensed format that doesn't require as much room. The **Bibliography** is printed at the end of a report and is a summary of all the master sources cited in the report and is shown in alphabetical order.

## The Parts of the Source Info Tab

**Field Examples** – Most input fields have some kind of instruction or example in grey lettering centered in the field. This text gives you a sense of what the field is for. When you click in a field (or tab to it), the example text disappears so that you can enter your information. **Note**: The example text is also shown as a tool tip when the cursor is held over the field label so that you can remember what the example was when you are filling in the field.

**Default Entries** – Some fields have default entries. In most cases, this is what should remain in the field. You can replace it if needed.

**Locked Fields** – Some fields have default text and are locked so that you cannot change the contents. They are actually part of the source citation output and are only shown so that you will know what part of the citation they are.

**Scrolling** – If there are more than ten input field, a scrollbar is shown allowing you to manually scroll up and down in the field list. When you are entering information and tabbing down the list, it scrolls automatically for you.

## Filling In the Source Template Fields

**Master Source List Name** – Enter a name for the master source record. This name will be used in the *Master Source List* whenever it is displayed. The source name is generally an abbreviation of the source title. For example, if you are working from a book called **"Gilbert**

**Radcliff Johnson of Wilderberry County, South Dakota and all Known Descendants Through 1945"**, you might want to name the source something like **"G.R. Johnson Descendants."**

**Template Fields** – Tab from field to field and fill in the information you have about the source. Locked fields with default text are skipped while tabbing. When the cursor enters a field, the example text disappears. (Again, you can see the example text as a tool tip when the cursor is held over the field label so that you can remember what the example was when you are filling in the field.)

**Text Tab** – Here you can record actual source text and comments about the source. The text box can be a word-for-word copy of any description contained in the source. Don't enter opinions about the source by you or the compiler. This should only include "what the original record keeper said" as opposed to any interpretations. The Comments box is used to record notes for each master source you enter. This is a good way to document how you found a particular source and other interesting and important information about it.

    **Embedding Formatting Codes into the Notes** – You can add formatting codes to your source text and comments so that portions print in bold, italics, underline and superscript. These codes are used when printing reports, producing word processing files and Web pages.

**Repository Tab** – Record the name and address of the place where this source is stored. It may be a cemetery, library, or archive. It can even be the address of another person who has a copy of the document.

**Multimedia Tab** – Used to attach graphic files and other files to the source. These may be scanned images such as birth certificates, obituaries, sound files, etc.

**Overrides Tab** – You can override any of the automatically formatted output that *SourceWriter* produces. You can pre-fill each override (Footnote Citation, Subsequent Citation, or Bibliography) section by clicking on the ⟳ button to its right. You can change the output to anything you want. To actually override the default output, you must also checkmark the option just below each section.

## Other Options

Below the tabbed sections of the template are two more fields and three options:

## Recorded Date

This is the date you recorded the source citation.

## File ID #

You can assign your own filing number if desired.

> **File ID Assistant** – To help you figure out the next available file ID number, click the
>
> Assistant button ⚞ . (See **File ID Number Assistant** on page 311 for more information.)

**Verified** – This checkbox is used when you have verified the source information. For example, if you receive information from another person, either through a GEDCOM import or by email or other means, you should verify that the source citations are true and accurate. As you check each citation, you can mark **Verified** to indicate your confirmation of the source information.

**Tag** – Sources can be marked with a tag so that later you have the option to print only the tagged sources when doing a source report.

**Exclude from reports** – Select this option to exclude this source from the footnotes, endnotes, and bibliographies when printing reports or books. Normally you will only want to print a few of your best and most reliable sources for each event on a report or book. You might have a dozen or more sources for a person's name, for example, but it doesn't make sense to include all of them on a report. The resulting footnotes end up very long and take too much space at the bottom of each page.

## Other Options

In the header at the top of the screen there is an **Options** button. From here you can set the Font size used for the *Output Preview* by using the **Zoom** option. You can also save a bookmark for the current template so that you can easily use it in the future. See **Bookmarks** a few pages back.

## Selecting a Different Template

If you are adding a new source (as opposed to editing an existing source) you can go back to Step 1 and select a different template if you wish by clicking the **Click here to select a different source template** link in the header section.

## Saving the Source

To save the source, click **Save**. If you are adding a citation, you will be taken next to the Detail screen where you can enter addition information pertaining to the particular citation of the source that you are making. This is usually a page number, item number, etc.

# Recording the Details

The third step in adding a source citation is to fill in the detail information. A particular master source of information may be an unlimited number of times within a Family File. You might have found a book or bible that contains hundreds of family members. The location of each piece of information for each individual should be recorded. Rather than record the entire source description hundreds (or thousands) of times, taking up huge amounts of storage space, it is much more efficient to enter a general source description once, point to it in the master source list and record just the unique information for each piece's place within that source.

The *Source Detail* window is where you enter information about a source that indicates where in a specific source the cited information was found. Most source templates contain additional detail fields, that when filled in, are incorporated into the final output of the footnotes or endnotes. A typical *Source Detail* screen might look like this:

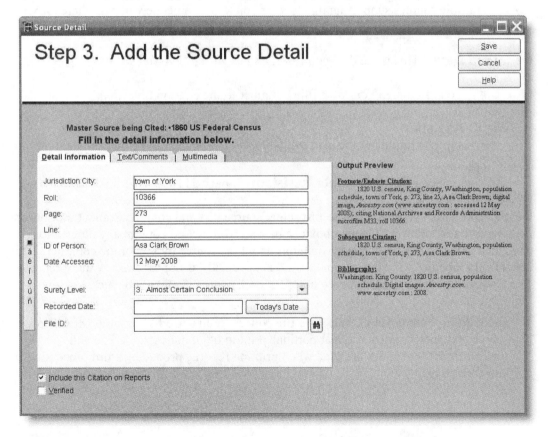

**Detail Fields** – Enter the requested information if you know it. These is usually page numbers, volume numbers, item numbers of a microfilm rolls, line numbers, etc.

**Surety Level** – While specifying the source detail, you can also indicate the *Surety Level* of the information. This number, from zero to four, shows how sure you are of the information.

**0** indicates that you have not yet made up your mind about how convincing this source of information is.

**1** indicates that there is a little evidence to support this fact but it is not too convincing.

**2** indicates that this is probably a true fact. You don't have any reason to doubt it but there is no other evidence that backs it up.

**3** indicates that this is almost certainly a reliable source with factual information.

**4** indicates that you are as sure as you can be about this piece of information. There are multiple sources supporting this fact, or you know someone who was there, or you were there yourself. You are convinced that it is true.

**Recorded Date** – This is the date you recorded the source citation.

**File ID #** – You can assign your own filing number to the citation if desired.

### File ID Assistant

To help you figure out the next available file ID number, click the Assistant button

 . (See **File ID Number Assistant** on page 311 for more information.)

**Detail Text Tab** – Here you can record actual source text and comments about the source pertaining to this citation. The text box can be a word-for-word copy of any description contained in the source. Don't enter opinions about the source by you or the compiler. This should only include "what the original record keeper said" as opposed to any interpretations. The **Comments** box is used to record notes for each source citation you enter.

**Embedding Formatting Codes into the Notes** – You can add formatting codes to your source text and comments so that portions print in bold, italics, underline and superscript. These codes are used when printing reports, producing word processing files and Web pages.

## Multimedia Tab

### Output Preview

To the right of the input section is the **Output Preview**. As you enter the information about the source detail, it is instantly processed and displayed in three different formats so that you can see how it will look when included on a report or book. The **Footnote/Endnote Citation** output is used for the first occurrence of a footnote (at the bottom of each page where a source is cited) or endnote (at the end of each generation, chapter, or book) on a report. The **Subsequent Citation** is used in the same places as the footnotes and endnotes but uses a condensed format that doesn't require as much room. The **Bibliography** is printed at the end of a report and is a summary of all the master sources cited in the report and is shown in alphabetical order.

**Verified** – This checkbox is used when you have verified the source detail information. For example, if you receive information from another person, either through a GEDCOM import or by email or other means, you should verify that the source citations are true and accurate. As you check each citation, you can mark **Verified** to indicate your confirmation of the source detail information. (Master Sources also have a **Verified** checkbox for the same reason.)

# Citing an Existing Source Using *SourceWriter*

- From the **Assigned Sources List** from an **Individual**, **Marriage**, or **To-Do** screen, click **Cite a Master Source**. The Master Source List appears.

# Master Source List

Select this box to exclude the source on reports.

Select this box when you have verified the source as reliable.

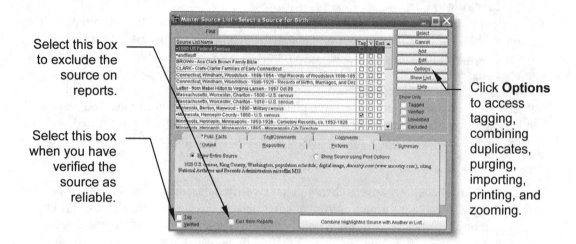

Click **Options** to access tagging, combining duplicates, purging, importing, printing, and zooming.

## What Is Included in the List?

The *Master Source List* shows all the sources being cited by any piece of information in your family file. If a source is referenced from more than one place, only one copy is recorded in the *Master Source List* and all references point to this one master copy. The lines showing in the *Master Source List* are the *Source List Names*. These names are displayed alphabetically.

## Showing Source Details

Below the *Source List Name* column, the details of the highlighted source are shown. This includes the Title, Author, Type, Publication Facts, Source Text, Comments, Repository, and Pictures. As you move the highlight bar up and down in the list, the details for the currently highlighted line are shown.

## Selecting a Source

To select a particular master source, highlight the desired line and click **Select**, or double-click on the line.

## Tagging a Source

You can tag Individual source lines in the *Master Source List* by either clicking in the *Tag* column of the desired source line, or by clicking the line to highlight it and then clicking the **Tag** checkbox. When a source line is tagged, a check mark appears in the

*Tag* column. The tags can be used to limit the included sources when printing a *Source Citation Report*.

## Excluding a Source

You can exclude an individual source from reports by either clicking in the *Excl* column of the desired source line in the *Master Source List* or by clicking the line to highlight it and then clicking the **Excl from Reports** checkbox. When a source line is selected for exclusion, a checkmark appears in the *Excl* column.

## Adding a New Master Source

▶ **To add a new source:**
1. Click **Add**. The *Define/Edit Source Listing* window appears. (For more information on filling in this window, see *Defining or Editing a Master Source* on page 55.)
2. Fill in the source definition.
3. Click **Save**.

(Help index: ***Define:Source citation***)

## Editing a Master Source

▶ **To edit an existing source:**
1. Highlight the source entry you want to change.
2. Click **Edit**. The *Define/Edit Source Listing* window appears.
3. Make the desired changes to the source definition.
4. Click **Save**.

## Deleting a Master Source

To delete a master source, all references to it must first be deleted. Legacy can tell you which records include references that you would like to delete.

▶ **To remove a master source from the *Master Source List*:**
1. Highlight the source line you want to erase.
2. Click the **Options** button and choose **Delete Master Source** from the popup menu. If the source is not being cited by any record in your family file, the source is removed from the *Master Source List*. If there are one or more records connected to the master source, a message is displayed indicating that the source cannot be deleted because it is in use. The message offers to display a list of the records currently using the source. Click **Yes** and a window with a list of all individuals who use the master source appears. If you still want to delete the master source, click **Delete this Master Source and All Citations to It**.

## Other Options

The **Options** button brings up a menu where you can choose the following:

**Delete Master Source** lets you erase a master source from the list. If you try to delete a source that is being used anywhere in your family file, you receive a message to that effect and you are offered the option to view all the records that use it.

**Tag/Exclude** brings up the *Tag/Exclude Option* window where you can quickly set or clear all general source or report exclusion tags.

**Change Surety Settings** lets you modify the surety level setting of the highlighted master source.

**Combine Duplicates** combines any sources that are identical in every way.

**Purge Unused Sources** removes any master sources that are not being cited from anywhere in the entire family file.

**Import Lists** lets you import various lists from other family files. These include *Locations, Surnames, Event Definitions, Temples, Marriage Status, Source Types, Child Status, Picture Locations*, and other *Master Source Lists*.

**Print** prints either a list of all the *Master Sources* or a *Source Citation List* that shows every individual and marriage that cites each source.

**Zoom** lets you vary the font size of the *Source List Name* column.

**Options for Non-Sources** lets you move information from master sources that doesn't belong there. This usually originates from imported material where other people have entered information that really belongs in a notes field instead of a master source record.

## Show List

The **Show List** button displays a list of individuals who use the highlighted master source(s).

(Help index: ***Who is using this***)

## Searching for a Specific Source List Name

If your list of master sources is extensive, you may have a need to search the list for a specific entry.

▶ **To search for a source list name:**

1. In the **Find** field above the *Source List Name* column, type the text you want to find. This should be the beginning of the source list name. As you type, Legacy displays the closest matching line in the list.

# Source Clipboard

The *Source Clipboard*™ is a feature in Legacy that can tremendously increase the efficiency with which you document the sources of the information you enter into your family file. The *Source Clipboard* holds copies of up to five source citations that you are currently working from. You can then record the sources of each piece of information by simply clicking one button.

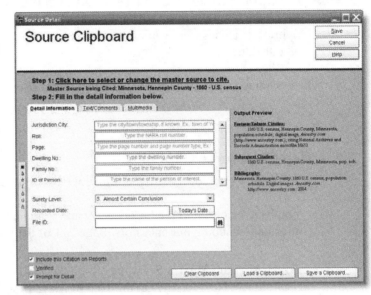

To get to the Source Clipboard, click the 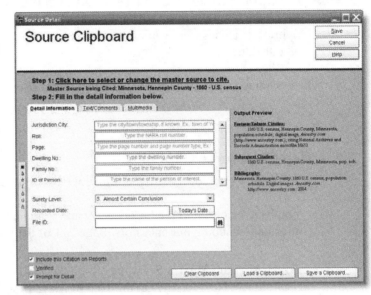 button on any form that contains sourceable information. These include the **Individual** and **Marriage** Information screens, the **Event** screen, the **Children** List, and many others.

You can add or change citations on the clipboard by clicking the **Set** button on each of up to five tabs. (See *Master Source List* on page 66 for more information.) The clipboard also holds the detailed information about where in each source the current information is coming from. This is usually a page number, microfilm item number, etc. The actual source text being cited can be entered in the large text box below the detail field. You can also set the surety level for each source information. This reflects your confidence in the accuracy of the information. (See *Recording the Details* on page 63 for more information.) In addition, you can enter a user file number to cross-reference the photocopies, extracts, and documents you find as you research your family.

▶ **To exclude source details on a report:**
Deselect **Add this Detail to Source Citation on Reports** on each of the tabs.

▶ **To exclude a source citation on a report:**
Deselect **Include this Citation on Reports**.

▶ **To include the actual source text in citations:**
Select **Add this Text to the Source Citation on Reports**.

▶ **To be prompted for the Source Detail each time you use the clipboard:**
Leave the **Current Source Detail** field blank and select **Prompt for Detail** to the right of it. This is a convenient way to cite sources that are on many different pages of a document.

When you have entered the current source information, click **OK** to return to the entry form.

## Using the Source Clipboard

Perhaps some examples will help to illustrate the value of this feature:

You have just been to the local library and found a book that contains a lot of information about your ancestors. Page 211 of the book contains the following text:

**James Michael Martin Sr.** was born on the 23rd of December, 1762, in Hackensack, New Jersey. On the 16th of May, 1784, Jim married Sarah Rebecca Gilbert somewhere in rural Bergen County, New Jersey, and they had the following children:

1. **James Michael Martin Jr.** Born 30 Apr 1785 in Hackensack. He married Ida Fredricks, daughter of Henry R. Fredricks and Millie Andrews, on 25 Dec 1806. Jim Jr. died in 1838 in New York, NY.
2. **Sarah Martin** Born 22 Jun 1786 in Hackensack, NJ. Died young and was buried in Hackensack.
3. **Rebecca Martin** Born 8 Sep 1788. Married William Demarest in about 1807. They had six children. Becky died 15 Oct 1867 and was buried in Ohio.

As you enter the information for each person on this page of the book, you should record the source of the information. Let's go through the steps:

1. On the *Individual's Information* window, enter the information for James Michael Martin Sr.
2. When you have finished, but before you click **Save,** set up the *Source Clipboard* with the source information. Click the **Source Clipboard** ▲ button.

3. First make an entry in the *Master Source List* about the book we are using. To do this, click **Click here to select or change the mastersource to cite** to bring up the *Master Source List* window.
4. Click **Add** to display the *Add a New Master Source* window.
5. Choose the source template to use and then click **Go to Step 2**
6. Enter the source information into the template fields.
7. **Save** the master source and **Select** it for use in the *Source Clipboard*.
8. In the Detail Information section, fill in the details fields.
9. Set the surety level to reflect your confidence in the accuracy of this information.
10. Click **Save** to close the *Source Clipboard* and return to the *Information* screen.

Now you are ready to assign the source citation to the information you have entered for James Michael Martin Sr. You have three choices from the *Individual's Information* window:

1. You can place the cursor in the **Given** field and click the ▬ button to assign the source to just that piece of information. Place the cursor in the **Birth** field and click ▬ again. Continue doing this in each field on the window to assign the source from the clipboard.

2. Or, you can click ≣ to have Legacy automatically assign the source to every field on the *Information* form that is not blank.

3. Or, you can click ■ and have the source assigned to the general *Unspecified* category for this person.

**Option 1** is used when you return to add a newly found piece of information to an individual at a later time and want to assign a different source citation to that entry specifically.

**Option 2** is generally the best and fastest method to use when entering information for an individual for the first time.

**Option 3** is used if you are not interested in keeping specific source information for each type of event for an individual, but just want to record the source in one place.

## Saving the *Source Clipboard*

If you find that you are reusing a particular source citation, you can save it to disk for use in the future. Up to ten different citations can be saved. To save a citation, click **Save** after loading the desired master source and filling in the detail fields. When the

*Save Source Clipboard* window appears, select one of the ten save positions by clicking it. Next, enter a name (up to 40 characters) in the **Name** field to describe the setup and then click **Save**.

### Loading a Saved *Source Clipboard*

If you have saved one or more *Source Clipboards*, you can quickly load one back in. Simply click **Load**. When the *Load Source Clipboard* window appears, highlight the entry you want to load and then click **Load**. (Or just double-click on the entry.) The citation is loaded from disk and is placed on the clipboard.

You can also load any of your saved clipboards by right-clicking on the [▲] button whenever it is visible. This pops up a small list of the saved clipboards where you can simply click the one you want to load.

### Erasing Saved Clipboards

To erase an entry from the list, highlight it and then click **Delete**.

# Source Template Conversion Tool

The *Source Template Conversion Tool* helps you convert your existing basic source citations to the new *SourceWriter* templates. Although you can continue to use your previous citations, converting them to the new style ensures that the citations are produced according to industry standards and allows the generation of bibliographic entries as well.

### Converting Your Source Citations

The *Source Template Conversion Tool* is reached from the Master Source List by clicking the **Options** button and then choosing **Source Template Conversion Tool** from the submenu.

A source citation consists of a master source and some detail information. Both of these two parts need to be converted into a *SourceWriter* template. This is done in the three steps described below. These steps take you through converting each master source and detail pair, to the appropriate template. The process cannot be automated because basic-style citations are not broken down into the individual pieces of information that are need to fill in the templates. So, you will need to copy bits of information from the basic citation to the template fields in order to make the conversion.

Some people only have a few citations to convert, other may have thousands. This isn't something that you need to do right away or all at once. Some people find it easiest to convert one family's citations at a time or to convert the sources that are used the most.

## Select a Citation to Convert

The first step is to select a basic-style master source and then start converting all the citations that use it.

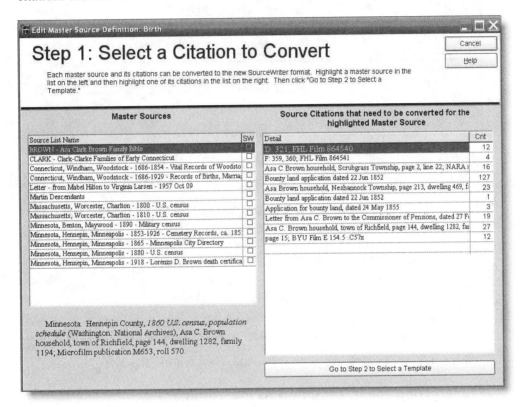

The **Step 1** screen shows all of your master sources that have not been fully converted yet. This list is shown on the left. When you highlight a master source, a list of all the citations that use it is shown on the right. The goal is to convert all the citations for a given master source. There might only be one citation or hundreds of citations that use a master source. As each citation is converted, it is removed from the list on the right. After all of the citations are converted, the master source is removed from the left-hand list.

1. Click on the master source you want to start converting.
2. Click on the **Go to Step 2 to Select a Template** button.

## Select a Source Template

The second step is to select the source template that matches the basic-style master source you are converting. There are several ways to select the *SourceWriter* template. See

*Choosing a Source Template* on page 56 for a complete description of how to select a template.

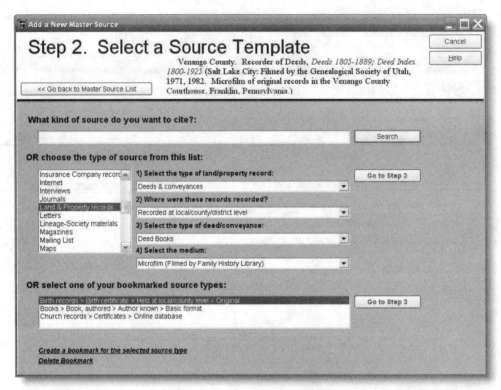

When you have selected the source template, click **Go to Step 3**.

## Transferring the Information to the Template

The third step is to transfer the bits of information from the basic source to the source template fields.

The basic information is shown on the right and the template on the left. To move the information, use copy and paste. (To copy information, highlight it with the mouse and then press **Ctrl-C**. To paste information, click in the field where you want to put it and then press **Ctrl-V**.) Using this method, copy all the information from the right to the left, from the basic-style source to the template fields. Usually, the upper information from the basic master source (Author, Title, and Publication Facts) goes into the Master Source Information template fields and the detail information goes into the Source Detail fields. There are cases, however, when some of your basic-style master source information will be put into details fields, and some basic-style detail information will be put into one or more master template fields. This all depends on how you had arranged your information in the basic-style citations.

When you have finished transferring the citation information, click the button called **Save, then display Next Citation for same master source**. The new master source and citation detail will be saved and then the next citation (if any) for the same master source will be displayed. The fields for the master template source will remain on the screen, the detail fields will be blanked, and the new basic-style citation information will be shown on the right.

## Continue to Convert Citations

After you have converted the basic-style master source to a new *SourceWriter* template source the first time, all you have to do for any remaining citations is to transfer the detail information to the detail fields. This is usually a very quick process. Continue to convert all the citations for the current master source until you have worked through all of them (pressing **Save, then display Next Citation for same master source** after each one). When you have completed all the citations, you will be returned to **Step 1** where you can select another master source and its citations to convert.

# Chapter 5

# *Lists and Tags*

Working With Master Information Lists

## The Name List

### What It Shows

The *Name List* displays a list of individuals. It can either contain all the individuals in the entire family file or just a search subset. The list has six columns: one for the RIN number (or the User File#), one for the individual's full name, one for the individual's sex, and three tag columns. The area to the right of the list contains information about the highlighted individual and his or her family. The information shown can be customized. (See *Displaying and Changing an Individual's Details* on

page 79.) The *Name List* is displayed by clicking the **Name List** icon on the toolbar.

The *Name List* can also include the alternate names that have been recorded for various individuals. This makes the list especially useful when trying to find a specific person whose name may have been spelled differently on different records or when a nickname has been used.

Click **#** to sort the list in record number order.

Enter a RIN here to jump to that person in the list.

Click **Given** to sort the list in order of given name(s).

Click **Surname** to sort the list in surname order.

Click **Select** to bring up the Information screen for the highlighted person.

Click **First** to jump to the beginning of the list.

These three columns show the tag settings for each individual.

Click **To-Do** to create a list of tasks needing to be done.

These tabs display additional information for the highlighted person. Click a tab to change the information shown.

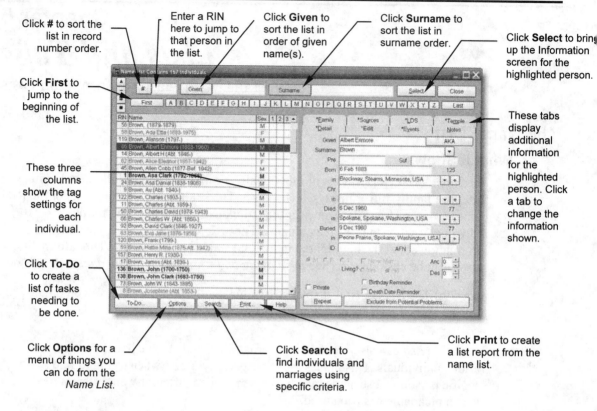

Click **Options** for a menu of things you can do from the *Name List.*

Click **Search** to find individuals and marriages using specific criteria.

Click **Print** to create a list report from the name list.

## Sorting the List

The *Name List* can be displayed in either surname order, given name order, or RIN order. Click **Surname, First** or **#** at the top of the window, or click in the **Surname**, **First** or **#** box.

## Finding an Individual

If the list is long, you can search for an individual in the list by RIN, given name, or surname. To search by surname, click in the **Surname** box and type the name you want to find. Enter the surname first, followed by a comma and then the given name(s). To search by given name, click in the **Given** box and type the given names, followed by a comma and then the surname if known. To search by RIN, click in the **#** field and type the number you want to locate. As you type, Legacy automatically jumps to the nearest matching name in the list.

## Selecting an Individual

To select an individual from the list, highlight the name and click **Select**, or double-click the name in the list.

## Editing an Individual

If you want to edit the information for any one person in the list, highlight the name and click the **Edit** tab. The individual's edit screen appears.

## Adding, Deleting, or Editing an Individual's Events

If you want to add, delete, or edit an individual's events, highlight the name and click the **Events** tab.

(Help index: *Events on Name List*)

## Displaying and Editing an Individual's Family

To display a list of an individual's family members, highlight the name and click the **Family** tab. The individual's parents, siblings, spouse, and children appear. You can edit a family member or marriage information by highlighting the family member and clicking the desired edit button below the list.

(Help index: *Family tab on name list*)

## Adding, Deleting, or Editing an Individual's Sources

If you want to add, delete, or edit an individual's sources of information, highlight the name and click the **Sources** tab.

(Help index: *Sources tab on name list*)

## Adding, Deleting, or Editing an Individual's Notes

If you want to add, delete, or edit an individual's notes, highlight the name and click the **Notes** tab.

## Displaying and Changing an Individual's Details

To display changeable details about an individual, highlight the name and click the **Detail** tab. There are up to eight lines on the *Detail* screen that can contain information. Each of these information lines can be changed to other pieces of information you might want to view instead. To change the lines, click any of the descriptive labels to the left of the lines (for example, "Born," "Chr," "Died," or "Buried"). The *Customize Name List Detail Information* window then appears where you can select the new information you want to see.

| Customize Name List Fields | | |
|---|---|---|
| **Customize Display** | | Close |
| | | Cancel |
| Field Name | Names to Display | Defaults |
| Birth Date/Place | ... Born | |
| Christening Date/Place | ... Chr | Load... |
| Death Date/Place | ... Died | Save... |
| Relationship | ... Relshp | |
| Father | ... Father | Help |
| Mother | ... Mother | |
| Marriage: Preferred, Spouse Name | ... *Spouse | |
| Marriage: Preferred, Date/Place | ... *Marr | |

▶ **To select the pieces of information to be shown on the Detail tab:**

1. Click [...] at the right of the item you want to change.
2. From the resulting *Field Names to Display* list, select the new item by highlighting it and clicking **Select**.
3. Continue with steps 1 and 2 until you have selected the information you want to display. If you want to display fewer than eight items, choose **blank – display nothing** from the *Field Names to Display* list.
4. When you are finished, click **Close**.

You can save up to ten arrangements of custom fields for future use. To save the current arrangement, click **Save**. To reload an arrangement that was previously saved, click **Load**. (You can also reload a saved arrangement by right-clicking on the field names back on the *Name List*. This pops up a small list of your saved arrangements where you can select the desired one.)

## Navigating

**Detail Tab** At the bottom of the **Detail** tab is a three-generation pedigree chart. The starting person on the chart is the highlighted person in the *Name List*. Use the pedigree chart to navigate along family lines. Click on anyone in the pedigree chart to navigate to that person in the *Name List*.

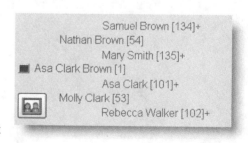

The chart is then redrawn for the new person.

**Family Tab**  The *Immediate Relatives* list shown on the **Family** tab can also be used for navigating through family lines. Double-click any name to navigate to that person in the *Name List*.

| Immediate Relatives |
|---|
| par-Nathan Brown [54] and Molly Clark [53] |
| self-+Brown, Asa Clark [1] (1792-1866) |
| sib-Brown, Rebekah [52] (1794-1796) |
| sib-Brown, Samuel Miller [51] (1795-) |
| sib-Brown, Alanson [119] (1797-) |
| sib-Brown, Frank [120] (1799-) |
| sib-Brown, Ruth [121] (1801-) |
| sib-Brown, Charles [122] (1803-) |
| par-William Brown [155] and Catherine Sabin [156] |
| sp-+Reynolds, Elizabeth [33] (1794-Bef. 1832) |
| ch-Brown, [21] (Abt. 1815-) |
| ch-+Brown, Nathan R. (Reverend ) [23] (Abt. 1817-1897) |

## Creating a To-Do List

To create a *To-Do List* of tasks (like finding a birth certificate), that need to be done, click **To-Do** in the lower-left corner. (See *The To-Do List* on page 105 for more details.)

(Help index: *To Do lists*)

## Searching for Individuals

You can search for individuals in your family file in many different ways by clicking **Search**. The type of searches you can do include: Query by Example, Detailed Search, and Miscellaneous Searches. (See *Searching for Individuals* on page 291 for more details.)

(Help index: *Search*)

## Printing a Name List Report

Whenever you create a list of individuals or marriages, you can also print a report containing those names. For example, if you search for all the people in your family file who have lived in New Jersey, a list is displayed containing the names found. This list can be printed by clicking the **Print** button on the bottom of the *Name List* window. The *List Report Options* window appears, where you can select the information you want to include on your report.

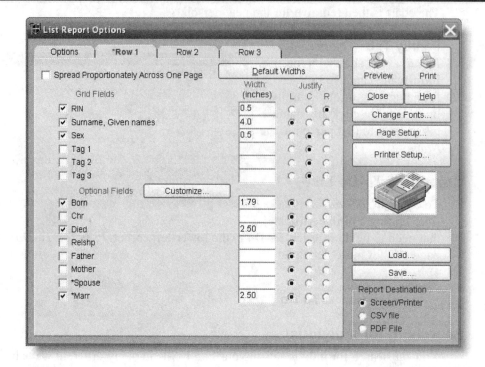

For complete information about printing list reports from the *Name List*, see the Legacy Help system and search the index for: **List report options**

## Other Options

Clicking **Options** displays a menu of options you can do from the *Name List*.

**Include Alternate Names (*Deluxe Edition* only)** includes the alternate name entries for each individual in your family file. When turned on, the alternate names, also known as AKAs, are shown in the list with a leading tilde (~) character.

**Show User ID Number in List (*Deluxe Edition* only)** toggles the RIN column in the *Name List* with User ID#. When the User ID#s are being displayed, typing in the # field at the top of the form searches for ID numbers.

**Edit an Individual** lets you make changes to the individual's information for any person highlighted in the list.

(Help index: *Information screen*)

**Delete Individual** erases the highlighted individual in the list.

**Advanced Deleting** allows you to delete tagged individuals.

(Help index: *Advanced deleting*)

**Advanced Tagging** lets you can tag an individual, their family, descendants, or ancestors. In addition, you can tag a focus group or everyone in the file. You can untag everyone in the file.

(Help index: *Advanced tagging*)

**Show Search List** displays the most recent *Search List*.

**Show All Tagged** displays a list of all individuals tagged on the selected level.

**Show All Untagged** displays a list of all individuals not tagged on the selected level.

**Set Living** allows you to set the **Living** status to **Yes** or **No** for multiple individuals at one time.

(Help index: *Set living*)

**Set Bookmark** lets you set a bookmark on the highlighted name so you can quickly and easily return to it later.

**Go to Bookmark** returns to the bookmarked name at any time.

**Customize Display** lets you select the fields shown on the **Detail** tab.

(Help index: *Customize name list detail*)

**Zoom** zooms in and out, which changes the size of the lettering in the list. You can choose a font size or have Legacy size the font automatically.

## Jumping Into the List

If you are in name-order mode, jump to the first name beginning with any letter by clicking the letter buttons above the list. You can also jump to the beginning or end of the list by clicking **First** or **Last**.

## Tagging Records

You can tag or untag records using any of the three tag numbers for an individual by double-clicking the appropriate tag column to the right of each name in the list.

Legacy also offers some advanced options for tagging records. (See *Advanced Tagging* on page 110 for more information.)

**Note**:  If a tab caption is preceded by an asterisk (*), it means that there is information to view on that tab.  If all the fields on a tab are blank, there is no asterisk shown.

# The Marriage List

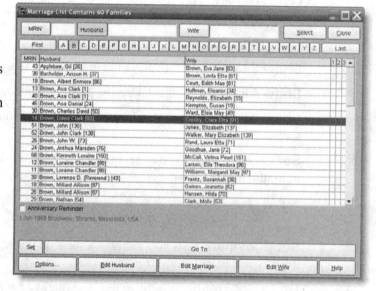

The *Marriage List* shows husband-wife combinations. If a person was married three times, there are three entries in the list. The *Marriage List* is displayed by clicking the **Marr List**

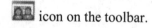 icon on the toolbar.

## Editing a Marriage

To edit the marriage information for a couple, highlight the names and click **Edit Marriage.** The *Marriage Information* window appears.

To edit either the husband's or wife's information, click **Edit Husband** or **Edit Wife** respectively. The *Individual's Information* window appears.

## Searching for a Husband or Wife

If the list is fairly long, you can search for either a husband's name or a wife's name by typing the name in either the **Husband** or **Wife** field, starting with the surname. As you type, the nearest matching name is displayed in the list. You can also search by marriage record ID number (MRIN) by typing the number into the **MRIN** box.

## Jumping Into the List

You can jump down into the list to names beginning with a certain letter by clicking the letter buttons above the list. This feature is available while the list is sorted by either the husband's or wife's name. If the list is sorted by MRIN, only the **First** and **Last** buttons are enabled.

## Selecting a Marriage

To select a marriage, either highlight the line and click **Select** or just double-click the line.

## Bookmarks

You can set a bookmark in the marriage list so that you can return quickly and easily to it later, by clicking **Set**. To return to the bookmark later, click **Go to**.

## Options

The following options are available by clicking **Options**:

**Sort by Given Name, Surname** changes the sort order of the Husband or Wife column and shows the given names before the surnames. When in this sort mode, this option changes to **Sort by Surname, Given Name** so that you can change back if desired.

**Print** displays the *Marriage Report Options* screen where you can print a *Marriage List* report.

**Remove Marriage Link** unlinks the husband and wife from each other and from any children.

**Untag All** lets you remove the marriage tags for any of the displayed tag numbers in the list.

**Zoom** zooms in and out, which changes the font size for the *Marriage List*.

# The Spouse List

The *Spouse List* shows all the spouses for the current individual along with the dates and locations of their marriages.

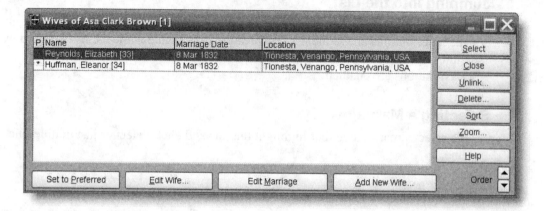

## Selecting a Spouse to Display

▶ **To change the currently displayed spouse:**
Highlight the desired spouse and click **Select**. You can also double-click on the desired spouse to select him or her.

## Changing the Sequence of Marriages

▶ **To change the order of the entries in the *Spouse List*:**
1. Highlight the line you want to move.

2. Click Up or Down ⬆⬇ in the lower-right corner of the window to move the line up or down in the list.

## Sorting the List

▶ **To sort the *Spouse List* by the marriage dates:**
Click **Sort**. All marriages with no marriage date are sorted to the beginning and the remainder are displayed in date order.

## Setting a Spouse to Preferred Status

A *preferred* spouse is the spouse that is automatically shown when that person's husband or wife is selected or displayed on the *Family View* or *Pedigree View* as you navigate through your ancestors and descendants. This avoids having to ask which spouse to display each time you change generations. The spouse that is currently set as *preferred* has an asterisk (*) in the **P** column of the *Spouse List*.

▶ **To move the *preferred* setting to a different spouse:**

Highlight the spouse you want to set as *preferred* and click **Set to Preferred** in the lower-left corner.

## Adding a New Spouse

▶ **To add a new spouse to the *Spouse List:***

1. Click **Add New Wife** (or **Add New Husband**) near the lower-right corner.
2. From the *Add* window, choose **Add a New Person**. The *Information* screen is displayed.
3. Fill in the new information and click **Save**.

## Linking to an Existing Spouse

▶ **To link the current individual as a spouse to another person in the family file:**

1. Click **Add New Wife** (or **Add New Husband**) near the bottom-right of the screen.
2. From the *Add* window, click **Link to an Existing Person**. The *Name List* appears.
3. Select an existing individual.

## Unlinking a Spouse

▶ **To remove the marriage link of the current individual from a spouse in the *Spouse List*:**

1. Highlight the spouse you want to unlink.
2. Click **Unlink** at the right side of the window. The *Unlink* window is displayed. This window shows the name of the current individual from whom the spouse will be unlinked, along with a list of any children who are currently linked to these two people. If you continue with the unlinking, the children will remain linked to the current individual but will be unlinked from the spouse.
3. If you are sure you want to unlink this spouse, click **Yes**. Otherwise, click **Cancel** to abort the command.

**Note:** Unlinking a spouse from a marriage does not delete the person from the family file. It just breaks the marriage tie. The unlinked person still shows up on the *Name List* and is available for linking to someone else.

## Deleting a Spouse

▶ **To delete a spouse from the *Spouse List*:**

1. Highlight the name of the spouse you want to delete.
2. Click **Delete** at the right of the window. The *Delete* window appears showing the names of those who will be affected by this deletion. These include the

parents of the person being removed (who will lose a child), the current individual who is the husband or wife of the person being deleted, and the children of the marriage (who will be losing a mother or father).

3. If you are sure you want to delete this person, click **Yes**. Otherwise, click **Cancel** to abort the deletion.

**Note:** When you delete an individual it totally removes that person from the family file and also removes any links between the individual and any other person in the file. Before completing this command, Legacy displays a window warning of the consequences and listing all the people from whom this individual will be unlinked. These include parents, spouses, and children. If you are sure that you want to continue, click **Yes**. If you want to abort the command, click **Cancel**.

# The Child List

The *Child List* shows all the children linked to the current parents. (To display the *Child List*, either choose **Child List** from the **View** menu, or right-click on any child's name in the list of children on the *Family* or *Pedigree Views*.)

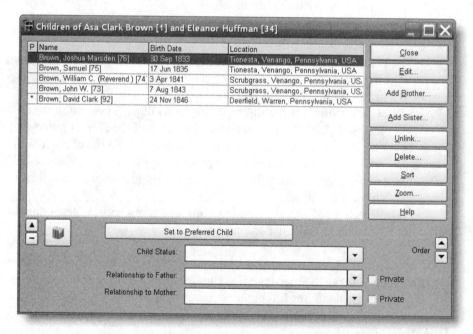

## Changing the Sequence of Children

The initial sequence of the children in the *Child List* is set by the order in which they were entered. If you want to change this order, highlight the child whose name you want to move, and then use the Up and Down ⬆⬇ arrows in the lower-right corner to move the name within the list.

## Setting a Child to Preferred Status

The *preferred* child is generally the child in your direct line and is indicated by an asterisk (*) in the **P** column of the list. Knowing who the *preferred* child is makes it much easier to move down your line from one descendant to the next. You can change the *preferred* child by highlighting the desired name and clicking **Set to Preferred Child** in the lower-left corner of the window. The asterisk in the left column of the list then moves to the new child's name.

## Sorting the List

If you would like to sort the list in ascending order by the birth dates of the children, click **Sort**.

## Child Status

You can tag each child with a special status if you like. Choose from Twin, Triplet, Stillborn, etc. You can also add new statuses. The default setting when a child is first added to the list is blank. To set a new status, highlight the child and then type the new status or click the **Down** ⬇ arrow on the **Child Status** field at the bottom and select the new status by clicking on it.

## Relationship to Father and Mother

The link between a child and his/her father and mother can be specified and sourced. Choose from such things as Biological, Adopted, Guardian, Sealed, Step, as well as a place to record Challenged and Disproved relationships. The default setting is blank, meaning Natural. To set a new status, highlight the child and then type the new status or click the **Down** ⬇ arrow on the **Relationship to Father** or **Relationship to Mother** fields at the bottom and select the new status by clicking on it. (These new fields are displayed on both Children List window as well as the Parents List window.)

## Private Relationships

You can mark the **Relationship to Father** or the **Relationship to Mother** as Private by putting a checkmark in the **Private** option to the right of the appropriate relationship status. The Private setting makes it possible to exclude these relationships on reports, web sites, and exports.

## Editing a Child's Information

You can edit the individual's information for any person in the list by highlighting the name and clicking **Edit**. The *Information* screen appears, where you can make changes.

## Adding a Brother or Sister to the List

You can add an additional brother or sister to the *Child List* by clicking either **Add Brother** or **Add Sister**. The *Add* window appears, where you can choose to **Add a NEW Person** or **Link to an EXISTING Person**.

## Unlinking a Child

▶ **To unlink a child from the list:**
   Highlight the name and click **Unlink**.

When you choose to unlink an individual from his or her parents, you are telling Legacy to break the tie that exists between that person and his or her parents and siblings (if any). Unlinking a person does not delete the individual from the family file. It simply disconnects him or her from having a child relationship to the current parents and a brother-sister relationship with any siblings.

Before completing the Unlink command, Legacy displays a window containing the name of the parents and a list of any siblings currently linked to the individual. You can then complete the unlinking by clicking **Yes**, or abort the command by clicking **Cancel**.

## Deleting a Child

▶ **To delete a child from the list:**
   Highlight the name and click **Delete**.

Deleting an individual totally removes that person from the family file and also removes any links between the individual and any other person in the file. Before completing this command, Legacy displays a window warning of the consequences, and lists all the people from whom this individual will be unlinked. These include parents, spouses, and children. If you are sure that you want to continue, click **Yes**. If you want to abort the command, click **Cancel**.

**Note:** Deleting a person can have several effects. The person will no longer be listed as a child of their current parents. The person will no longer be listed as a parent to children. Any children currently linked will no longer be connected to their grandparents. Before deleting a person, make sure it is what you really want to do.

Once a person is deleted, the only way to get that individual back is to re-enter a record from scratch.

# The Parents List

This is a list of all the names who are currently linked to an individual as parents. A person might have more than one set of parents if an adoptive family line is being tracked, for example.

### Setting Parents to Preferred Status

The *preferred* parents are shown in the list with an asterisk (*). These parents are shown on the *Family View* and *Pedigree View*.

▶ **To assign *preferred* status to other parents:**
1. Highlight the line by clicking on it.
2. Click **Select**. The window closes and the new preferred parents are displayed.

### Adding New or Additional Parents

You can also add a new set of parents by clicking **Add New Parents**. This adds a new set of "Unknown" parents to the list. Click **Add Father** and **Add Mother** to fill in their information. (See *How to Add > Additional Parents* in Legacy Help.) If you want to attach a set of parents who are already in the family file, click **Link to Existing**. The *Marriage List* appears, where you can select the couple to add.

### Unlinking a Set of Parents

▶ **To unlink a set of parents in the list:**
1. Highlight the line by clicking on it.
2. Click **Unlink From Child**. The *Unlink* box appears, showing the parents and siblings who will be unlinked by this action.
3. Click **OK** to confirm your intent.

### Zooming the Parents List

If you would like to have the font size in the *Parents List* made larger or smaller, click **Zoom**. The *List Font Size* window appears, where you can select a different font size. When you return, the list redisplays in the new size.

# Master Location List

The *Master Location List* contains all the location names that are being used in the current Family File. Legacy only records one copy of each different location and points any use of it to its entry in the list. This saves a lot of disk storage space by eliminating duplications.

To the right of the list of locations is the **People using this location** box. The box shows which individual in your family file are using the currently highlighted location.

Below the list of locations is a map of the current location. To see the map you must have Internet access and be online.

## Selecting a Location from the List

To select a particular location, click on it and click the **Select** button. You can also select a location by double clicking.

## Adding New Locations

When you enter a location in a Place field, Legacy checks to see if the name is already in the *Master Location List*. If it is not found, it is added to the list. Depending on the setting in *Options*, you may or may not be prompted for confirmation. When the *Master Location List* is displayed, you can add new locations by clicking the **Add** button below the list. This pops up a form where you can type in the name of the new location, a short name, notes and latitude and longitude coordinates, which is then added to the list.

(Help index: ***Adding or Editing Master Locations***)

## Editing Locations

You can change the spelling of any location in the *Master Location List* by selecting it and clicking the **Edit** button. Remember, however, that a change to a location in the master list affects all references to it.

## Tagging Locations

You can tag locations so that you can filter the *Location Report* to a certain subset. To tag a location, click the checkbox in the **Tag** column to the right of the desired location name.

(Help index: ***Location Report***)

## Verifying Locations (Deluxe Edition only)

From time to time you need to do some cleanup on your *Master Location List*. This includes combining locations that are really the same, getting rid of locations that are no longer used, things like that.  Sometimes you will run across various locations that appear to be in conflict with each other.  For example, **New Barbadoes, Essex, New Jersey** and **New Barbadoes, Bergen, New Jersey**.  Which one is right?  Well, after doing a little research you find that they are both correct.  New Barbadoes was in Essex County from 1693 to 1710 and was then transferred to Bergen County (and even later became the city of Hackensack).  You want to keep them both but somehow you need a way to mark them as such.  This is where the **Verified** tag comes in.  Simply click on the checkbox column to mark them as verified, thus indicating to you later that they are "keepers." (You can also put a comment in the **Notes** fields, describing this.)

# Notes

If you have added a note to a location (by using the **Edit** feature), an **X** shows in the **N** column in the list.

# Other Options

Clicking the **Options** button displays a shortcut menu where you can choose from the following options:

### Deleting a Location

If a location in the master list is not being used, you can remove it from the list by highlighting it and then choosing the **Delete** option.  Legacy confirms that the location is not being used and removes it from the list.  If one or more records are referencing the location, it cannot be removed. In this case, Legacy offers to display a list of all records currently using the name.

### Tag and Untag

You can tag **All Records** in your location list or just the **Highlighted Records**.  (You can highlight more then one location in the list by holding down the Ctrl key while you click the locations.)

### Combining Duplicate Locations

When correcting misspelled place names, you may find that you end up with duplicates within the *Master Location List*.  To remove these duplicates and clean up the list, choose the **Combine** option.  Legacy then goes through the list, combines the duplicates and moves the links.

### Purging Unused Locations

To remove unused locations from the *Master Location List*, choose the **Purge** option. Legacy checks each name to see if it is being used.  If not, it is removed from the list.

## Importing a Locations List

You can import a list of locations from a different Family File by choosing the **Import** option. Legacy prompts for the name of the other Family File and then loads its list. (If you end up having duplicate master locations that only differ by format, you should combine them together. See Combining Multiple Locations below in this topic.)

## Printing the List or the Map

You can print the contents of the list in two different formats by clicking **Print...** Choosing **Location List** from the submenu prints a simple report listing the locations in the current sort order. Choosing **Location Report** opens the *Location Report* options screen where you can print a report showing who uses each location and where they use them. Choosing **Virtual Earth Map...** prints the map for the current location. (See **Mapping My Places** on page 98 for more information.)

## Page Setup

You can change page orientation, margins, paper size, and font size before printing a report.

## Zoom

You can change the font size of the master list grid.

## Options for Non-Locations

If you have entries in your list that are not actual places but are valuable information that you would like to keep, you can move these entries into the Notes fields of the individuals and marriages that use them.

(Help index: *Moving Non-Locations Out of the Location List*)

## Jump with Edit Sorting

When you edit a location name, it is immediately resorted into its new position in the *Master Location List*. Sometimes this moves the edited location far away from the current position. You can choose to have the current position move to the new point in the list or to just stay where you were and move to the next location name. If there is a checkmark next to the **Jump with Edit Sorting** option, the current position will move to the next location name after the newly sorted position of the edit name. If there is no checkmark next to the option in the shortcut menu, the current position will just move down to the next location. Clicking the option toggles the checkmark on and off.

## Bookmarks

If you are working your way down the *Master Location List* cleaning it up by combining variations of the same location name, correcting comma locations, etc., you can drop a bookmark to save your place until you return to resume the process. Click **Set Bookmark** to drop a bookmark. Click **Go To Bookmark** to return to the previously set bookmark.

## Contract/Expand Location Parts

Legacy can automatically expand and contract state, province, and country names within your master locations.

(Help index: *Contract/Expand Location Parts*)

# Who is Using This Location

The list to the right of the locations shows a list of all the individuals who are using the current location. As you highlight each name in the list, you can see which events use the current location. These are shown below the list, under the Edit button.

### Editing a Person in the List

To edit a person in the list, click the Edit button to diplay their Information screen.

### Options

Click the **Options** button for the following commands:

### Create Search List

You can create a new search list of names (replacing whatever is in the current search list) or add the names to the current search list.

### Print the List

You can print a report list showing the names that use the current location.

### Tag or Untag All the Records in the List

If you have just the records in the list tagged on a certain number, you can quickly jump to each of them by clicking the right or left tag arrow on the *Family/Pedigree View*. You can then edit each record and remove or change the list reference.

**To tag the records in the list:**

1. Select the tag # you want to use by using the UP and DOWN arrows. To make sure all the other records in the Family File are untagged first, click the **UnTag Everyone in File** button.
2. To tag all the entries in the list, click **Tag Everyone in List**.
3. Click **Close**.

Now, when you return to the *Family/Pedigree View*, you can rotate through all the tagged records and make the needed changes.

(Help index: ***Tagging Records***)

# Adding a Picture to a Location

Click the **Picture** ![Picture icon] icon to add pictures, sounds and video clips to the event.

# Deleting a Location

You cannot easily remove a location from the master list if it is being used by one or more individuals or marriages. If you are sure you want to delete a location, you will have to remove the references to it shown in the list of individual who are using the location.

# Sorting the List

You can display the *Locations List* in different sorted orders for the purpose of finding duplicate entries by clicking the **Sort** button.

(Help index: ***Sort Location List***)

# Combining Multiple Locations

Often, through entering information and by importing records from other people you will end up with two or more variations of the same location, spelled a little bit differently. For example, you might end up with:

Pompton Pl., Morris, NJ
Pompton Plains, Morris, NJ
Pompton Plains, Morris Co., NJ
Pompton Plains, Morris, New Jersey
Pompton Plains, Morris, New Jersey, USA

All of these locations are obviously the same place and should be combined into just one, "good", location name. This is very easy to do in Legacy. To combine multiple locations:

1. Choose one of the locations that you want to keep. If it isn't exactly like you want it formatted, use the **Edit** button to fix it. This is now your "good" location name.
2. Highlight all the other locations in the group. If the group is contiguous, you can highlight the top location and then hold down the **shift** key while you click on the bottom location. The entire group will then be highlighted. If the various locations are not in a continuous block, highlight the first one and then press and hold down the **Ctrl** key while to click on each of the other locations in the group. Each one will remain highlighted as you click the others.
3. Click the **Combine** button at the bottom of the list. The caption on the button will now change to read **Combine With**.
4. Highlight the "good" location line by clicking on it.
5. Click the **Combine With** button at the bottom. All the "bad" locations are then combined with the "good" one and all the records in your family file that were pointing to the "bad" ones now point to the "good" one... (saving you potentially hours of editing).

# Distance and Bearing Calculator

If you have the **Deluxe Edition** of Legacy you have access to the *Distance and Bearing Calculator*. Using this calculator you can figure the distance between any two cities in your family file that have latitude and longitude coordinates. To do this, you can highlight the two cities (click on the first city to highlight it and then find the second city and hold down the **Ctrl** key while you click on it. This will leave both cities highlighted) and then click the [button] button and choose **Distance and Bearing Calculator**. You can also figure the direction to travel to get from one to the other.

(Help index: *Distance and Bearing Calculator*)

The *Master Locations List* is reached by clicking the **down arrow** next to any location field. It can also be displayed by choosing **Master Lists / Locations** from the **View** menu.

# Mapping My Places

When all the locations where a family lived and worked are plotted on a map together, you can easily see the overall area in which the family spent their lives. You can visualize how the family members migrated from place to place as they grew older. (Or you can see if they stayed in one place their entire lives.) New research opportunities come to light as you see the surrounding cities, counties, provinces, and countries.

With Legacy Mapping you can see an overall view of a family's territory spanning the entire earth if necessary. You can also zoom right into the street level of anywhere in any country in the world.

There are two places in Legacy where mapping is available, the *Master Location List* and the *Map of Places* for an individual.

**Note**: An active Internet connection is required in order to use the mapping feature in Legacy. If you are not online, the maps will not be displayed. Virtual Earth also requires that you are using Internet Explorer, version 7.

# Master Location Mapping

Whenever the *Master Location List* screen is displayed, the current location in the list is shown on a map in the lower half of the window. (Unless you have the **Show Map** option unchecked or you are not connected to the Internet.) As you highlight locations in the list, the map is drawn for that place. If the location has an **X** in the **L** column (which stands for Latitude/Longitude) the map is drawn for the coordinates in the latitude and longitude fields for that location. If there is no **X**, Legacy submits the place name to *Virtual Earth*[TM] over the Internet where it is matched with a location in its worldwide database. The resulting latitude and longitude coordinates are then recorded in Legacy for future use. Sometimes an acceptable close match in *Virtual Earth* cannot be found for a place name. In this case, a small window is displayed with two or more location names to choose from. For example, Peone Prairie, Spokane, Washington results in the following five possibilities:

If you find one that is acceptable, click on it. If none of the choices are correct, click the close button in the upper-right corner.

If no possibilities are found by *Virtual Earth*, which is rare, a message is shown telling you that you will have to use other tools to figure out the real location name.

---

**Location Not Found**                                                    close

**Dixville, Morrison, Minnesota, USA**
Virtual Earth could not find a match for this location. Please check your spelling. You may have to edit your location to complete the name including country. You could also try clicking the globe icon above and looking for the location in the Geo Location List.

---

Since *Virtual Earth* only looks for current locations, a historically accurate place name that no longer exists may trigger a Place Not Found message.

*Virtual Earth* is even smart enough to find US Zip Code locations. If you only know a person's Zip Code, enter it into a master location. The map will display the location. Once this is done, you can change the zip code location to the actual city name found.

Sometimes *Virtual Earth* returns some really ridiculous possibilities as it tries to find a place name match. Look them over carefully before accepting one.

# Geo-coding Your Locations

Geo-coding is a process that runs through all your locations and tries to find a match in the Virtual Earth location database. Upon finding a match, the latitude and longitude coordinates are then recorded in Legacy. As you highlight any location in your *Master Location List*, this geo-coding is automatically attempted. You can have Legacy run through all of your locations automatically geo-coding what it can by clicking the **Geo-Code** button and then choosing **Geo-code all unresolved locations through Virtual Earth**. As each location is resolved, an **X** is shown in the **L** column. At the end of the process, any location without an **X** will have to be looked at so see if you can figure out where they refer to.

If you would like to redo the geo-coding for a specific location, highlight the place name, click the **Geo-Code** button and then choose **Geo-code current location again through Virtual Earth**.

# Working With the Maps

Here is a typical map, in this case showing Paris, France:

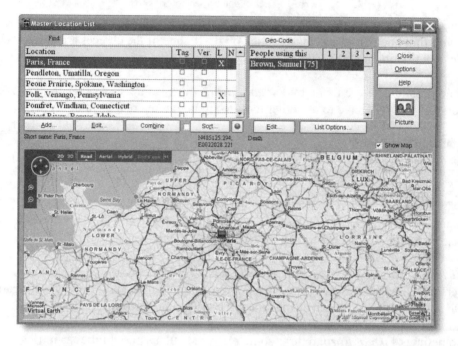

Notice the 📌 pushpin on the map at the location. The map only shows the current location. If you hover the mouse over the pin, the location name is displayed in a popup.

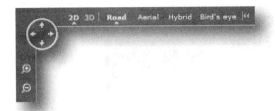

In the upper-left corner of the map is the *View Control*. The *View Control* lets you zoom in and out, pan the map up and down and sideways, switch from **Road** (drawn map) to **Aerial** (satellite view) to **Hybrid** (a combination of **Road** and **Aerial**) and **Bird's eye** (an angled airplane view).

You can hide the *View Control* by clicking the button at the upper-right corner. To display the *View Control* again, click .

If you double-click anywhere on the map, the point where you clicked will move to the center of the map and the map will zoom in one setting. You can also drag the map in any direction with the mouse.

The 2D view is a rendered (drawn) view.

The 3D view of the map starts with a globe of the world and then allows you to zoom in, tilt, and twist it to add perspective. New York City, New York looks like this:

When you zoom in a ways, it looks like this:

You can then use the tilt buttons, ⬚ and ⬚, to change the perspective:

In some parts of some countries, major buildings are rendered in three dimensions. If you zoom into New York City, you can see some of them. Here is a 3D Road view:

While in 3D view, if you also change to Aerial view, the buildings and landscape become almost real:

There may not be large, major buildings where your ancestors lived, but it might be fun to look and see.

# Printing a Map

If you would like to print the map, click the **Options** button near the upper-right corner of the window and choose **Print > Virtual Earth Map** from the submenu. If you would like to print the map in landscape mode, click **Preferences** from the Print dialog box and change the **Orientation** to **Landscape** and then click **OK**. Click **Print** to send the map to your printer.

# How to Make a Graphic File From the Map

If you would like to save the map as a graphic file that can be attached to a person, event, location, source, etc., you can use any good screen capture program, or you can use the following steps:

1. Create the map as you would like to see it. You can zoom in or out and pan from side to side to get the map positioned correctly.
2. Click the ▌« button to close up the View Control in the upper-left corner of the map.
3. Capture the Master Location Screen, including the map, by pressing **Alt-PrtScn**. This puts a copy of the current window on the Windows Clipboard. (If you have an **F Lock** key on your keyboard, make sure it is turned off before pressing **Alt-PrtScn**.)
4. Open the Microsoft Paint program.
5. Paste the screen capture by pressing **Ctrl-V**.
6. Drag the map portion of the window up into the upper-left corner of the Paint window.
7. Click on the Pencil ⟦✎⟧ tool and then drag the bottom-right corner handle up to the lower-right corner of the map portion, thus clipping off everything but the map. The map should now be the only thing showing in the Paint window.
8. Choose **File > Save As...**
9. From the Save As screen, navigate to where you want to save the map file, enter a file name for the map, choose a **Save as type** (JPEG format is generally good enough for a map, although Bitmap is sharper – and ten times bigger) and then click **Save**.
10. The map picture file can now be attached to any appropriate item in Legacy.

# Event / Repository Addresses

The *Event Address* and *Repository Address* screens provide researchers a place to record addresses where key events took place (for example a church) or where important records are located (for example an archive or library). The *Event Address* and *Repository Address* screens look and behave like the *Mailing Address* screen, except that they do not build a name and do not have *Mailing List* options.

▶ **To open an event address:**

1. Click the ⊞ button to the right of a birth, christening, death, or burial event on a person's *Information* screen and then choose the **Address** option from the popup menu. The *Event Address* window appears. It can also be reached by clicking the

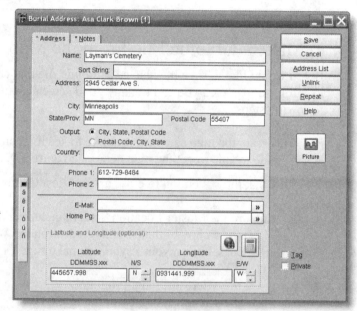

**Address** 🏠 icon in the *Add* or *Edit Event* window for an individual. In addition, the screen can be opened by selecting **Master Lists > Address Lists** from the **View** menu, then choosing **Event**.

2. Select an address from the *Master Event Address List*.

▶ **To open a repository address:**

1. Select **View > Master Lists > Address Lists > Repository**. The *Master Repository List* appears.
2. Select an address.

You can enter a name, address, and up to two phone numbers for each event or repository address. You can also include e-mail and Internet addresses, plus latitude and longitude, notes, and pictures.

▶ **To add a repository address:**

1. Click **Add** on the *Master Repository List* window.
2. Fill in the address, phone number(s), e-mail address, and Internet address.
3. Click the 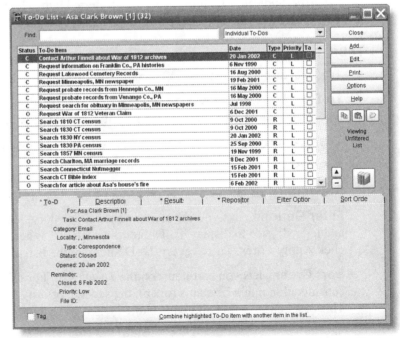 button at the right of e-mail and Internet addresses to send a message or connect to the Internet without leaving Legacy.
4. You can include the latitude, longitude, and notes about the address.
5. When you are finished, click **Save**.

### Other Address Options

**Save**   saves the address.

**Cancel**   closes the window without saving any entries or changes.

**Address List**   opens the *Master Mailing, Event, or Repository Address* lists.

**Delete**   removes an address from an individual or event.

**Repeat**   repeats the entry made in the same field of the last address you entered during the current session. If the current field already contains an entry that would be overwritten by the **Repeat** option, Legacy asks for permission before replacing it. You can also use **F8** to repeat a field. Clicking on the line labels also repeats the entries. Clicking the **Address** label repeats both address lines. Clicking on any other box label repeats just that line (including the "Name" label). You can repeat an entire address by right-clicking **Repeat**.

**Help**   opens Legacy Help.

**Picture** opens the *Picture Gallery,* where pictures can be added.

## The To-Do List

The *To-Do List* makes it easy to track research and other tasks that need to be done. Legacy allows you to create *General* and *Individual* To-Do Lists. For example, you can create a General *To-Do*

*List* of books and microfilm to search when visiting a library; or create an Individual *To-Do List* for your great grandfather by listing your need to find his obituary, his World War I service record, and his birth certificate. *To-Do Lists* can be printed out for research trips or used as research logs to be placed with your transcriptions, photocopies, and correspondence.

**Find**   Type the first few letters of a To-Do Item name to jump to it in the list.

**To-Do Type**   By default, **General To-Do Lists** display when opening the *To-Do List* from the toolbar or from the **View** menu. By default, **Individual To-Do Lists** display when opening the *To-Do List* from an *Individual's Information* screen, the **Husband** or **Wife** box in the *Family View*, or when the primary individual is selected in *Pedigree View*. To select the type of To-Do item you want to view, click the **Down** ▼ arrow (to the left of the **Close** button) and choose from the list.

## The To-Do Item List

**Status**   indicates whether the task has been completed or not (**O** = Open, **C** = Closed).
**To-Do Item**   is the name of the task.
**Date**   is the opening date of the task.
**Type**   is the type of task (**R** = Research, **C** = Correspondence, **O** = Other).
**Priority**   indicates the importance of the item: High, Medium, or Low.
**Tag**   indicates whether the To-Do items has been tagged for printing.

## Tabs

Tabs that display an asterisk (*) contain information.

**To-Do**   shows who or what the highlighted item is for, as well as the task name, task type, status, open date, closed date, priority, and filing reference number.

**Task Description**   is the detailed description of the task to be done.

**Results**   shows the outcome of the task.

**Repository**   is the location or repository to visit or contact to accomplish a task.

**Filter Options**   lets you choose the criteria (category, locality, status, type, priority, and tagged) used to display To-Do items on the list. When your selection is complete, click **Apply Filter**. To see every To-Do item on the list, click **Show All**.

**Sort Order**   lets you sort items on the *To-Do List*. For example, the primary consideration might be status (open), the second, priority, and the third, open date. This order ensures that all items marked Open go to the top of the list, sorted by priority, then date. After selecting the three sort levels, click **Apply** for your choices to take effect.

## Buttons

**Close**  exits the window.

**Add**  adds a new To-Do item.

**Edit**  allows you to edit a highlight item on the list.

**Print**  prints a *To-Do List*.

**Options**  gives you a choice to **Delete, Combine Duplicates, Import, Tag, Untag,** and **Zoom**.

**Combine Highlighted To-Do Item to Another To-Do Item in the List**
allows you to select a To-Do item on the list that you want to combine with another item. Click this button and the button face changes to **Highlight Destination To-Do Item. Then Click This Button**.

## Sources of Information

To attach a source to the to-do item, click the **Sources**  icon. (See *Citing Your Sources* on page 53 for more information.)

## Source Clipboard

The *Source Clipboard* is a feature in Legacy that can tremendously increase the efficiency with which you document the sources of the information you enter into your family file. (See *Source Clipboard* on page 69 for information on how and why to use this feature.)

(Help index: *Source clipboard*)

## To-Do Clipboard (*Deluxe Edition* only)

You can copy To-Do items to the clipboard and then paste them again where desired.

▶ **To copy a To-Do item to the clipboard:**
  1.  Highlight the item you want to copy.

  2.  Click the 🗒 button.

▶ **To paste an item from the clipboard to a list:**
  1.  Open the To-Do list you want to add the item to.

2. Click the 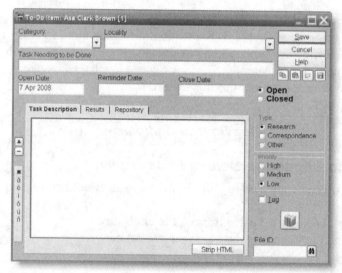 button.

▶ **To load a clipboard item previously saved:**

1. Click the button.

## Tag Checkbox

The *To-Do List* contains a **Tag** column. You can tag a To-Do item by clicking its checkbox, or by highlighting the item and selecting the checkbox in the lower-left corner of the window.

## Creating a New To-Do Item

▶ **To create a To-Do item:**

1. To create a general To-Do item, click the **To-Do** icon on the toolbar or select **To-Do List** from the **View** menu.
   Or

   To create an individual To-Do item, click the **To-Do** icon associated with the individual in *Family View* or *Pedigree View*, or open the *Information* screen and click the **To-Do** icon.

2. In the *To-Do List* window, click **Add** to create a new To-Do item.

3. In the *To-Do Item* window, select a category for the task in the **Category** field.
4. Enter the locality of the task in the **Locality** field.
5. Enter a task name in the **Task Needing to be Done** field.

6. Note that the **Open Date** defaults to the current date and the **Status** defaults to Open when adding a new item.
7. If you want to be reminded of this To-Do item on the Legacy Home tab, enter a reminder date. The reminder will start showing on the Home tab when the advanced reminder time arrives.
8. If the task involves visiting or writing to a specific place, click **Add** on the **Repository** tab to enter it on the *Master Repository List*. Type the name, address, phone number(s), plus e-mail and Internet addresses. If the location is already on the list, click **Select** and choose it from the *Master Repository List*.
9. Indicate the Type of task to be done by selecting **Research**, **Correspondence**, or **Other**.
10. Indicate the Priority of the task by selecting **High**, **Medium**, or **Low**.
11. Click the **Task Description** tab to enter a brief explanation of the task.
12. Click the **Results** tab to enter a summary of the results.
13. Click **Save** when finished.

### Editing an Item

▶ **To edit a To-Do item:**
1. From the *To-Do List* screen, highlight the To-Do item to be edited.
2. Click **Edit** to modify the selected item.
3. Edit the To-Do item.
4. Click **Save** when done.

# Tagging Records

You can tag individuals and marriages to mark them for various reasons. For example, you might want to tag some people to be included in a report, or tag some individuals whom you are currently researching so you can find them quickly when you get more information. There are nine tag numbers you can use for each individual and for each marriage. (If you are using the *Standard Edition*, only three are available.) This allows you to use different tag numbers for different purposes. Perhaps you want to export all #3 tagged individuals, print an ancestry report for all #2 tagged people, and use #1 tags for names you are currently working on.

To tag an individual, click the desired tag number in either the *Husband* or *Wife* box. To tag a marriage, click the desired tag on the *Marriage* bar.

When an individual or marriage is tagged, the tag box is filled with a color other than gray (blue for #1, red for #2 and black for #3, etc.). When it is untagged, it is filled with gray. (You can set the tag colors in the *Customize* section.)

# Advanced Tagging

The *Advanced Tagging* window is used to quickly tag or untag families and other larger groups of related people. Entire ancestral or descendancy lines can be tagged (or untagged) with the click of a button. This window is activated by right-clicking one of the three **tag** boxes. The *Advanced Tagging* window appears.

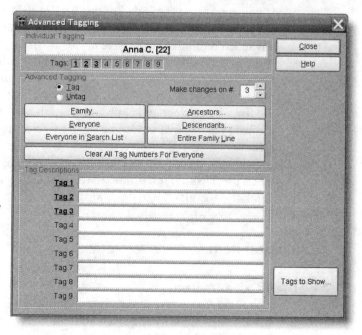

The person whose name appears in the box at the top is considered the current individual. All tagging actions (listed below) are done with this individual in mind. If you want to change to a different person, close the window, navigate to the new person, and then right-click on the **Tag** box again.

The Tag number (1 through 9) boxes under the name show the current status of each of the nine tags (three in the *Standard Edition*). You can tag or untag any of these by clicking on them.

## Tagging or Untagging

Select either **Tag** or **Untag** to specify the type of action you want to accomplish. All further actions will follow this command.

## Tag Number

Use the Up and Down ⬍ arrows to the right of **Make changes on #** to select the tag number to work with. All further actions will affect this number.

## Tagging an Individual

To tag (or untag) a specific individual, select (or clear) the desired **Tag** boxes under the name box. You generally don't come in here just to tag an individual. It is much easier just to click their **Tag** box on the *Family View* or *Pedigree View*, but the option is included here just in case.

## Tagging a Family

A family is considered to be the selected individual and his or her spouse(s) and all the children from the individual and his or her spouse(s). To tag (or untag) a family, click **Family**. The *Spouse List* for the current individual appears.

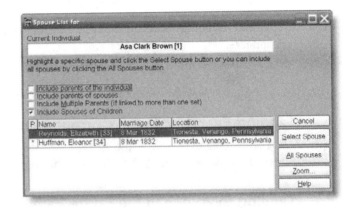

If the individual has more than one spouse, you can select one of them or all of them by clicking the appropriate button on the right side.

You can also use the four checkboxes above the spouse list to expand the scope of the family. You can include:

- The parents of the current individual.
- The parents of the selected spouses.
- Multiple parents, if any.
- The spouses of the children.

## Tagging a Person's Ancestors

You can tag (or untag) all the direct-line ancestors of the selected individual for a specific number of generations and even include the descendants of those ancestors if you want to include an entire branch of a family.

To tag (or untag) ancestors, click **Ancestors**. The *Ancestor Options* window appears.

(Help index: ***Tag:Ancestors***)

## Tagging Everyone in the Entire Family File

You can tag (or untag) every person in the entire family file by clicking **Everyone**.

## Tagging a Person's Descendants

A person's descendants include the individual's children from every marriage, their children from all of their marriages, and so on.

To tag (or untag) descendants, click **Descendants**. The *Descendants Options* window appears.

(Help index: *Tag:Descendants*)

## Tagging Everyone in the Current Search List

You can tag everyone in the current search list by clicking **Everyone in Search List**. (If there is no current search list, this button is disabled.)

## Tagging Everyone in the Entire Family Line

You can tag (or untag) everyone connected to the current person by clicking **Entire Family Line**. This means all of the individual's ancestors and descendants. It also includes all the descendants of the ancestors, ancestors of the descendants, and all their spouses. Everybody linked in any way to the starting individual is included. This is a great way to separate one line from another in a family file.

## Clear All Tags on All Numbers, For Everyone

You can clear all tags on all tag numbers for everyone in the entire family file, by clicking **Clear All Tags, All #s, For Everybody**. This is a good thing to do before tagging individuals and lines using different criteria.

## Naming the Tags

You can enter a description in the **Tag Level Descriptions** fields for each of the nine tag numbers to remind you what they are being used for. These descriptions are optional and for your own information.

## Selecting the Tag Numbers for the *Family View* and *Pedigree View*

The *Family View* and *Pedigree View* show only three of the available nine tag numbers for the current individuals (only three are available in the *Standard Edition*). You can choose which three tag numbers to show by clicking on **Tag #'s to Show** in the lower-right corner. This brings up the *Select Tags to Show* screen where you can select the desired tag numbers by choosing them from the drop-down lists.

# Chapter 6

# *Creating and Printing Reports*

## What Goes In Can Come Out

There are several different report formats available within Legacy. They are accessed by clicking the **Reports** icon on the toolbar or by selecting the **Reports** menu.

## Select a Report

Click the **Reports** icon to open the *Select a Report* window. In this window are eight tabs, each representing a different report. Illustration of the *Family Group Records* report is shown as an example for all of the screens.

This screen is representative of the other available screens which can be selected by clicking on each respective tab at the top of the window.

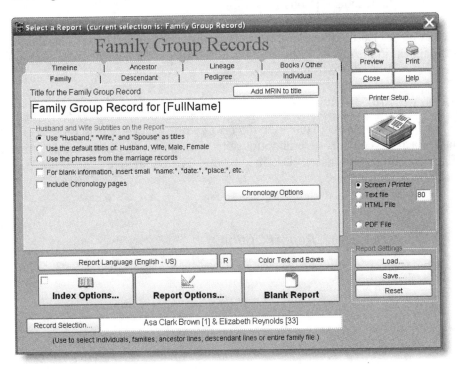

## Report Language

For many of the reports in Legacy, you can choose from different languages when generating them. For example, you might want to produce a Family Group Record in German to send to a cousin there. To select a language, click the **Report Language** button and choose the language file to be used when generating the report. There are many language files available. These can be found on the www.LegacyFamilyTree.com web site. To reset the language selection back to the default value, click the **Reset** button.

## Color Text and Boxes

When printing reports that included boxed information, you can select from three different coloring styles (or none at all). Color all text and boxes the same, male/female color, or 4-line color.

## Options

Some screens have a **Report Options** button. There are also **Index Options** from which you can choose index style, number of columns, and border lines. A Location index is also available. (See *Index Options* on page 119 for a complete description of all the available index options.)

Selecting or clearing the appropriate checkboxes and option buttons establishes what will appear in the report. If an option is not available for a particular report, the check box or option button will be disabled.

## Report Options

Click **Report Options** to open the *Report Options* window where there are eight tabs. Each tab contains several options that you can use to customize the printout. Each tab and its options are described below. For a complete explanation of what each option means see:

(Help index: ***Report Options***)

# Include Tab

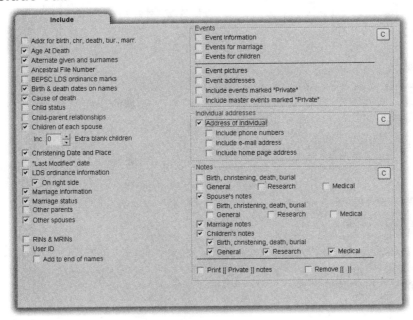

# Format Tab

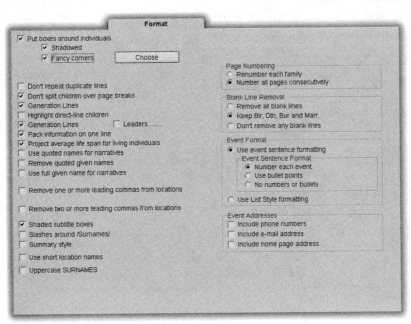

# Privacy Tab

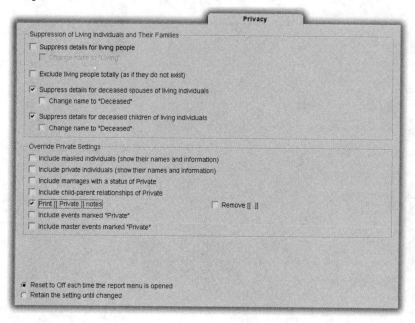

# Sources Tab

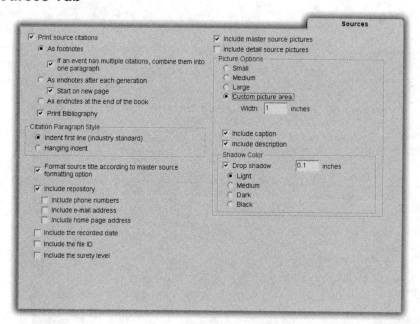

## Pictures Tab

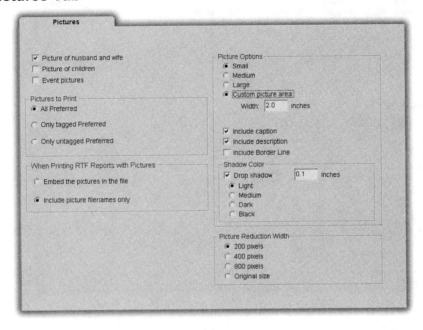

## Page Setup Tab

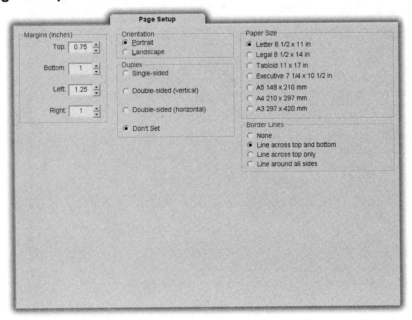

## Header/Footer Tab

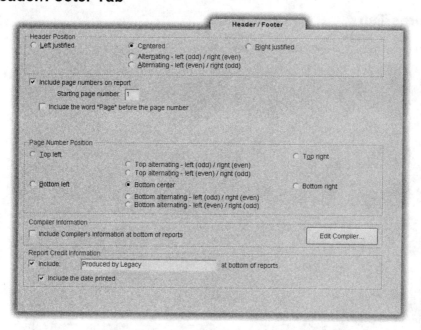

## Fonts Tab

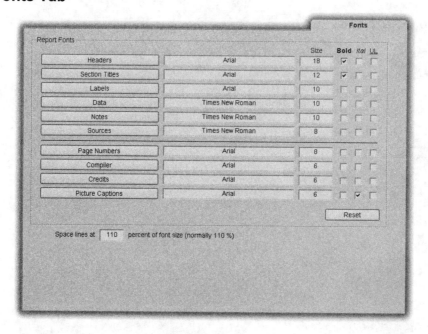

## Index Options

### Name Index

**Birth & Death Years on Names** includes birth and death years in parentheses after names.

**Include Alternate Names** to include each individual's alternate names in the report index, select this option. The alternate names are shown with a leading tilde character (~).

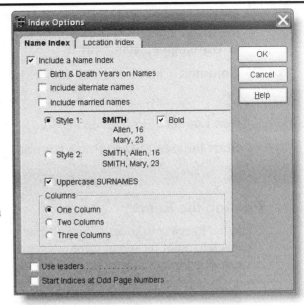

**Include married names** to include the married names of the individuals in the name index. (Married names are entered on the Marriage Information screen, either manually or automatically, depending on the married name rule setting.)

**Style 1** shows each surname only once in the index, with associated given names arranged under it.

**Style 2** shows each individual by surname and given name in the index.

**Uppercase SURNAMES** formats surnames in uppercase.

**Columns** chooses one, two, or three index columns per page.

### Location Index

**Include a Location Index** adds a Location Index after the regular index.

**Include Latitude and Longitude** includes these values in the index entries.

**Include Notes** includes the location notes (if any) along with the index entries.

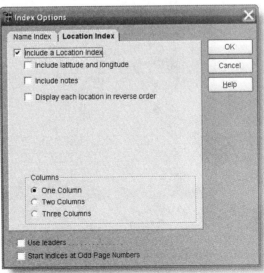

**Display each location in reverse order**   causes the locations to be printed from the largest jurisdiction to the smallest.  **Seattle, King, Washington** would be printed as **Washington, King, Seattle**.

**Columns**  Choose one, two or three index columns per page.

**Use Leaders**  adds leaders (. . . . . . .) between the name and its page number(s).

**Start Indices at Odd Page Number**   starts an index on an odd page number.

## Printing the Report

Click **Preview** to generate and display the report on the screen. This step should be taken to proof the report prior to printing, as it can keep you from wasting paper and can help you save time.

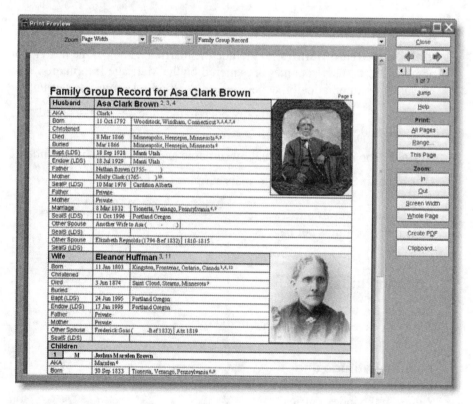

For complete information about previewing reports, see the Legacy Help system and search the index for: ***Print Preview***

# Individual Report

The *Individual* tab is used to build a report on all items related to the personal information of the person. These items include names, dates, event information, parents, children, notes, pictures, etc. Select the items you want to include in the report.

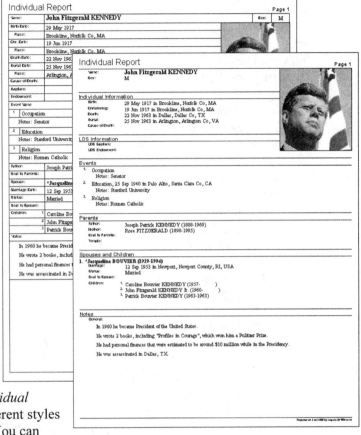

There are many options that can be set on the *Individual Report*, including two different styles (Regular and Summary). You can also print a blank *Individual Report* form by clicking the **Blank Report** button.

# Ancestor Chart

The *Ancestor* tab is used to create a report listing the ancestors for any given individual selected from the family file. Birth dates, RINs, generation-level numbers, and the number of generations to show are controlled here.

▶ **To create an Ancestor chart:**

1. From the *Family View* or *Pedigree View*, highlight the person you wish to begin with.
2. Click the **Reports**  icon to display the *Select a Report* screen.
3. Click on the **Ancestor** tab.
4. Set the desired options.
5. Click **Preview** to view the report on the screen before printing, or click **Print** to send the report directly to the printer.

(Help index: ***Ancestor reports***)

# Descendant Chart

The *Descendant* chart is very much like the **Ancestor** chart but the design of the page is different. In this report, the individual is placed at the top of the page and each successive generation is indented to the right. All members of each family are listed.

▶ **To create a Descendant chart:**

1. From the *Family View* or *Pedigree View*, highlight the person you wish to begin with.

2. Click the **Reports**  icon to display the *Select a Report* screen.

3. Click on the **Descendant** tab.

4. Set the desired options.

5. Click **Preview** to view the report on the screen before printing, or click **Print** to send the report directly to the printer.

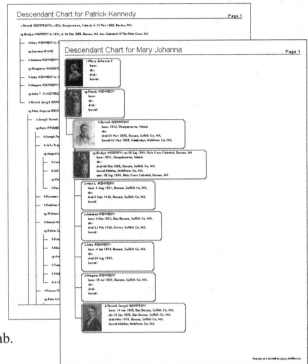

(Help index: ***Descendant chart***)

# Family Group Records

The *Family Group Record* report provides information about a particular family and includes excellent detail concerning the parents and their children.

▶ **To create a Family Group Record:**

1. Highlight the Husband or Wife on either the *Family View* or *Pedigree View*.

2. Click the **Reports** icon to display the *Select a Report* screen.

3. Click on the **Family** tab.

4. Set the desired options.

5. Click **Preview** to view the report on the screen before printing, or click **Print** to send the report directly to the printer.

(Help index: **Family group records**)

There are many options that can be selected when printing a Family Group Record. You can also print blank Family Group Records by clicking **Blank Report**.

# Pedigree Chart

A *Pedigree Chart* includes an individual and his or her direct ancestors (parents, grandparents, great grandparents, etc.).

▶ **To create a Pedigree Chart:**

1. Click the **Reports**  icon on the toolbar. When the *Select a Report* screen is displayed, click the **Pedigree** tab.
2. Set the desired options.
3. Click either **Print** or **Preview** to view the report.

(Help index: ***Pedigree charts***)

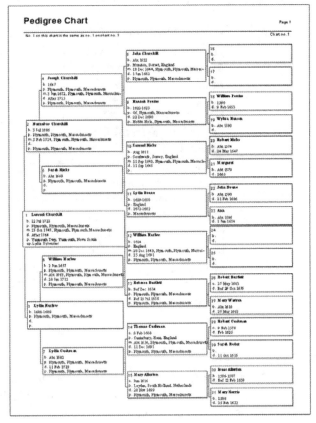

There are many options that can be selected when printing a Pedigree Chart. You can also print blank *Pedigree Charts* by clicking **Blank Report**.

# Timeline Report

The *Timeline* Report is designed to show an overview of dates and people in the family file.

▶ **To create a Timeline report:**
1. Highlight the person you want to start with on either the *Family View* or *Pedigree View*.

2. Click the **Reports**  icon to display the *Select a Report* screen.
3. Click on the **Timeline** tab.
4. Set the desired options.
5. Click **Preview** to view the report on the screen before printing, or click **Print** to send the report directly to the printer.

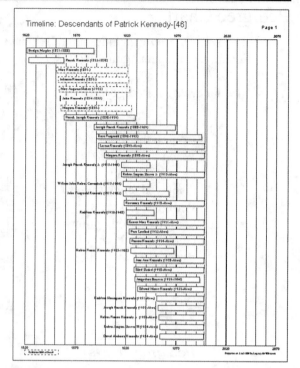

(Help index: *Timeline reports*)

Dotted lines forming the boxes on the *Timeline* report are placed around the name when there is an *estimated* birth or death. Legacy estimates the birth or death if one or the other date is missing in the individual's data. The default number of years is 70. The number of years printed across the page and the average life span can be changed. If the individual's name is longer than the life box (as determined by the birth date and death date), the name is placed to the right or left of the box.

# Lineage Report

The *Lineage* Report is a very simple report showing the direct ancestry line from the selected individual along with the siblings.

▶ **To create a Lineage report:**

1. Highlight the person you want to start with on either the *Family View* or *Pedigree View*.

2. Click the

   **Reports**  icon to display the *Select a Report* screen.

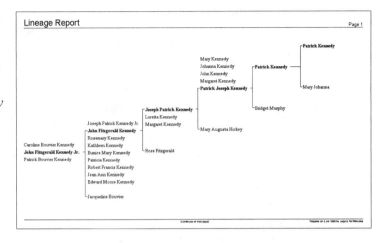

3. Click on the **Lineage** tab.
4. Set the desired options.
5. Click **Preview** to view the report on the screen before printing, or click **Print** to send the report directly to the printer.

(Help index: ***Lineage reports***)

# Chronology Report (Deluxe Edition only)

The **Chronology Report** is produced from the *Chronology View* screen. (See *Chronology View* on page 12 for more information.) This report shows an individual and all the surrounding events associated with that person. These include the person's birth, christening, death and burial information, his or her individual events, marriages and marriage events, parents, the birth of children, and the individual and marriage notes. All these events are arranged on the view in sorted order so you can see what affected this person throughout his or her life.

## Options

You can include and exclude many items in this report, including a timeline chart and an ages column to further illustrate the life events of the individual. These options are all selected on the *Chronology View Options* screen (page 18).

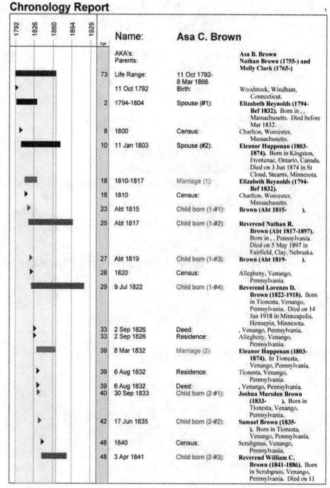

# Family Tree Picture Report (Deluxe Edition only)

The "Family Tree Picture Report" is reached by choosing **All Reports (books and others)...** from the **Reports** menu and then clicking the **Family Tree Picture Tree** button.

This report produces a one- to four-generation picture pedigree chart superimposed on an optional background picture.

The following options are available:

## Include Tab

**Report Title** - The default title is Family Tree for [Name]. [Name] is replaced by the starting person's name. If you would like something different, you can edit the title. You can embed replaceable fields within the title text.

### Names

**Wrap wide names** - Prints long names on multiple lines.

**Make all pictures the same size** - Prints all pictures same height even if some of the names wrap around to additional lines.

**Shorten wide names by using initials** - Shortens the names in the given names to their initials in order to shorten the name enough to fit on one line. Benjamin Franklin Brown would appear as Benjamin F Brown or B F Brown.

**Remove Quoted Names** - Excludes quoted names from the given names. **William "Bill" Martin** appears as **William Martin**.

### Caption

**Include life years** - Adds the lifespan years of each individual under their pictures. For example: **(1912-1963)**.

**Suppress for Living** - Omits the lifespan years for persons marked as Living.

## Design Tab

**Borders** - Prints a border line around each picture. You can choose from several different border styles and colors.

**Shadow** - Adds a shadow behind each picture box. You can also select a shadow color.

**Box Background Color** - Selects the picture box background color.

**Text Color** - Sets the picture caption text color.

## Layout Tab

**Generations** - Choose from one to four generations. The picture size and layout will be adjusted accordingly.

**Horizontal Spacing** - Adjusts the horizontal spacing of pictures to Tight, Normal, or Loose.

**Vertical Spacing** - Adjusts the vertical spacing of pictures to Tight, Normal, or Loose.

**Picture Box Width** - Adjusts the relative picture box width to Narrow, Normal, or Wide.

**Picture Box Height** - Adjusts the relative picture box height to Short, Normal, or Tall.

## Background Picture Tab

**Print a Background Picture** - Includes a background picture. Several pictures are included with Legacy, or you can select any other picture you might have by clicking **Choose**.

## Page Setup

Click the **Page Setup** button to change page margins, print orientation, line spacing, paper size, border lines, heading and page numbering options, and footer options.

## Font Size

Click the **Change Fonts** button to select a different font or font size for the report.

When you are ready to print, click either the **Preview** or **Print** button.

## Printer Setup

Lets you change the page size before generating the report. You can also change the target printer and its specific settings.

## Save and Load

You can save and reload any set of Family Tree Picture Report settings using the **Save** and **Load** buttons.

(Help index: *Family Tree Picture Report*)

# Books and Other Reports

The **Books / Other** tab on the *Select a Report* screen allows you to print many other kinds of reports. These reports can also be reached from the **Reports** menu.

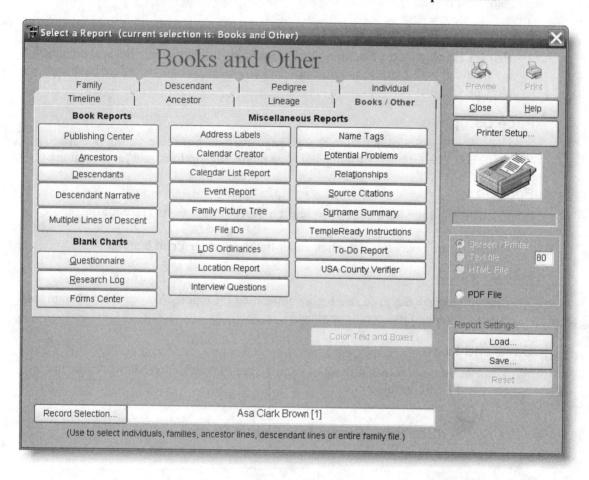

# Ancestor Book

An Ancestor book (also known as an *Ahnentafel* report) is a book-style report beginning with a specific person and moving back through the person's ancestors for a given number of generations. (Ahnentafel means *ancestor table* in German.) This type of report describes each person in a narrative format and gives each person a unique ahnentafel number. The starting individual is given a number of 1. From then on, an individual's father is assigned a number that is two times the number of the individual. The mother is assigned a number that is twice the individual's plus 1. If you are number 1, your father is 2, your mother is 3, your father's father and mother are 4 and 5, and your mother's father and mother are 6 and 7, and so on. If a person is missing, their number is skipped.

### Ancestors of John Fitzgerald KENNEDY

#### First Generation

**1. John Fitzgerald KENNEDY-[52]**  (1) was born 29 May 1917 in Brookline, Norfolk Co, MA (1, 2). He was christened 19 Jun 1917 in Brookline, Norfolk Co, MA. John died 22 Nov 1963 in Dallas, Dallas Co, TX (1, 2). He was buried 25 Nov 1963 in Arlington, Arlington Co, VA (1).

Notes: In 1960 he became President of the United States.

He wrote 2 books, including "Profiles in Courage", which won him a Pulitzer Prize.

He had personal finances that were estimated to be around $10 million while in the Presidency.

President Kennedy
While travelling around the country, President Kennedy urged people to serve their country.

He was assassinated in Dallas, TX.

Medical: He suffered from many physical ailments, including a weak spine, Addison's disease, being underweight, severe allergies, periodic asthma, and a weak stomach. He also suffered scarlet fever, measles, appendicitis, tonsillitis, frequent colds,

Later on in life he faced serious back surgery two times, one of the operations almost claimed his life.

Noted events in his life were:

1. Occupation. (1)Senator
2. Education; 25 Sep 1940; Palo Alto, Santa Clara Co, CA.  (1)Stanford University
3. Religion.  (1)Roman Catholic

John married Jacqueline BOUVIER-[53] [MRIN:13], daughter of John Vernou BOUVIER III-[48] and Janet Norton LEE-[49], on 12 Sep 1953 in Newport, Newport County, RI, USA.

Children from this marriage were:

1. Caroline Bouvier KENNEDY-[54] (1957-)
2. John Fitzgerald KENNEDY Jr.-[55] (1960-)

▶ **To create an Ahnentafel (or Ancestor) book:**
1. From the **Reports** menu, choose **All Reports (Books and others)**.
2. Click **Ancestor Book** under the **Book Report** column.
3. Set the desired options.
4. Click **Preview** or **Print**.

(Help index: ***Ancestor book reports***)

The *Ahnentafel (Ancestor) Book/Report Options* window has four tabs and three buttons that you can use to customize the printout. Each tab and button is described below:

## Options Tab

**Insert Underlines** inserts an underlined space so that missing given names or surnames can be filled in later.

**Total Generations** sets the number of generations to include in the report. A three-generation report would include an individual, his parents, and his grandparents.

**Table of Contents** generates a table of contents, listing the starting page for each generation included in the report. You can specify the format of the table.

### Other Report Options

Click **Index Options**, **Report Options** , and **Title Page** at the bottom of the **Options** tab to open up additional screens where you can select many more customization features. Click **Help** on these screens to read all about the options available.

## Page Layout Tab

**Start New Page After Each Generation** starts each generation on a new page.

**Print Names in Bold** puts each name in bold-face type.

**Paragraph Indents** set the distance to indent each type of paragraph included in the report.

**Custom Report Spacing** choose blank space to be included above the report sections.

## Heading Layout Tab

**Title for Page 1** prints the title only at the top of the first page of the report.

**Headings** prints the title at the top of all the pages after the first page.

**Subtitles** specifies the type of generation subtitles printed. These can include the generation number (Generation One, Generation Two), or the relationship of the generation (Parents, Grandparents), or both (Generation Two, Parents). You can also specify the position of the subtitles as being left-justified or centered.

## Wording Tab

You can specify phrases when creating narrative paragraphs of the report.

## Print the Book

The book can be printed in different ways. These are controlled by the settings in the *Report Destination* box in the lower-right corner of the window. The output can be set to:

- Screen/Printer
- Text File
- HTML File
- Rich Text File
- PDF File

## Produce the report in a print preview window

Using the **Screen/Printer** option in the *Report Destination* box, click **Preview** to see the report before committing it to paper. You can view each page and see how it looks. If you find something you want to change, simply close the preview window, change the desired option(s), and then preview it again. When everything looks correct, print it on paper.

## Print directly to your printer

When you are confident of the output format, send the report directly to the printer by clicking **Print**.

## Send the output to a text file

The **Text File** option in the *Report Destination* window causes Legacy to send just the text of the report to a file. The resulting file contains no formatting such as bold print or centering. After Legacy has produced the text file, you are prompted to view it in your default text editor.

The **Line Length** box lets you set the number of characters per line. The higher the number, the longer a line of text is before it wraps to the line below. The default is set at 80.

## Send the output to an HTML file

Legacy can generate an HTML document that you can upload to the Internet. After Legacy has produced the HTML file, you will be prompted to view it in your web browser.

## Send the output to a Rich Text Format file

Legacy can produce a specially formatted file that can be loaded into a word processor. All the original formatting of the output is retained. In addition, all necessary text is marked so that you can produce a table of contents and a complete index of all names. All report options are retained and used for these reports. After Legacy has produced the RTF file you are prompted to view it in your word processor.

## Send the output to a PDF file

This generates the report, displays it in the Print Preview window and then creates an Adobe PDF (Portable Document File) file. This file can be viewed with the free Adobe Acrobat Reader and easily sent to other people by e-mail. (This feature is part of the *Deluxe Edition* only.)

When this option is selected, the ⟦Print⟧ button changes to ⟦Create⟧. When you click **Create**, Legacy asks for an output filename and then sends the report to this location.

(Help index: ***Ancestor Book Report***)

# Descendant Books

A Descendant Book is a book-style report that begins with a specific person and moves forward through the person's descendants for a given number of generations. Descendant Books are available in both Modified Register and Register formats. The Modified Register format describes each person in a narrative format and gives each person a number. The starting individual is given a number of 1. From then on, each person encountered is assigned the next higher number. Children with an upcoming main entry are displayed with a "+" to the left of the child number. The Register format is similar to the Modified Register

### Descendants of Patrick KENNEDY

#### First Generation

1. **Patrick KENNEDY-[46]** was born in 1823 in Dunganstown, Ireland. He died on 22 Nov 1858 in Boston, Suffolk Co, MA. Patrick was buried on 23 Nov 1858 in Cambridge, Middlesex Co, MA. Cause of death was He died of an outbreak of Cholera.

Notes: The potato famine of 1845-48, plagued the country of Ireland and pushed many Irishmen to flee to the land of promise, the USA. Patrick Kennedy was among those to leave his home in Wexford County, Ireland, in 1848, in hopes of finding a better life in the US. Once he arrived in the US, he settled in East Boston, where he remained for the rest of his life. life.

Upon Patrick's arrival in Boston, he immediately became involved in politics. He was known as a Ward Boss in Boston, looking out for the other Irish immigrants and trying to improve the conditions in the community.

HIST Dunganstown, Ireland
HIST Liverpool St., East Boston, MA

Noted events in his life were:

1. Occupation. Cooper, Ward Boss
2. Religion. Roman Catholic

Patrick married Bridget MURPHY-[47] [MRIN:10], daughter of Richard MURPHY-[85] and Mary-[86], on 28 Sep 1849 in Holy Cross Cathedral, Boston, MA.

Notes: After her husband died, she opened up a "Notions Shop" to provide for her family.

HEAL Suffered from heart trouble in her old age (67).
HEAL
HEAL Her death was caused by a cerebral hemorrhage.

They had the following children:

+ 2 F i. **Mary L. KENNEDY-[60]** was born on 9 Aug 1851 in Boston, Suffolk Co, MA. She died on 7 May 1926 in Boston, Suffolk Co, MA.
  3 F ii. **Johanna KENNEDY-[61]** was born on 4 Dec 1852 in East Boston, Suffolk Co,

except that only individuals that have children are assigned a number.

▶ **To create a Descendant book:**
1. From the **Reports** menu, choose **All Reports (Books and others)**.
2. Click **Descendant Book** under the **Book Report** column.
3. Choose either **Modified Register** or **Register** format.
4. Set any other desired options.
5. Click **Preview** or **Print**.

 (Help index: *Descendant book report*)

## Report Options

There are four tabs and three buttons that you can use to customize the printout. Each tab and button is described below:

## Options Tab

**Insert Underlines** inserts an underlined space so that missing given or surnames, or date or places can be filled in later. You can also have spaces reserved for death information even though the person is marked as living.

**Total Generations** Sets the number of generations to include in the report. A three-generation report would include an individual, his parents, and his grandparents.

**Table of Contents** generates a table of contents listing the starting page for each generation included in the report. You can specify the format of the table, including the option to include leader lines (.........) between the chapter names and the page numbers.

**Include Main Entries For** includes individuals with children but no spouses (standard format), or individuals with children *or* spouse(s). You can also choose to show the family line back (in parentheses) to the starting ancestor after the name of main individuals.

## Other Report Options

Click **Index Options, Report Options** , and **Title Page** at the bottom of the **Options** tab to open up additional screens where you can select many more customization features. Click **Help** on these screens to read all about the options available.

## Page Layout Tab

**Start New Page After Each Generation**  starts each generation on a new page.

**Print Names in Bold**  puts each name in bold-face type.

**Paragraph Indents**  sets the distance to indent each type of paragraph included in the report.

**Custom Report Spacing**  choose blank space to be included above the report sections.

## Heading Layout Tab

**Title for Page 1**  prints the title only at the top of the first page of the report.

**Headings**  prints the title at the top of all the pages after the first page.

**Subtitles**  specifies the type of generation subtitles printed. These can include the generation number (Generation One, Generation Two) or the relationship of the generation (Parents, Grandparents), or both (Generation Two, Parents). You can also specify the position of the subtitles as being left-justified or centered.

## Wording Tabs

You can specify phrases when creating narrative paragraphs of the report.

## Print the Book

The book can be printed in different ways. See page 135 for the various options.

# Descendant Narrative Book

A Descendant Narrative Book is a book-style report that begins with a specific person and moves forward through the person's descendants for a given number of generations. It is similar to the Modified Register (Descendant) Book, but more abbreviated in its style. This type of report describes each person in a narrative format and may or may not give each person a number.

▶ **To create a Descendant Narrative book:**
1. From the **Reports** menu, choose **All Reports (Books and others)**.
2. Click **Descendant Narrative Book** under the **Book Report** column.
3. Set the desired options.
4. Click **Preview** or **Print**.

### Descendants of John Alden

1-John Alden (1, 2) was born in 1598-1599 in possibly Harwich, Essex, England and died on 12 Sep 1687 in Duxbury, Plymouth, Massachusetts, USA.

John married Priscilla Mullins, daughter of William Mullins and Alice _____, about 1623 in Plymouth, Plymouth, Massachusetts, USA (3).

2-Elizabeth Alden (1) was born about 1624 in Plymouth, Massachusetts, USA and died on 31 May 1717 in Little Compton, Newport, Rhode Island, USA.

LDS Baptism. 13 Dec 1973, Mesa, AZ. Endowment. 16 Jan 1974, Mesa, AZ.

2-John Alden was born about 1626 in Plymouth, Plymouth, Massachusetts, USA and died on 14 Mar 1702 in Boston, Suffolk, Massachusetts, USA.

2-Joseph Alden was born after 22 May 1627 in , , Massachusetts, USA and died on 8 Feb 1697 in Bridgewater, Plymouth, Massachusetts, USA.

2-Sarah Alden was born after 22 May 1627 in , , Massachusetts, USA and died before 13 Jun 1688.

2-Jonathan Alden was born about 1632 and died on 14 Feb 1697 in Duxbury, Plymouth, Massachusetts, USA.

2-Ruth Alden was born about 1636 and died on 12 Oct 1674 in Braintree, Norfolk, Massachusetts, USA.

2-Mary Alden was born about 1641 and died after 13 Jun 1688.

2-David Alden was born about 1646 and died in 1671-1676.

2-Priscilla Alden was born about 1648 and died after 13 Jun 1688.

2-Rebecca Alden was born before 1649 and died after 13 Jun 1688.

1                                                    Printed by Legacy on 8 Feb 2000

(Help index: ***Descendant narrative report***)

The *Descendant Narrative Book Options* window has four tabs and three buttons that you can use to customize the printout. Each tab and button is described below:

## Options Tab

**Insert Underlines** inserts an underlined space so that missing given or surnames can be filled in later.

**Total Generations** sets the number of generations to include in the report. A three-generation report would include an individual, his parents, and his grandparents.

**Table of Contents** generates a table of contents listing the starting page for each generation included in the report. You can specify the format of the table, including the option to include leader lines (.........) between the chapter names and the page numbers.

## Other Report Options

Click **Index Options**, **Report Options**, and **Title Page** at the bottom of the Options tab to open up additional screens where you can select many more customization features. Click **Help** on these screens to read all about the options available.

### Page Layout Tab

**Print Names in Bold** puts each name in bold-face type.

### Heading Layout Tab

**Title for Page 1** prints the title only at the top of the first page of the report.

### Wording Tab

You can specify phrases when creating narrative paragraphs of the report.

### Print the Book

The book can be printed in different ways. See page 135 for the various options.

# Multiple Lines of Descent Book

A Multiple Lines of Descent Book Report is a book-style report that begins with various specified people and moves forward through their descendants for a given number of generations. This type of report describes each person in a narrative format and gives each person a number. The starting individual is given a number of 1. From then on, each person encountered is assigned the next higher number. The multiple lines usually intersect at some point. These intersections are indicated in the report.

**To create a Multiple Lines of Descent Book Report:**

1.  From the *Report* menu, choose **Multiple Lines of Descent Book.** The *Options* window is displayed.
2.  Select two or more couples to include in the report.
3.  Set the options, as described below.
4.  Click either **Print** or **Preview** to view the report.

## Choosing the Multiple Lines for the Report

To select the various marriage records from which to start each line of descent in the report, click the Change button in the lower-left corner of the screen. The Multiple Lines of Descent screen appears. Enter the Marriage Record ID Numbers (MRINs) of the couples at the tops of each line you want to include in the report. (See *Selecting Multiple Lines of Descent* on page 144 for more information on how to select the couples.)

## Options Tab

**Missing Information Space** Inserts an underlined space so that missing information can later be filled in for given names, surnames, dates and places.

**Number of Generations** Number of generation to include in the report. A 3-generation report would include an individual, his parents and his grandparents.

**Book Format** Choose between Register or Modified Register.

**Table of Contents** Legacy will generate a Table of Contents listing the starting page for each generation included in the report. You can specify whether or not you want to have leaders on the page numbers.

**Main Entries** Normally, only **individuals who have children** are given their own main block of information. Otherwise, they are just listed as children of their parents. You can also specify that **individuals with either children or spouses** be listed in a main information block or that **all individuals** have a main entry. You can also choose to include the direct line back to the starting ancestor. This might look like this:

**James R Wilson** (Robert[26], James[14], Robert[6], Brigham[1])

You can also choose to **show the spouses for children who will have a main entry.**

## Page Layout Tab

**New Generation On Each Page**  Starts each generation on a new page.

**Starting Page Number**  The number of the first page.

**Paragraph Indents**  The distance to indent each type of paragraph included in the report.

**Custom Report Spacing**  chooses blank space to be included above the report sections.

## Heading Layout Tab

**Title for Page 1**  The title that is printed only at the top of the first page of the report, after the title page.

**Headings**  The title that is printed at the top of all the pages after the first page. You can also embed replaceable fields within the title text.

By default, when you open this window, the two title fields will default to "Descendants of [Fullname]". You can customize either title by adding [replaceable field names].

(Help index: ***Report Title Options***)

The fields will be saved and restored each time you open the Book Report window.

**Subtitles**  Specifies the type of generation subtitles printed. These can include the generation number (Generation One, Generation Two) or the Relationship of the generation (Parents, Grandparents) or both (Generation Two, Parents). You can also specify the position of the subtitles as being left- or center-justified.

## Wording Tab

You can specify phrases when creating the narrative paragraphs of the report. These include:

**Individual Events**  For example, **Noted events in [his/her] life were:**

**Marriage Events**  For example, **Noted events in their marriage were:**

Children (if couple was married).  For example, **Children from this marriage were:**

**Children** (if couple was not married)   For example, **Their children were:**

**Notes**   General, Research, Medical, Marriage, Birth, Christening, Death, and Burial Notes

The Individual and Marriage Event and the Children wording may include embedded fields that are replaced during the generation of the report.  For example, **The events for [firstname] were:.**

(Help index: *Report Title Options*)

## Report Options

Click **Index Options**, **Report Options**, and **Title Page** at the bottom of the Options tab to open up additional screens where you can select many more customization features. Click **Help** on these screens to read all about the options available.

## Index Generation

By selecting the checkbox in the upper-left corner of the **Index Options** button, you can have Legacy generate an alphabetical index for the report and an optional Location index.  This is particularly useful when you are printing a large number of consecutively numbered reports.  The index includes each person who is shown on each page and what position they occupy on that page.  The index can be lined or unlined and printed in one, two or three columns.  Click the **Index Options** button to make changes in the index format.

## Title Page

By selecting the checkbox in the upper-left corner of the **Title Page** button, you can have Legacy generate a title page for the report.  Click the Title Page button to set the title page options.  These include:

**Title**   The title on the Title Page.
**Subtitle**   The subtitle that prints at the bottom of the Title Page.
**Lines**   Dividing lines across the top, bottom and sides.
**Picture**   You can specify to print a specific picture on the Title Page.

**Caption**  The caption you want to print under the picture.

**Size**  The picture can be printed small, medium or large.

**Shadow**  You can have a drop-shadow behind the picture.

## Where to Send the Report

Descendant Charts can be output to various formats.  Make your choice by clicking on the appropriate option button in the lower right corner of the Report Menu window.  The choices are:

**Screen / Printer**  Sends the report to either the Print Preview window or directly to your printer depending on whether you click the Preview or Print button.  (See Printing below.)

**Rich Text File**  Sends the report to a disk file containing all the formatting options such as bolding, indents, fonts and font sizes.  It also contains all the index and table of contents marks.  This file can then be loaded into your favorite word processor for further editing and formatting.

**Text File**  Sends the report to a text file on either your hard drive or a floppy disk. You will be prompted for a drive and path.

**HTML File**  Sends the report to a HTML file that can be used on a web site or sent as an e-mail message. You will be prompted for a drive and path.

## Printing

The book can be printed in different ways. See page 135 for the various options.

## Selecting Multiple Lines of Descent

You can either enter the Marriage Record ID Numbers (MRINs) in the field at the bottom of the screen by hand, or you can click the **Marriage List** button to display the *Marriage List* from which you can select the couples.  Any couple selected from the *Marriage List* will be inserted into the MRIN line where the cursor is located.

If you want to start a line with the wife (female) instead of the husband (male), add a plus sign (+) to the left of the MRIN.  For example, **+286**.

# Legacy Publishing Center

You can create professional-looking books by assembling the various reports and charts available in Legacy into one single document. This can include ancestor and descendant book reports, pedigree charts, family group records, picture scrapbooks and much more. You can also add a table of contents, other introductory sections and an overall index and list of source citations.

When you create a book, you select from the various items available and effectively add chapters to your new book arranged in the order of your choice.

## Getting Started

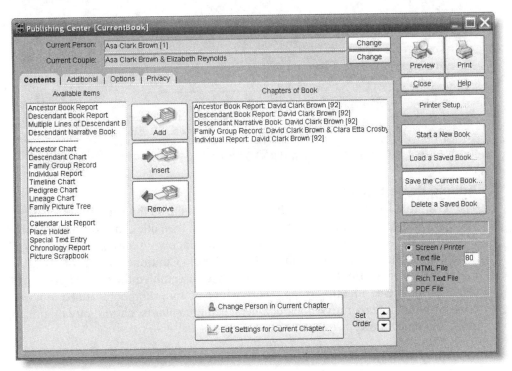

### To create a new book:

1. Open the *Publishing Center* from the **Report** pulldown menu.
2. Click the **New Book** button.
3. Enter a name for the new book. Select the file name and path to save the book files.
4. Select the various sections to include in the book. Click **Preview** to generate and view the book.

## The Contents Tab

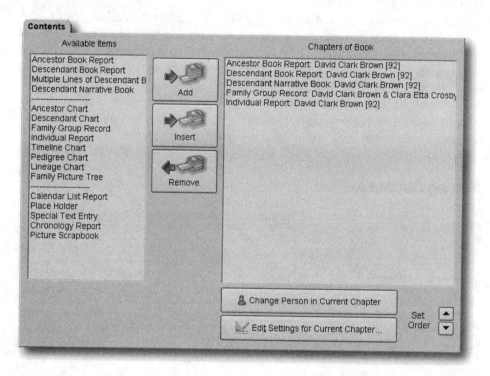

### Adding Items to your Book

The **Available Items** list on the left of the window shows the various reports from which you can choose. To select an item, highlight it and then click the **Add** button. This adds the item to the bottom of the **Chapters of Book** window on the right. (You can also drag an item from the left window to the right window.) Continue adding (or dragging) items into the Chapters of Book window until you have assembled the desired document. This can be as simple as a family group record with a picture scrapbook added to it or a large book with multiple narrative book chapters, pedigree charts, chronology reports, picture trees, and much more.

### Inserting an Item

If you want to select an item and place it between two existing items in the **Chapters of Book** window, highlight the item in the right window just below where you want to insert the new item. Then highlight the item in the left window and click the **Insert** button. The items in the right window are moved down to make room for the new inserted item.

### Rearranging Items

If you want to move an item in the **Chapters of Book** window, highlight the item to move and then move it by using the up and down **Set Order** arrow buttons ⬆⬇ below the window.

### Removing Items

To remove an item from the right window, select the item and click **Remove**.

### Adding Place Holders

At times you may want to reserve space in your publication for insertion of external pages. Perhaps you have a copy of a three-page handwritten letter from an ancestor. To create space for this, add a **Place Holder** item to your publication. When you add a **Place Holder**, Legacy asks for a Place Holder name and how many blank pages to insert. When the book is printed, you then remove the place holder pages and replace them with the letter.

### Adding Text Items

You can add a text chapter to your book by inserting a **Special Text Entry** item. Adding this item displays a Note window where you enter text. This might be a family story, notes about your research efforts and conclusion, or anything else you want to add.

### Editing Items

All of the reports, charts, etc. in the **Available Items** list have options associated with them. Most are also connect to individuals as the subject of the report or the starting person for an ancestor or descendant line. To change the starting person for a report that has one, highlight the section name in the **Contents of Book** window and then click the **Person** button below the list. To change the report options for any item in the list, highlight it and click **Edit**.

## The Additional Tab

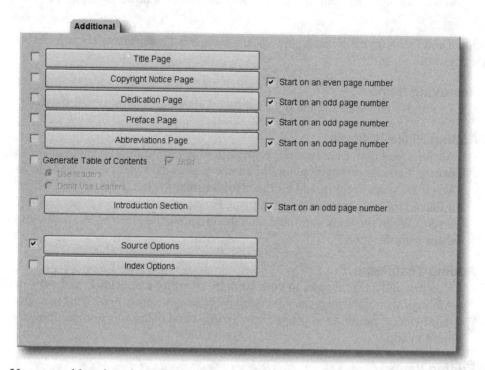

You can add various introductory sections to your book, including a title page, preface, dedication page, copyright notice, introduction and an abbreviations page. To include one or more of these sections in your book, put a checkmark in the checkbox to the left of each desired item. To create the item, click the appropriate button. The **Title Page** button displays the *Title Page Options* screen where you can layout the page. The other buttons display a notes-type window where you can enter the contents of each page. When the book is produced the items selected on this page are included in the order shown on the tab: Title page, Copyright, Dedication, Preface, Abbreviations, Table of Contents, and Introduction. The Copyright Notice page can be forced to start on an even-numbered page by selecting the **Start on an even page number** option. This puts the copyright notice in its customary position on a left-hand page, opposite the dedication or preface page. All successive sections can be started on an odd-numbered page by selecting the **Start on an odd page number** option.

### Table of Contents

Legacy can generate a Table of Contents listing the starting page for each section included in the report. You can specify whether or not you want to have leaders on the page numbers.

### Source Options

To include source citations throughout the book, select the checkbox to the left of the **Source Options** button. To set (or change) the options, click the button to see the *Source Options* screen.

### Index Options

By selecting the checkbox to the left of the **Index Options** button, you can have Legacy generate an alphabetical index and an optional Location index for the entire book report. The index includes each person who is shown on each page. The index can be lined or unlined and printed in one, two or three columns. Click the **Index Options** button to make changes in the index format.

## The Options Tab

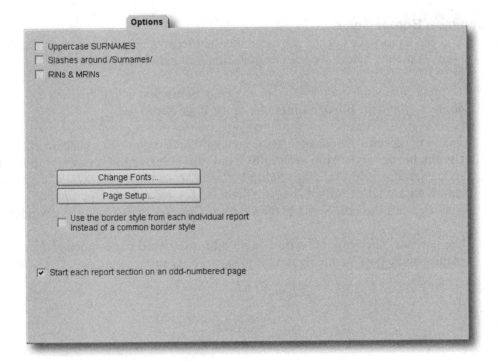

### Uppercase SURNAMES

If this option is selected, surnames are set off in uppercase letters ("SMITH" instead of "Smith").

### Slashes Around /Surnames/

If this option is selected, surnames are set off with slashes ("/Smith/" instead of "Smith").

### RIN & MRIN Numbers

The Record Identification Number (RIN) of each individual and the Marriage Record Identification Number (MRIN) of each marriage.

### Fonts

You can select the font and font size to use in the book by clicking the **Change Fonts** button.

### Page Setup

Click the **Page Setup** button to change page margins, orientation, paper size and border style.

### Common Border Style

You can either have Legacy use a common border style (the border around each page) or use the border style associated with each individual report.

To use a common border style, click the **Page Setup** button and then select the desired style in the **Border Lines** box of the **Page Setup** tab.

To use the specific border style associated with each report, put a checkmark in the **Use the border style from each individual report instead of a common border style** checkbox below the **Page Setup** button. (To set the border style of a specific report, click on the **Contents** tab, highlight the desired report in the *Chapters of Book* window, click the **Edit Settings for Current Chapter** button below the window.)

Use the **Start each report section on an odd-numbered page** option to start each chapter of the book on the right-hand side, which is customary.

# The Privacy Tab

Privacy

Suppression of Living Individuals and Their Families

☐ Suppress details for living people
   ☐ Change name to "Living"

☐ Exclude living people totally (as if they do not exist)

☐ Suppress details for deceased spouses of living individuals
   ☐ Change name to "Deceased"

☐ Suppress details for deceased children of living individuals
   ☐ Change name to "Deceased"

Override Private Settings

☐ Include masked individuals (show their names and information)
☐ Include private individuals (show their names and information)
☐ Include marriages with a status of Private
☐ Include child-parent relationships of Private
☐ Include [[ Private ]] Notes       ☐ Remove [[ ]]
☐ Include events marked "Private"
☐ Include master events marked "Private"

● Reset to Off each time the report menu is opened
○ Retain the setting until changed

Privacy is of great concern when printing reports and books. Legacy provides many options so that you can suppress and eliminate sensitive information, individuals, and marriages.

## Suppression of Living Individuals and Their Families

### Suppress Details for Living People
Select this option to remove all details from living persons, except their name. This protects the privacy of living individuals who may not want personal information made public.
**Change Name to "Living"**- To provide complete anonymity, you can have the names changed to "Living" when suppressing the details of living people.

### Exclude Living People Totally
Removes the person from the report all together. They are treated as if they are not in your family file at all. If you are doing an ancestor style report, any ancestors of the living person are also left out. In like manner, any descendants of a living person are also excluded. Non-direct-line spouses of a living person would not be included.

### Suppress Details for Deceased Spouses of Living Individuals
This option removes the detail information from all dead spouses or partners of living individuals. Only their names are shown.
**Change Name to "Deceased"** - To provide complete anonymity, you can have the names changed to "Deceased" when suppressing their details.

### Suppress Details for Deceased Children of Living Individuals

This option removes the detail information from all dead children of living individuals. Only their names are shown.

**Change Name to "Deceased"**- To provide complete anonymity, you can have the names changed to "Deceased" when suppressing their details.

## Override Privacy Settings

### Include Masked Individuals

If you have marked one or more individuals in your family file as **Masked**, they are included in the report but their detail information is suppressed and their names are shown only as "Private." If you would like to include their names and information, select this option.

### Include Private Individuals

If you have marked one or more individuals in your family file as **Private**, they are excluded from reports by default. It is as if they do not exist. If you would like to include them, select this option.

### Include Private Marriages

If you have set the **Marriage Status** of a marriage or partnership to **Private**, it is excluded from reports by default. It is as if they the marriage does not exist. If you would like to include these marriages, select this option.

### Include Private Child-Parent Relationships

If you set the **Child-Parent** relationship status between a child and a father or mother to **Private**, the relationship is excluded from reports by default. It is as if it doesn't exist. If you would like to include them, select this option.

### Include [[ Private ]] Notes

Include any parts of notes that have been marked as private using the double opening [[ and closing ]] square brackets. You also have the option to remove the double brackets.

### Include Events Marked "Private"

Include individual events that are checkmarked **Private**.

### Include Master Events Marked "Private"

Include all individual events based on master events that are checkmarked **Private**.

### Automatically Resetting Privacy Options

The default setting for printing Private information on reports is **Off**. In other words, you have to specifically check the **Include Private ...** options to have private individuals and information included on a report. If you would like to have your setting for printing Private information saved when you leave the report menu and restore then next time you open it, choose **Retain the setting until changed**. If you want the printing of Private information turned back **Off** each time you exit the report menu, choose **Reset to Off each time the**

**report menu is opened**. (This is the safest setting to use as it is easy to forget that you had temporarily turned it **On**.)

## Saving a Book Format

After you have formatted your publication, you can save it for future use by clicking the Save button in the lower-right corner of the window.

**Note**: A book format is closely associated with the individual of the family file from which it was created. If you load a book format into another family file, the results will most likely not be what you expected because the RIN numbers saved with the report point to different people.

## Printing Your Book

### Where to Send the Report

The book publication can be output to various formats. Make your choice by clicking on the appropriate option button in the lower right corner of the Publication Center window. The choices are:

**Screen / Printer** Sends the report to either the Print Preview window or directly to your printer depending on whether you click the **Preview** or **Print** button. (See Printing below.)

**Rich Text File** Sends the report to a disk file containing all the formatting options such as bolding, indents, fonts and font sizes. It also contains all the index and table of contents marks. This file can then be loaded into your favorite word processor for further editing and formatting.

**Text File** Sends the report to a text file on either your hard drive or a floppy disk. You are prompted for a drive and path. (Note: The Index, Table of Contents, and Title Page options are not included when using the Text File output format.)

**HTML File** Sends the report to a HTML file that can be used on a web site or sent as an e-mail message. You will be prompted for a drive and path. (**Note**: The Index, Table of Contents, and Title Page options are not available when using the HTML File output format.)

**PDF File** Generates the report, displays it in the Print Preview window and then creates an Adobe PDF (Portable Document File) file. This file can be viewed with the free Adobe Acrobat Reader and easily sent to other people by e-mail. (This feature is part of the Deluxe Edition only.)

**Note**: Not all of the available report items can be printed all of the output formats. For example, the chart-type reports (ancestor, descendant, timeline, pedigree, and lineage) are not printed to HTML or RTF output. The Family Picture Tree is also not produced in these formats. When a report section is encountered that cannot be produced in the selected format, it is skipped. (A message is displayed at the beginning of the printing process telling you that one or more sections will be skipped.)

When you have set all the options, click either the **Preview** button to see an on-screen view of the report before it is actually printed, or click **Print** to have the report sent directly to the printer.

# Blank Forms, Questionnaires, and Research Logs

## Forms Center

The *Forms Center* is reached by clicking the **Forms Center** button on the **Books / Other** tab of the **Reports** menu.

The *Forms Center* is the central repository for the many blank forms that are available in Legacy. These include a multitude of census forms, relationship diagrams, research forms, and more. As new forms are added, you can download them from our web site and they will automatically be added to the *Forms Center*. Many forms are available in several different languages.

### The Forms List

The list of available forms is built from the names of the form files in the Forms folder. By default, Legacy installs the initial group of forms into the Forms folder off of the Legacy folder (for example: C:\Legacy7\Forms).

When the list is first displayed, it is in a compressed format showing only the top-level categories. For example:

&#x2610; Census
&#x2610; Relationship Chart
&#x2610; Research

This example shows three groups of forms, Census, Relationship Chart, and Research.

## Expanding and Contracting Sections

To expand a group, click the plus sign to the left of it (or press the plus key on your keyboard when the line is highlighted). The sub-categories are then shown. For example, if you click the plus sign to the left of Census, you will see:

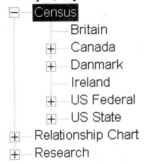

This shows that there are several types of **Census** forms available. If a sub-category has a plus sign to the left of it then an additional level of choices can be opened up by click it. In the example above, **Britain** does not have a plus sign but **Canada** does. Therefore, **Britain** has only one **Census** form available and **Canada** has more than one. Clicking the plus sign next to **Canada** opens up the list to show the two available forms:

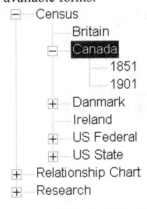

Any available individual form is shown without a plus sign or minus sign next to it. In the example above, **Britain** is a form and **1851** and **1901** are Canadian census forms.

To contract a section of the list, click the minus sign to the left of the section (or press the minus key on your keyboard when the line is highlighted). To quickly expand all the sections in the list, click the **Expand All Sections** button. To contract all section down to just the main groups, click **Contract All Sections**.

## Selecting a Form to Print

To select a specific form to print, click the form name to highlight it and then click the **Preview** or **Print** button to produce the form.

## Selecting Groups of Forms to Print

You can also print groups of forms. In the example above, **Canada** consists of a group of two forms, **1851** and **1901**. To print both of these forms together, click **Canada** to highlight it (as shown in the example). Clicking **Preview** or **Print** will generate both forms on two different pages. If you were to click **US Federal**, all the US Federal census forms would be printed as a group.

If you click another level up, for example the **Census** line,

all the groups of forms below it will be printed. In the example above, this would include all the British, Canadian, Danish, Irish, and US Federal and State census forms.

## Selecting Multiple Forms to Print

You can also select random (non-consecutive) individual forms or groups of forms to print. To do this you must first select the **Select Multiple Forms** option. When you do, empty checkboxes are added to each line in the list:

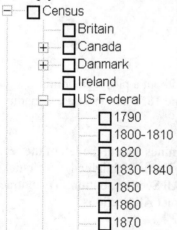

You can then select the specific forms you want to print:

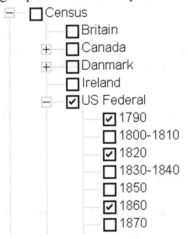

In the above case the **US Federal** census forms for **1790**, **1820** and **1860** will be printed.

If you select a higher level group by placing a checkmark in its checkbox, the entire group below it will be printed.

☐ Census
    ☐ Britain
    ☐ Canada
    ☐ Danmark
    ☐ Ireland
    ☑ US Federal
        ☑ 1790
        ☐ 1800-1810
        ☑ 1820
        ☐ 1830-1840
        ☐ 1850
        ☑ 1860
        ☐ 1870

In the above example, all of the **US Federal** census forms will be printed even though there are some specific forms left unchecked within the group.

Checking a main group, like **Census**, will cause all the forms within that group to be printed.

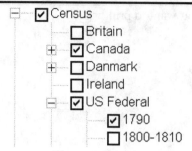

In the example above, all the census forms for all the countries will be printed whether checked or not – because the main **Census** group line has been selected.

### Changing to a Different Forms Folder

Again, by default, Legacy installs all the form files into the Legacy7\Forms folder. Any additional forms that you download from the Legacy web site would normally be placed in this folder as well.

If you find that you eventually have more form files than can easily managed from one folder, you can split them into multiple folders. For example, you might create three folders under the Forms folder called Census, Relationship Charts, and Research and then move the appropriate form files into these subfolders.

To change to a different folder, click the **Browse...** button and select the desired folder. The *Form Center* will read the list of form files and create a new, smaller list for you. The current folder path is always displayed at the bottom of the window.

### Page Setup

The Page Setup screen allows you to change margins, paper orientation, paper size, borders, headers, page numbering and footers.

### Change Fonts

You can specify the font name, size, and style to be used in each section of the chart.

When you have set all the options for the relationship chart printout, click either **Preview** to see an on-screen view of the chart before actually printing, or click **Print** to have the chart sent directly to the printer.

### Printing

When you have set all the options, click either the **Preview** button to see an on-screen view of the report before it is actually printed, or click **Print** to have the report sent directly to the printer.

## Questionnaires

The Questionnaire is used when you want to get information about your family from another person. It is easy for another family member to simply fill in the blanks with what they know. You can customize the questionnaire to include specific information you want and how many children to prompt for.

▶ **To print a questionnaire:**
1. From the **Reports** menu, choose **All Reports (Books and others)**.
2. Click **Questionnaire** under the **Blank Charts** section.
3. Set the options and fonts you want.
4. Fill in the Opening and Closing paragraphs.
5. Click **Preview** or **Print**.

## Opening Paragraph

The customized text for the opening paragraph is printed at the top of the first page and serves as an introduction to the questionnaire. You can include the purpose for which you are seeking information and a return address where the form is to be returned.

## Closing Paragraph

The customized closing paragraph is printed at the end of the questionnaire and can be a summary of the information requested, a plea for the return of the form and a "thank you" for their time.

 For complete information about Questionnaires, see the Legacy Help system and search the index for: *Questionnaire*

## Research Log Blanks

A *Research Log* is simply a form where you can organize your research efforts. Use it to keep track of things you want to do when you go to different places in the future. You can track where things were found and where you want to look in the future.

**Note:** Legacy also has a powerful To-Do List that you can use to record and keep track of all the research tasks you want to do as you gather more information about your ancestors. See *To-Do List* on page 105 for more information.

▶ **To print one or more blank research logs:**
1. From the **Reports** menu, choose **All Reports (Books and others)**.
2. Click **Research Log** under the **Blank Charts** section.
3. Click **Preview** or **Print**.

(Help index: ***Blank research logs***)

# Relationships Report

Legacy can show you how people are related to each other. The relationships are figured for the blood relatives of a source person. The spouses of aunts, uncles and cousins are also shown although they are not actually related. Once you initially build the relationships, Legacy tries to update new additions as you go. Before you can print a *Relationships* report, you must first make sure that the **Relationships** have been set:

▶ **To calculate relationships to a specific individual:**
1. From the *Family View*, make sure the individual you want to be the source person is in either the *Husband* or *Wife* box. From the *Pedigree View*, highlight the desired person.
2. From the **Tools** menu, choose **Set Relationships**. The *Set Relationships* window appears. Make sure the correct individual is shown as the *Source*.
3. Click **Set Relationships**. Legacy calculates the relationship of all blood relatives to the *Source* person. The relationship is shown above the *Husband* and *Wife* boxes on the *Family View* and at the middle right of the *Pedigree View*.
(If you import individuals, or link to a family line, you will have to rebuild the relationships in order for them to all be updated.)

▶ **To print a Relationships report:**
1. From the **Reports** menu, choose **All Reports (Books and others)**.
2. Click **Relationships** under the **Miscellaneous Reports** column.
3. Check the settings.
4. Click **Preview** or **Print**.

(Help index: ***Report printing options***)

(Help index: ***Relationship Report***)

# Potential Problems Report

To create a *Potential Problems Report*, Legacy runs through your family file and checks the information it contains for some common and sometimes unnoticed discrepancies. Some of the possible problems it finds may not be problems at all but they are not normally seen. If you are sure that a particular situation is correct, you can mark the record, telling Legacy to not report on it in the future.

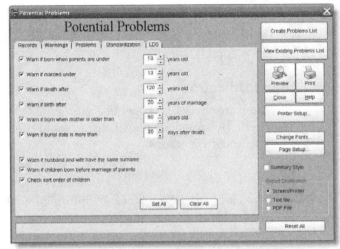

> ▶ **To print a Potential Problems report:**
> 1. From the **Reports** menu, choose **All Reports (Books and others)**.
> 2. Click **Potential Problems** under the **Miscellaneous Reports** column.
> 3. Check the settings on the *Records, Warnings, Problems, Standardization,* and *LDS* tabs.
> 4. Click **Preview** or **Print**.

(Help index: ***Potential problems***)

## Records to Check

Specifies which records you want Legacy to check. See the online Help for more information on each option.

**Tagged Records**  limits the problem checking to only the specified tag number.
**Tagging Records**  tags all the problem records on any of the three tag numbers.

## Warnings

These are situations that are probably problems with your dates, but in a few cases, may not be. For example, having a birth records before the parents were 13 years of age, or recording a death after the age of 120 years of age. Many of the warnings that Legacy checks for have a day or year range associated with them. You can change these settings by using the **Up** and **Down** arrows to change the associated value.

## Problems

Checks for situations that are wrong, like recording a birth that is after the person's death date, or a burial that is before a death. Checking invalid dates is also done in this section.

## Standardization

These are checks to ensure that you are not entering your information in non-standard ways. These include illegal characters in names, incorrectly formatted names, and other incorrect entries.

## LDS

If you are keeping track of LDS information, these checks verify temple operational dates, and ordinance completion order.

## Creating the List

When you have set all the options, click either **Preview** to see an on-screen view of the report before it is actually printed, or **Print** to have the report sent directly to the printer.

## Print the Report

When you have set all the options, click either **Preview** to see an on-screen view of the report before it is actually printed, or **Print** to have the report sent directly to the printer.

(Help index: ***Problems report***)

# Creating a Problems List

Instead of printing the Potential Problems report, you can also create an interactive list of the problems found. This is done by clicking the **Create Problems List** button which displays the *Potential Problems List*.

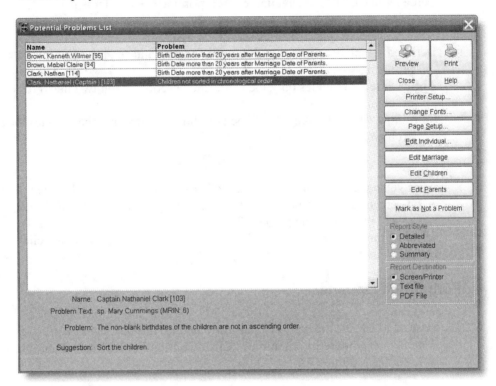

This list shows the names and abbreviated descriptions for all of the problems found in the last problems search. As each name/problem is highlighted, the full problem description and suggested action is shown under the list at the bottom of the window. The list is interactive in that you can edit the individuals and marriages right from the list to correct the problems or exclude them from future checking.

If a problem involves individual information for a person and you would like to edit that information, highlight the person's name and problem in the list and then click the **Edit Individual** button. The person's Individual Information screen appears where you can make changes. If the problem has to do with marriage information, click the **Edit Marriage** button to display the Marriage Information screen.

If you find that a reported problem is not really a problem, you can mark it as "Not a Problem" and have it excluded from lists generated in the future. Make sure the desire problem is highlighted in the list and then click **Mark as Not a Problem**. The marked and removed from the list.

## Printing a Report

Three report formats are available when printing the problems list:

**Detailed** – Includes the name, description, dates, and suggested action for each problem.
**Abbreviated** – Includes only the name and description (on two lines) for each problem.
**Summary** – Includes only the name and short description (on one line) for each problem.

After you have select the desired report format, click either the **Preview** button to see an on-screen view of the report before it is actually printed, or click **Print** to have the report sent directly to the printer. The report can also be sent to a text file by selecting the **Text file** option in the *Report Destination* box and then clicking the **Create** button to specify a file name and location.

## Formatting Options

You can customize the look of the report by setting the format options. Click **Page Setup...** to change the margins, page orientation, line spacing and print size. (See Page Setup for more information.) Click **Change Fonts** to select the font size and style for the report.

## Saving the List

The Potential Problems List is kept from session to session so that it doesn't have to be generated each time you want to view it. To display the list, click the **View Existing Problems List** button on the previous *Potential Problems Report* screen.

## Creating a New List

If you want to create a new problems list, either for a different set of individuals or with different options selected, click the **Create Problems List** button on the previous *Potential Problems Report* screen. Any previous list is erased and the new list takes its place.

# LDS Ordinance Reports

The *LDS Ordinance* reports show each selected individual along with each individual's ordinance information. This includes the individual ordinances of baptism and endowments, as well as all sealing information for spouses, children, and parents.

▶ **To print an LDS Ordinances report:**
1. From the **Reports** menu, choose **All Reports (Books and others)**.
2. Click **LDS Ordinances** under the **Miscellaneous Reports** column.
3. Select the **Records to Include**.
4. Set any other desired options.
5. Click **Preview** or **Print**.

(Help index: ***LDS ordinance reports***)

## Records to Include

The following record groups can be included in the report:

**All Records**   prints all the records in the family file, including those that have some, all, or no ordinance dates.

**Records With One or More Missing Ordinance Dates**   prints the records of individuals with one or more missing ordinance dates or marriages with no sealing date.

**Records With All Ordinance Dates Filled**   prints the records of individuals or marriages that have all the ordinance dates filled in.

**Records With One or More Dates Filled**   prints the records of individuals or marriages that have at least one ordinance date filled in.

**Records Currently Qualified for TempleReady Submission**   prints the records of individuals with "Submitted" or "Sub" in one or more ordinance fields.

**Records With Missing Sealed to Spouses Dates**   prints the records of marriages with missing sealing information.

## Options

**RINs** prints the record ID number with each name on the report.

**Include Living Individuals** lets you include individuals marked as "Living" on the report.

**Include Alternate Names**

**Show Children of Each Individual** includes the spouses and children of each individual. This is very helpful when trying to determine who a particular individual is.

**Temple Name List Appendix** prints a list of all the temples included in your records as an appendix at the end of the report, beginning on a new page.

**Shading** print lightly shaded bars behind every other line, to enhance your report. This often makes reading the report easier because you can follow across wide blank areas to dates listed on the right side and see which name they belong to.

**Lines** prints vertical lines between columns, and/or horizontal lines between rows by checking the appropriate box.

## Printing

When you have set all the options, click **Preview** to see an on-screen view of the report before it is actually printed, or **Print** to have the report sent directly to the printer.

(Help index: *LDS Ordinance Report*)

# Calendar Creator

Create your own calendars, complete with pictures, birthdays, and anniversaries. There are options to include a cover picture (front and back), picture pages above each calendar month, and complete control over color, layout, shadows, fonts, page size, etc. Create complete yearly calendars suitable for gifts. The calendars can be blank or include the birthdates and anniversaries of your family file members.

The Old Homestead

The following options are available:

## Include Tab

### Records to Include

**Only Living Individuals** Includes only people who are marked as still being alive. (This marking is done on the *Information* window.)

**All Individuals, Living or Dead** Includes all individuals, whether living or dead. If your Family File is large, this can result in large calendars.

**Only Dead Individual** Includes only people who are marked as not living. . (This marking is done on the *Information* window.)

**Only Tagged Living Individuals** Includes only people who are alive and who have a given tag level set.

**All Tagged Individuals, Living or Dead** Includes anyone in the Family File, whether living or dead, who has a given tag level set.

**Only Tagged Dead Individuals** Includes only people who are marked as dead and who have a given tag level set.

**Only Individuals from the following Address Lists** You can choose from Newsletter, Fam. Assoc., Birthday, Research, Christmas, and Holiday groups.

## Options Tab

### Name Format

You can have the names on the calendar printed as either **Surname, Given name(s)**, **Given name(s) Surname**, or **First name Surname**. Select the appropriate option button.

### Include RIN & MRIN Numbers
Check this option if you want to have the individual and marriage record ID numbers included on the calendar.

### Married names for females
Uses the surnames of the husband when printing a wife's name.

## Type of Calendar

### Birthdays
When printing a birthday calendar, you can choose to include the birth year and age.

### Anniversaries
When printing an anniversary calendar, you can choose to include the marriage year, anniversary number, and to skip divorced couples.

### Report Language
You can choose from different languages when generating the Calendar report. To select a language, click the **Report Language** button and choose the language file to be used when generating the report. There are many language files available. These can be found on the www.LegacyFamilyTree.com web site. To reset the language selection back to the default value, click the **R** button.

## Fonts Tab

You can choose the font, font size, and style for nearly every part of the calendar.

## Format Tab

### Borders
-Selects the border style (if any) to be printed around each calendar and picture page. You can select the line and background colors.
Shadow-Prints a drop-shadow behind the border.

### Month Name
You can choose the justification (left-, center-, or right-justified) of the month names, and the print color.
Shadow behind month name-Prints a drop-shadow behind the names of the months.

### Content Font Color
The color of the printing used for birth date and anniversary entries.

Shadow Color-The color used for all drop-shadow effects.

**Day Name**   You can choose the font color for the day names, the background color for the day name strip, whether to print a drop-shadow behind the day name strip, and whether to abbreviate the names of the days.

**Day Box Style**   You can choose to have a box printed around each day of the month or to have grid lines printed between each day.  You can also choose to have a drop-shadow printed behind each day box.  Line colors and background colors can be selected.

**Position of Day Numbers**   The number of each day can be printed left-, center- or right-justified.  The color of the day numbers can also be selected.

## Pictures Tab

Pictures can be printed on their own pages between each calendar page or included on each calendar page.

**Include Picture Page**   Prints pictures with the calendar pages.  You can choose to print the pictures Between Calendar Pages or On Calendar Pages.  If printing on each calendar page, you can choose to have a Dividing Line printed between the picture and the calendar.

**Main title on cover page**   The text to be included on the cover page printed before the first calendar month.

**Subtitle**   The text to be printed as a subtitle on the cover page.

**Front Cover Picture**   The name of the graphic file to be printed on the cover page.

**Front Cover Caption**   The text to be printed below the picture on the cover page.

**Individual Month Pictures and Captions**   The pictures and captions to be included before (or on) each monthly calendar from January to December.  If you want to omit a picture or caption for any particular month, just leave the appropriate fields blank.

**Back Cover Picture and Caption**   The picture and caption to be printed after the last monthly calendar.

**Note**: To select a picture files, click the ... button and navigate to the desired file. To clear a picture name from a month, click the **C** button.  To remove a caption, blank out any existing text in the field.

**Picture Options**   You can choose to print the pictures in Small, Medium, or Large size.  The size of each picture will depend on the page size and margins selected. You can also choose to have a drop-shadow printed behind each picture rectangle.

## Months Tab

**Print Front Cover**  Prints a page (with or without a picture and caption) before printing the first monthly calendar page.

**Months to Print**  Place a check mark in the boxes for which you would like to print a calendar.  You can clear all the check marks by clicking the **Clear All** button.  You can select all the months by clicking **Select All**.

**Print Back Cover**  Prints a page (with or without a picture and caption) after the last monthly calendar page.

### Surrounding Months

**Mini Previous Month Block**  Prints a small version of the calendar month prior to the current month's calendar at the top or bottom of the current page.  This is a quick way to check dates in the previous month without having to turn the page back.

**Mini Following Month Block**  Prints a small version of the calendar month following the current month's calendar at the top or bottom of the current page.

**Position of small calendars**  Prints the small calendars at the Top of Page or Bottom of Page.  You can also choose to have a drop-shadow printed behind the small calendars.

**Text and Background Colors**  You can select the small calendars and the color of the text.

**Subtitle under month name on each calendar page**  As each monthly calendar is printed, the name of the month is printed at the top.  You can specify an additional line of text to be printed below the month names if desired.  For example, you might want to include a subtitle line of, "Birthdays and Anniversaries" or "The Anderson Family."

**Title**  If the calendar report is going to be part of a larger report, you can specify a Title line to be printed at the top of each page.

## Year of Calendar

Select the year you would like to print the calendar for.

The *Calendar Creator* screen can be reached by choosing **All Reports (Books and others)** from the **Report** menu and then clicking on **Calendar Creator**.

## Page Setup

Click the **Page Setup** button to change page margins, print orientation, paper size, heading and page numbering options, and footer options.

## Printer Setup

Lets you change the page size before generating the report. You can also change the target printer and its specific settings.

## Save and Load

You can save and reload any set of report settings using the **Save** and **Load** buttons.

## Printing

When you have set all the options, click either the **Preview** button to see an on-screen view of the report before it is actually printed, or click **Print** to have the report sent directly to the printer.

(Help index: *Calendar Creator*)

# Calendar List

A *Calendar List* report can be printed to show selected birth dates and anniversaries.

▶ **To print a Calendar List report:**

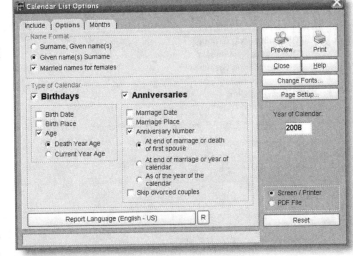

1. From the **Reports** menu, choose **All Reports (Books and others)**.
2. Click **Calendar List Report** under the **Miscellaneous Reports** column.
3. Select the records you wish to include.
4. Set any other desired options.
5. Choose the year to print.
6. Choose the months to print.
7. Select the type of calendar to print, and which fields to include.
8. Click **Preview** or **Print**.

(Help index: *Calendar List report options*)

# Interview Report

The Interview Report contains over 1200 questions in thirteen different categories that can be used when you interview a family remember. They are great at jogging the memory of the person being interviewed and elicit more in-depth responses.

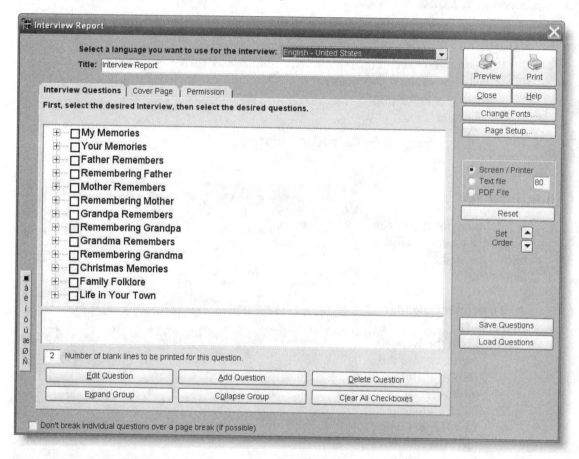

## Interview Language

The interview questions are available in English and several other languages. To select a different language, click the down arrow to the right of the combo box labeled, **Select a language you want to use for the interview**. If the desired language is not in the list, you can download any of the available files from the Legacy web site.

## Interview Title

In the Title field, enter the name of the interview. This title prints at the top of the report.

## Interview Types

There are thirteen interviews to choose from. Each interview type represents several subtopics, and each subtopic contains anywhere from 18 to 25 specific questions. To expand an interview type so that you can see its topics, click the plus sign ⊞ to the left of the interview name.

- ⊞ ☐ My Memories
- ⊞ ☐ Your Memories
- ⊞ ☐ Father Remembers
- ⊞ ☐ Remembering Father
- ⊞ ☐ Mother Remembers
- ⊞ ☐ Remembering Mother
- ⊞ ☐ Grandpa Remembers
- ⊞ ☐ Remembering Grandpa
- ⊞ ☐ Grandma Remembers
- ⊞ ☐ Remembering Grandma
- ⊞ ☐ Christmas Memories
- ⊞ ☐ Family Folklore
- ⊞ ☐ Life in Your Town

## Interview Topics

Interview topics break a specific interview into manageable pieces and deal with only a specific part or aspect of a person's life. Each topic contains one or more questions about the topic. To expand a topic to show its questions, click the plus sign ⊞ to its left.

- ⊟ ☑ My Memories
  - ⊞ ☑ All About Me
  - ⊞ ☑ An Apple a Day
  - ⊞ ☑ As Time Goes By
  - ⊞ ☑ Children in the Family
  - ⊞ ☑ Dating
  - ⊞ ☑ Faith
  - ⊞ ☑ Family Folklore
  - ⊞ ☑ Family Time
  - ⊞ ☑ Favorite Things
  - ⊞ ☑ Teenage Years
  - ⊞ ☑ Graduation and After
  - ⊞ ☑ Getting Married
  - ⊞ ☑ Holidays and Celebrations

## Interview Questions

- ⊟ ☐ Learning Responsibility
  - ☐ Chores I was responsible for when I was young?
  - ☐ Where I got spending money from and how I would spend it?
  - ☐ Did my family have enough money, or did I worry about family finances?
  - ☐ My first job for pay and what I liked about it?

The interview questions are meant to spark the memories of the person being interviewed so that he or she remembers many of the interesting details of his or her life.

**Selecting the Questions to Include**

You can include all the questions that come with a topic or you can pick and choose the ones you want. (You can also add your own questions. This is described a little further on.) To select all the questions in a specific topic, check the box to the left of the topic title.

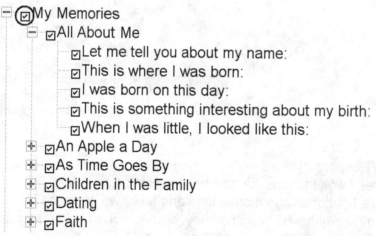

When you do this, all the questions within that topic are also checked. You can then uncheck specific questions individually if you want to. If you uncheck the box of a topic, all the questions for that topic are unchecked.

If you know that you want all the questions for small group of topics, it is easiest to just click the topic title boxes.

If you want all the questions for all the topics of a particular interview type, just click the checkbox to the left of the interview type name.

You can then uncheck any topics or questions that you don't want to include on the report.

**How Many Blank Lines?**

When an interview report is printed a certain number of blank lines are printed for each question. Legacy has set the default number of blank lines for each question. This is displayed below the question list as you highlight each question. You can change the number for any question.

## Adding Your Own Interviews and Questions

If you would like to add your own interview types, topics or questions, you can easily do so.

To add a new **interview type:**

1. Click on any existing interview type and then click the **Add Interview Type** button. You are prompted for the name of the new interview. The new type is then added to the bottom of the current list. You will notice that there is no plus sign to the left of it.
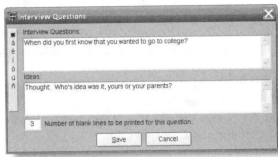

2. Highlight the new interview type and then click **Add Type or Topic**. This pops up a submenu where you choose **Add New Topic**.

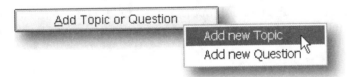

3. Enter the topic name.
4. To continue adding more topics, highlight the topic name you just added and then click **Add Topic or Question**. From the submenu, choose **Add new Topic**.

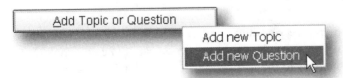

5. When you have finished adding topics, click on the first new topic and then click the **Add Topic or Question** button. From the submenu, choose **Add new Question**.

6. On the *Interview Questions* screen, type in your question in the upper text box and any ideas or prompts in the lower box.

   If you want more than the default 2 blank lines, change the number as desired. When you are finished, click **Save**. The new question is added to the list.

```
⊟  ☐My College Days
   ⊟  ☐Pre-College
         ☐When did you first know that you wanted to go to college?
      ☐Moving In
```

7.  You can now continue adding questions to the topics of your new interview type by repeating steps 5 and 6 above.

## Editing the Questions

You can change the wording of any question or any idea prompts by highlighting the question and then clicking **Edit Question**.

## Deleting a Question

To delete a question, highlight it and then click the **Delete Question** button.

## Expanding and Collapsing the Interview Groups

If you want to quickly expand all the interview types so that you can see the topics for all of them, click the **Expand Group** button.  To close all the topics and only show the interview types, click **Collapse Group**.

## Cover Page

When you print the interview report, it is nice to have a cover sheet that indicates who is being interviewed, who is doing the interviewing, and when and where it is being done.

To create a cover page, click the **Cover Page** tab.  Fill in the desired fields and comments.  Be sure to put a checkmark in the **Include Cover page on report** options.

## Permissions Page

Another important consideration before doing the actual interview is to obtain permission to use the information you collect during the interview.  By means of a simple release form, you insure both the integrity and continuity of an oral history project and safeguard each interviewee's rights.

To include a Permissions page on your report, click the **Permission** tab.  A default permission form is included with Legacy that you are welcome to use.  You can make any changes you feel appropriate.  (If you have made changes to the form and want to go back to the default wording, click the **Reset** button.)  Make sure you put a checkmark on the **Include Permission page on report** option.

## Saving Sets of Questions

You can save your interview questions in two different formats.

1. The first is the format Legacy uses to store the questions so that they can be reloaded and used again the in future. To save this format, click the **Save Questions** button and then enter a name and where you want to store them. The file extension for this type of format is **.ivw**.

2. The second format is as a standard text file. It can be loaded into a word processor or text editor (or a Legacy event note field) where you can then type in the answers that are given for the questions. To save this format, choose the **Text File** option in the *Output Options* box. Then click the Create button in the upper-right corner of the window and then enter a name and where you want to store them. The file extension for this type of format is **.txt**.

   If you want to save the results of your interview in an event for the person in your family file:
   1. Save the interview to a text file.
   2. Conduct the interview, either by typing the replies into your word processor or text editor as you go, or my transcribing the answers later into your word processor.
   3. Open your interview file with either a word processor or text editor.
   4. Highlight the entire interview document (usually by pressing **Ctrl-A**) and then Copy it to the Window Clipboard (usually by pressing **Ctrl-C**).
   5. Open your family file and navigate to the record of the person interviewed.
   6. Start a new event and call it something like Interview.
   7. Click in the **Notes** field and Paste the interview text there (usually by pressing **Ctrl-V**).
   8. Save the event.

## Loading Sets of Questions

To load a set of questions that you have previously saved, click the **Load Questions** button and specify the set of questions you want to load.

## Print the Interview Report

The interview report can be printed in different ways. These are controlled by the settings in the *Report Destination* box in the lower-right corner of the window. The output can be set to:
- Screen/Printer
- Text File
- PDF File

## Produce the report in a print preview window

Using the **Screen/Printer** option in the *Report Destination* box, click **Preview** to see the report before committing it to paper. You can view each page and see how it looks. If you find something you want to change, simply close the preview window, change the desired option(s), and then preview it again. When everything looks correct, print it on paper.

## Print directly to your printer

When you are confident of the output format, send the report directly to the printer by clicking **Print**.

# Surname Summary Report

A *Surname Summary* report summarizes all the surnames in the current family file, showing how many times each name is used and what date range it spans.

▶ **To print a Surname Summary report:**
1. From the **Reports** menu, choose **All Reports (Books and others)**.
2. Click **Surname Summary** under the **Miscellaneous Reports** column.
3. Set the Soundex Code option if desired.
4. Click **Preview** or **Print**.

(Help index: ***Report printing options***)

# Source Citation Report

The *Source Citation* report displays each master source, followed optionally by the individuals who have cited them. The specific events that use each source can also be included in this report, along with the citation detail and surety level. You can print all master sources or just those that are tagged or untagged.

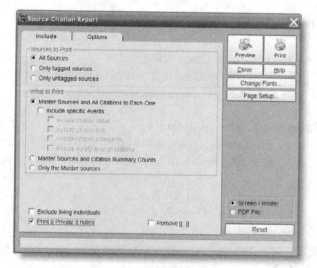

▶ **To print a Source Citation report:**
1. From the **Reports** menu, choose **All Reports (Books and others)**.
2. Click **Source Citation** under the **Miscellaneous Reports** column.
3. Choose which sources to include.
4. Set any desired options.
5. Click **Preview** or **Print**.

(Help index: ***Source citation report***)

# Age Report

The *Ages* report shows how old individuals are at certain events in their lives. The display shows three columns: Date, Day of Week, and Age. The *Date* column shows the date of the event, the *Day of Week* column shows what day of the week the event occurred, and the *Age* column shows how old the person was when the event occurred. The *Marriage* box at the bottom shows how long the couple was married. The earthly marriage is considered at an end when either of the persons has died, or on the date entered in the *Marriage Status Date*, if any. This is usually due to either a divorce or annulment.

▶ **To view the Ages window:**
From the **View** menu, choose **Ages**.

## Age Report

Husband: **Asa Clark Brown [1]**

| | Date | Day of Week | Age |
|---|---|---|---|
| Birth: | 11 Oct 1792 | Thu | 215 years, 5 months, 15 days ago |
| Christening: | | | |
| Marriage: | 1810-1815 | | 18 years |
| Death: | 8 Mar 1866 | Thu | 73 years, 4 months, 26 days |
| Burial: | Mar 1866 | | 73 years |

Wife: **Elizabeth Reynolds [33]**

| | Date | Day of Week | Age |
|---|---|---|---|
| Birth: | 1794-1804 | | 213 years ago |
| Christening: | | | |
| Marriage: | 1810-1815 | | 16 years |
| Death: | Bef. Mar 1832 | | <37 years |
| Burial: | | | |

Marriage:
Length: <21 years at death of Wife

**To print the Ages report:**

1. Click **Print Report** at the bottom of the *Ages* window.
2. Set any desired options.
3. Click either **Preview** or **Print**.

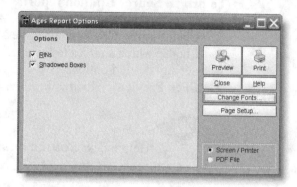

(Help index: **Ages**)

# Address Labels

You can print address labels in Legacy. The mailing labels are handy for holiday mailings and research contacts at archives and libraries.

**To print address labels:**

1. From the **Reports** menu, choose **All Reports (Books and others)**.
2. Click **Address Labels** under the **Miscellaneous Reports** column.
3. Choose which records to print.
4. Choose which fields to print on the labels.

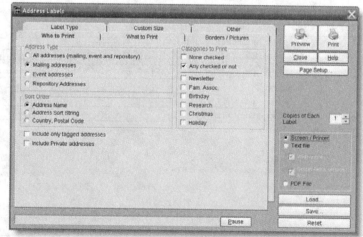

5. Select borders and pictures, if desired.
6. Select a label type, or set the specifications for a custom-size label.
7. Make other adjustments as needed for margins, indentations, and line spacing.
8. Click **Print** or **Preview**.

(Help index: *Name tags and address labels*)

# Name Tags

You can print name tags in Legacy for family reunions and clan gatherings. The labels can include the name of the event, a picture of each individual (or a common picture), the date, and the guest's name with a miniature pedigree chart to help others see how they are related.

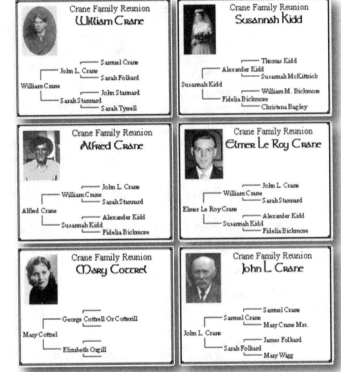

▶ **To print name tags:**
1. From the **Reports** menu, choose **All Reports (Books and others)**.
2. Click **Name Tags** under the **Miscellaneous Report** column.
3. Choose which records to print.
4. Select which fields you want to print on the tags.
5. Select borders and pictures, if desired.
6. Select a name tag type, or choose the specifications for a custom-size name tag.
7. Make other adjustments as needed for margins, indentations, and line spacing.
8. Click **Print** or **Preview**.

(Help index: *Name tags and address labels*)

# To-Do Report

▶ **To view the To-Do Report window:**

1. From the **View** menu, choose **To-Do List**. This displays the *To-Do List* window.

2. Click **Print**. The *Print To-Do List Report Options* window appears.

3. On the **Record Selection** tab, choose the type of To-Do items you want to print.

4. On the **What to Include** tab, choose the pieces of information you want to include on the report.

5. On the **Filter Options** tab, choose the types of To-Do items you want to limit the report to.

6. On the **Sort Order** tab, choose how you would like the report arranged.

7. To print the report, click **Preview** or **Print**.

The To-Do Report can also be reached from the Reports menu. Choose All Report (Books and Other) and click on To-Do Report.

(Help index: ***Print To-Do list***)

# Event Report

▶ **To Print the Events Report:**

1. From the **Reports** menu, choose **All Reports (Books and others)**.

2. Click **Event Report** under the **Miscellaneous Reports** column.

3. On the **Include** tab, choose who and what you want to print.

4. On the **Options** tab, select from the various formatting styles.

5. On the **Filter** tab, choose any options you want in order to narrow down the events printed.

6. To print the report, click **Preview** or **Print**.

(Help index: *Event report*)

# File ID Number Report

There are four types of records in Legacy that accept a File ID#. These are Master Sources, Source Citation Details, To-Do items, and Multimedia items (picture, sound, and video files). You can use these fields to create a filing system linking your family file records with printed source documentation, printed pictures, and other physical items that you want to store for the future.

The File ID Number Report lists all the numbers that you have in your family file and shows where they were used.

**To generate the File ID Number Report:**

1. Choose **All Reports (books and others)** from the **Report** pulldown menu.
2. Click **File ID Numbers**.
3. Select the desired reports options (described below).
4. Click either **Print** or **Preview** to view the report.

(Help index: *File ID Number Report*)

# Location Report

The Location report displays each master location, followed by the individuals and marriages that use them.

**To print the Location Report:**
1. Choose **All Report (books and other)** from the **Reports** pulldown menu.
2. Click **Location Report**
3. Select locations to print and who uses them from the **Include** tab
4. Check the pieces of information to be added to the report on the **Options** tab.
5. Click either **Print** or **Preview** to view the report.

# TempleReady Instructions

The TempleReady Instruction reports show you the steps you should take when submitting one or more individuals or marriage for temple work.

**To print the TempleReady Instructions Report:**
1. Choose **All Reports (books and others)** from the **Reports** pulldown menu.
2. Click on **TempleReady Instructions**.
3. Check the reports you want to print.
4. Click either **Print** or **Preview** to view the report.

# Chapter 7

# *Wall Charts*

Full-Color Masterpieces that you can be proud of

## Legacy Charting Overview

You have spent many long hours collecting and entering your family history. A feat that few other people even attempt, let alone accomplish in their lifetimes. Now you can experience the enjoyment of showing off your family tree by producing stunning full-color wall charts. Use them for your next family reunion or for a deserving wall in your home. Wall charts make great gifts for any holiday, birthday, or anniversary. They also make your own continuing genealogy research easier by having a large, easily readable working chart nearby to refer to.

Wall charts tell a story that can be seen at a glance. They are a graphical representation of your family that can extend forward or backward for many generations. Large charts are often a gathering place for conversations that bond your family together. They become family heirlooms of great importance that will be passed on into the future. So, show off all your hard work – print some wall charts!

### Starting the Wall Chart

When Legacy Charting is installed, a shortcut is placed on your Desktop to make it easy to start the program. Simply double-click the Charting icon to open the program. You can also click on the **Start** button on your desktop and then choose **Legacy Charting** from the menu to start the program.

When you first start Legacy Charting, the *Welcome to Legacy Charting* window appears where you can open an existing chart or start a new one.

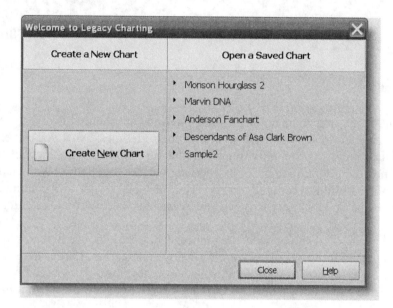

## Opening a Saved Chart

If you have previously saved some chart files, a list of up to the last ten charts are displayed on the right side of the Welcome screen. To open one, click on the name of the file. Legacy Charting opens the chart file and displays it on the screen.

## Starting a New Chart

To start a new chart, click the **Create New Chart** button. This starts the *Chart Creation Wizard*.

# Chart Creation Wizard

The *Chart Creation Wizard* consists of three easy steps: First, find the family file or GEDCOM file you want to create the chart from. Second, choose the individual from that file to start the chart from. And third, choose the type of chart you want to create.

## Step 1: Select a genealogy file to chart

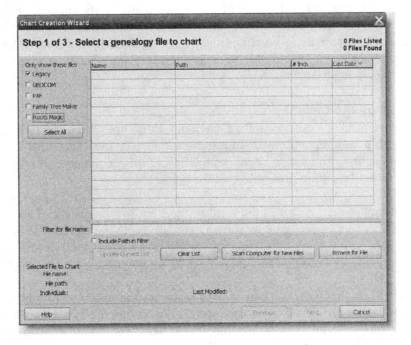

You can either have Legacy Charting scan your entire computer to find files to load, or you can browse for them yourself.

### Scanning Your Computer

Legacy Charting can create charts from several different types of files. These include Legacy Family Tree, Personal Ancestral File, Family Tree Maker, RootsMagic and GEDCOM files. To begin, click **Scan Computer for New Files**. The scanning process can take several minutes to search your entire computer. The time involved depends on the speed of your computer, the size of your hard drives, and how many qualifying files are found. When the process is complete, a list of the files found is displayed in the grid. While scanning, Legacy Charting collects all the file names for all the supported file types. When the resulting list is displayed, the file types shown depend on the filtering options you have selected. Please see **Filtering the List** below to see how this works.

The file list includes the name of the file, the path where it is located on your computer, how many individuals are contained in the file, and the date the file was last accessed.

The list of files is retained even when you quit Legacy Charting. When you start again, the list is still there. If you create additional family files or receive new GEDCOM files, you can have them added to the list by clicking **Scan Computer for New Files** again.

## Sorting the List

You can sort the file list by any of the four columns by clicking on the desired column heading. The first time you click the column, the list is sorted in ascending order as indicated by a small up-pointing triangle next to the column name. If you click the column heading a second time, the sort order is changed to descending, as shown by a down-pointing triangle.

## Filtering the List

Use the checkbox options in the **Genealogy File Types** box to include specific types of chartable files in the file list. To just display Legacy files, select the **Legacy** option and clear the rest. To include Legacy and GEDCOM files, put checkmarks in both options. To show all possible files, select all the types.

In the upper-right corner of the window there are two indicators. The top line shows how many files are currently being shown in the list (with the current filters) and the lower line shows how many files Legacy Charting found when it did its last scan. As you change filter options you can quickly see how many files are in the list.

There is another filter that can be used to narrow the list down further and help you to find specific file names. You can type characters into the **Filter for file name** text box to limit the list to file names containing those characters. There are two options below the text box, **Starts With** and **Include Path in Filter**. If neither of these options is selected, the file names included in the list will have the filter characters located anywhere within the names of the files. For example, if you enter "er" then files with names like **Ernhart**, **Rymer**, and **Fern** are included. If you select the **Starts With** box, only **Ernhart** is displayed. Selecting the **Include Path in Filter** option expands the search to include the **Path** column as well as the **Name** column.

## Update File List

When Legacy Charting scans your computer for chartable files, it looks at each file to see how many individuals it contains. If you later add new individuals, or delete some, you can have Legacy Charting recheck the files in the list to update the numbers by clicking the **Update File List** button.

## Clearing the List

If you would like to clear the file list, click **Clear List**.

## Selecting a File to Chart

To select one of the files in the list to chart, click on the name to highlight the line and then click the **Next** button. You can also double-click the file to choose it and automatically move to the next step.

## Browsing for a File Yourself

If you don't want to use the scanning feature of Legacy Charting, or if you don't want to wait for a new scan to pick up a new file (on a flash drive for example), you can find the file manually by clicking **Browse for File**. This opens a standard **Open** dialog box where you can select the drive, folder, and file you want to chart. When you select a file in this manner, you are then taken to step two.

# Step 2: Select an individual

The second step of the *Chart Creation Wizard* is to select the starting individual for the chart. A list of all the individuals in the file is displayed.

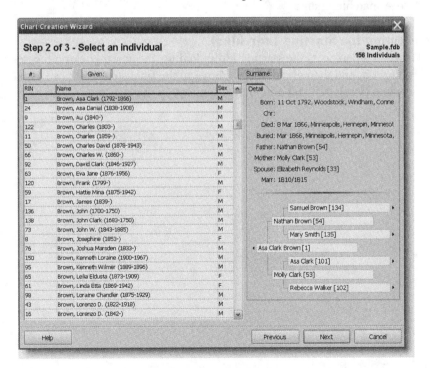

## What is Shown

The name list shows the record identification number (RIN), the name, and the gender of each individual in the file. To the right, on the **Detail** tab, dates and location are displayed for the individual along with the names of the parents and spouse. Below this information is a three-generation pedigree chart that begins with the current person and includes his or her parents and grandparents (if they are in the file).

### Navigating the Pedigree Chart

The pedigree chart can be navigated up and down. Clicking on any name moves that person to the starting position in the middle. You can navigate down by clicking the left-arrow to the left of the starting person. The first child of that person is displayed. You can also move to the right (to older generations) by clicking the right-arrows to the right of the four grandparents.

### Sorting the Name List

The name list can be sorted into RIN, Given Name, or Surname ascending order by clicking the #, Given, and Surname buttons at the top.

### Searching for a Name

You can search for a name in the list by entering a RIN, Given Name, or Surname into the appropriate text box at the top. As you type, the highlight in the list jumps to the nearest matching name.

### Selecting the Starting Individual

To select a person as the starting individual for the chart, click on the desired name to highlight it, and then click **Next** to move to the final step. You can also double-click on the name to select it and automatically move to the last step.

## Step 3: Select the type of chart to create

Legacy Charting offers several different styles of charts to choose from. These include Ancestor, Descendant, DNA, Fan, Hour Glass, and Bow Tie charts. Many of these charts have variations in spacing and layout giving you eighteen distinct charts.

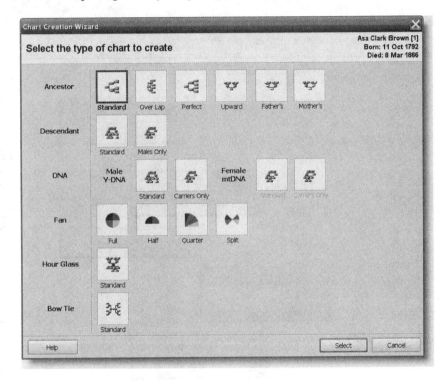

To select a chart type, click on the desired format and then click the **Select** button. You can also just double-click on a chart button to select it.

After selecting a chart, Legacy Charting generates the chart, starting with the person you selected and automatically selecting 5 generations. From here you can change many aspects of the chart, including size, color, spacing, content, and much more.

# The Legacy Charting Screen

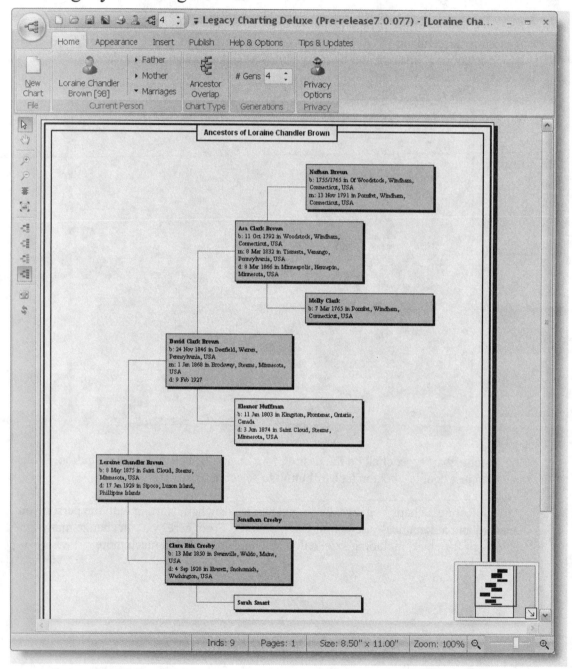

The main charting screen displays the chart you are working on. It is shown in the central portion of the window. Besides showing the current chart, the Legacy Charting screen offers many tools, options and commands that you can use to change and enhance the chart you are creating. You can change the starting person of your chart as well as the chart type. Charting has built-in themes that you can use to quickly change the look and feel of your chart. Many pre-defined color schemes are also available along with various borders and shadow effects. Pictures can be placed within the individual boxes as well as on the background of the chart. You can print your chart on your own printer or export a file that can be printed on a large-format plotter to create professional wall charts.

## The Home Tab of the Ribbon

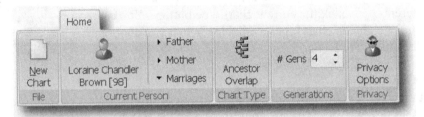

### Home Tab
The **Home** tab is part of the main Ribbon of Legacy Charting. (See The Ribbon for more information on how to use this main toolbar.)

#### File

##### Starting a New Chart
Click **New Chart** to create a new chart. This starts the three-step *Chart Creation Wizard* taking you through the process of selecting a file, starting individual, and chart type. If you have been working on a chart, you are prompted to save it before the new chart is created. (See Chart Creation Wizard for complete instructions on using the wizard.)

#### Current Person

##### Selecting the Starting Person
If you want to change the starting person of your chart, click **Select Individual** in the *Current Person* section. This is the button on the left side of the section with the

icon. This opens the *Chart Creation Wizard* where you can change to any person in the family file you are working with. When you return, the chart is redrawn with the new starting person. Note that if you have customized the chart by moving boxes around and resizing them, the new chart will revert to the default layout. Any color changes that you have made will remain in effect.

### Changing the Starting Person by Navigating

You can change the starting person of your chart to the father, mother, spouse, or child of the current starting person by clicking on **Father**, **Mother**, or **Marriage**. Clicking **Marriage** displays the spouses and children of the current person where you can select who you would like to change to.

### Changing the Chart Type

The current chart type is shown above the **Chart Type** label. To select a different type, click the current chart type button. You can choose from the eighteen chart types available. When you choose a new type, the chart is redrawn.

### Changing the Generations

When first displayed, your chart is built out to five generations. If you want more or fewer generations, you can change the setting by using the up and down arrows or by typing the desired number of generations and pressing **Enter**.

### Privacy

#### Suppress private individuals

Selecting this option removes any person who is marked as Private from the chart. Any line of people extending from the Private person is also removed.

#### Suppress private information [[Private]]

Any information that is marked as **Private**, using the [[ and ]] markers, is removed from the boxes.

#### Suppress details for living people

If a person is marked as being alive, only their name is shown in the box. If you would like to have the name changed to "**Living**," select the **Use "Living" instead of their name** option.

# The Appearance Tab of the Ribbon

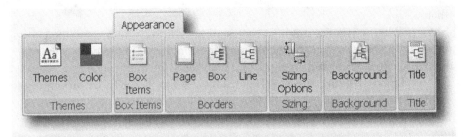

The **Appearance** tab is part of the main Ribbon of Legacy Charting. (See The Ribbon for more information on how to use this main toolbar.)

### Themes
### Themes

Legacy Charting has many pre-defined themes that you can use to format your chart. A theme includes a coordinated combination of fonts, colors, and borders to achieve a certain look. You can load a theme, alter it to your liking and then save it as a new theme. Themes include box colors, box gradients, box spacing, line colors, box content, borders, and fonts. Box sizes, generation settings, rearrangement of boxes or generations, and starting individuals are not included in a theme.

Because of the different layouts of each kind of chart, themes are specific to each chart type. A theme from one type of chart cannot be applied to a different chart type.

 To select a theme, click the **Themes** option to open the *Chart Themes* box. You can select any existing theme by either clicking on the theme name to highlight it and then clicking on **Apply Theme to Chart** in the **Actions** section below the theme list, or by double-clicking the theme name. When you select a new theme, the chart is immediately redrawn with the new options.

#### Actions

**Apply Theme to Chart** – Applies the currently selected theme to the current chart.
**Create New Theme** – Prompts you for a theme name and then creates a new theme

with the current chart layout and settings.

**Edit Theme Name** – Prompts you for a new name for the currently selected theme.

**Save to Theme [theme name]** – Saves all the currently settings to the current theme. This is how you change the setting for a theme in the list – Select the theme, make any desired changes, and then **Save** the theme again.

**Delete Theme [theme name]** – Deletes the current theme (after prompting for confirmation).

## Colors

Legacy Charting has many pre-defined color themes you can choose from while formatting your chart. These include themes for coloring by generation, ancestral line, and by gender.

To select a color theme, click the **Color** option to open the *Color Themes* box. Click the type of color formatting you want to use – either **By Generation**, **4 Colors**, or **Gender**. Click the specific color theme you want to use and then click **Apply Color Theme to Chart** in the **Actions** section. (You can also just double-click the desired color theme.) The selected theme is then instantly applied to your chart.

**Actions**

**Apply Color Theme to Chart** – Applies the currently selected color theme to your chart.

**Edit Color Theme Name** – Prompts for a new name for the currently selected color theme.

**Save to Color Theme [theme name]** – Saves all the current color settings to the current color theme. This is how you change the colors for a theme in the list – Select the theme, make any desired changes, and then **Save** the theme again.

**Delete Color Theme** – Deletes the current theme (after prompting for confirmation).

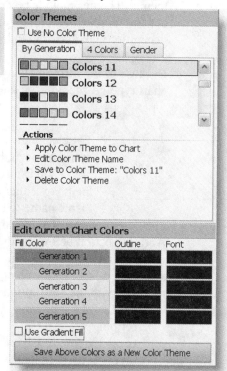

### Gradient Fill

You can change the solid colors to gradient filled colors by selecting the **Use Gradient Fill** option. This fills the boxes with the color fading from left to right.

## Box Items

The default information to be included in a chart box is the name, birth date and place, marriage date and place, and death date and place. In addition to these fields, you can also include the christening and burial information as well as the lifespan of the individuals.

### Adding an Item

To include a new item of information in the chart boxes, highlight the desired item in the **Available Items** list and then click the > button to copy it to the **Items to Display** list.

### Deleting An Item

To remove an item, highlight it and then click the < button. You can also delete all the items at once by clicking the << button.

### Moving an Item in the List

You can move an item up or down in the list to rearrange the order of the items in the chart boxes. To do this, highlight the item you want to move and then use the up ▲ and down ▼ arrows to move it.

### Formatting the Items

Each item that you include in boxes can be customized using the *Item Options* to the right of the *Items to Display* list. Names can be formatted in several different orders; birth, christening, death, and burial information can exclude the locations; items can be preceded by labels; and the fonts and font sizes can be changed.

### Settings

Each item can be placed in one of three columns within a box. If everything is placed within one column, that column will expand to occupy the entire width of the box. If items are placed in the left column and right column with nothing in the center column, the two used columns will expand to each occupy half of the width of the box. If items are placed in the left and middle columns, the middle column will expand to occupy two-thirds of the box. And finally, if only the middle and right columns have items, the middle column will expand to take up the left two-thirds.

## Borders

### Page Borders

Select from five chart borders by clicking on the desired style. (If you don't want a border, select the **No page border** checkbox.) The borders are fancy lines that encircle the entire chart. The borders can either be out at the page edges (select the **Align to the page** checkbox) or held in close to the actual chart itself. When held close to the chart, you can choose the margin distance. You can also select the line color of the border by clicking the color box below **Line Color**.

### Box Borders

The lines surrounding each person's box can be selected from the four available styles (or turned off). You can select different box styles for males, females, and people of unknown gender. Box shadows can be added.

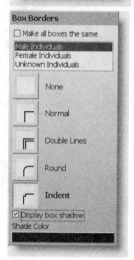

### Lines

The width and color of the lines that connect the boxes together can be changed.

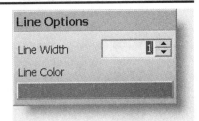

### Sizing

### Box Width

You can change the width of all the boxes by dragging the slider control to the left or right. This changes all the boxes on the chart. Boxes can be sized from 1/2 of an inch up to six inches wide which is desirable when creating large wall charts.

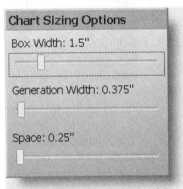

### Sibling Spacing

If you are creating a descendant chart, you can adjust the spacing between adjacent siblings.

### Generation Width

The horizontal spacing between the generation columns can be increased or decreased, varying from 1/8 of an inch up to six inches.

### Box Spacing

The vertical spacing between the boxes can be increased or decreased from 1/16 of an inch up to six inches.

## Background

You can select a solid-color to fill the background of the chart or any image can be used. When using an image, you can adjust the transparency to fade the picture lighter.

When adding an image to the background, you have several options as to its placement:

**Tile** – The image is repeated at its full size until the entire background if filled. This best used with a background image that was meant to fit together as a continuous pattern.

**Center with no stretching** – The picture is placed at its full image size once in the middle on the chart.

**Center and stretch** – The picture is enlarged proportionally until it is either the same width or same height as the chart.

**Stretch to Frame** – The picture is stretched both ways until it fills the entire chart background area. This option is used the most when placing a background image. You should take into account the shape of the picture so that you don't place a tall, narrow picture on a short, wide chart, as the stretching effect will be very noticeable. In most cased, however, the stretching is visually acceptable.

## Picture Resolution

Keep in mind that pictures used on a wall chart are generally larger than those you might see in a book or other page-sized report. If your pictures are low-resolution, they will probably look very grainy and jagged when enlarged on your wall chart. You should use the highest resolution you can when selecting pictures. This is especially important for pictures that are being enlarged for use as the background of the chart.

You can also use both a color and an image. The color will colorize the image more and more as you adjust the transparency more to the right.

### Title & Legend
You can add, change, or remove a title and legend to the chart.

## The Insert Tab of the Ribbon

### Insert Tab
The **Insert** tab is part of the main Ribbon of Legacy Charting. (See The Ribbon for more information on how to use this main toolbar.)

### Picture
One or more pictures can be placed in the background of the chart. These pictures lie in a layer that is behind the chart boxes. You can stretch these pictures to any size, even filling the entire background area of the chart. Pictures can be cropped, rotated, converted to black and white, and faded. Adjustments can be made to the brightness, contrast and saturation of the pictures. Drop shadows can also be added. (When you make these types of changes, you are working with a copy of the picture. The original is not changed.)

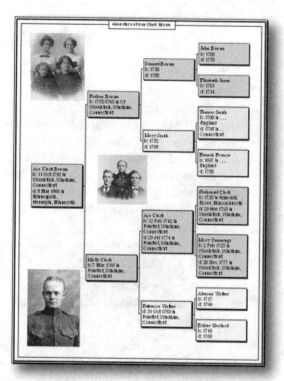

### Picture Resolution
Keep in mind that pictures used on a wall chart are generally larger than those you might see in a book or other page-sized report. If your pictures are low-resolution, they will probably look very grainy and jagged when enlarged on your wall chart. You should use the highest

resolution you can when selecting pictures. This is especially important for pictures that are being enlarged for use as the background of the chart.

### Stretching a Picture
When you click on a picture, eight handles appear around the edge of the image that you can use to change its size. The handles in the corners, when dragged, increase or decrease the picture size while maintaining the current aspect ratio (width and height proportions). The handles on the middle of each side are used to stretch the image vertically or horizontally. In other words, it will pull the picture out of its original proportions, making the picture, and the things or people within it, fatter or taller.

### Text
One or more text boxes can be placed and moved to any position to enhance and describe the various parts of your chart. The fill and text color can be changed and the box border lines can be adjusted or removed. Drop shadows can also be added.

Mother's Sisters

## The Publish Tab of the Ribbon

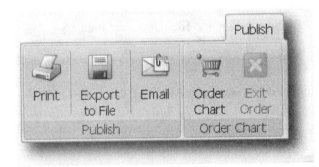

### Publish Tab
The **Publish** tab is part of the main Ribbon of Legacy Charting. (See The Ribbon for more information on how to use this main toolbar.)

The ultimate goal of creating a large chart is to print it and hang it up for all to see and enjoy. Charts can range from a single letter-sized page to a hundred square feet or more. Simple charts with only a few generations can often be sized and positioned so as to only take one small sheet of paper and be easily printed on your personal printer. Large charts can oftentimes require dozens or even hundreds of letter-sized pages to print. These are better reserved for output on a plotter where they can be printed on a single sheet of paper that can generally be up to 42 inches wide and twelve feet long. Plotters are often found at larger copy centers. Charting also has a built-in and affordable chart printing service.

Your chart can be printed on your personal printer at any time. Depending upon the size of your chart, it might span many pages that you would have to cut and tape together. The total number of pages that your chart will print upon is shown in the **Status** bar along the bottom of the window. Sometimes it is more efficient, taking fewer pages, to orient your paper to landscape rather than portrait mode before printing. (To make this change, go to the **Home** tab and choose **Page Setup**.)

### Printing Your Chart On Own Printer

To print your chart, click **Print** on the **Publish** tab (or on the **Quick Access Toolbar**). From the **Print** dialog box, make sure the correct printer is selected. If you only want to print a range of pages, set the **from** and **to** values accordingly. (The pages of the chart, as shown by the dashed red lines, are numbered left to right, and top to bottom.) When you are ready to print, click **OK**.

### Exporting to a File

You can export your chart to a graphic file in several different formats. These include PDF, Bitmap, Jpeg, PNG, Tiff, and PSD. PDF files are a great way to send charts to people by way of email. The other formats are useful when including charts in books and other publications.

To export your chart, click the **Export to File** button on the **Publish** tab. Choose the desired format, select the export folder and file name, and then click **OK**.

### Email

When you have produced a nice chart and you want to share it with another family member or friend, it is convenient to be able to email it to him or her. You can attach a PDF version of the chart or convert the chart to one of the other available file formats and send that.

To send a chart by email, click the **Email** button on the **Publish** tab. Choose the file format (PDF File is usually the best)

### Ordering a Printed Wall Chart

There are two modes for laying out charts in the program. The first one is used for charts that you will be printing on your own printer. The second is for layout charts that will be printed on a plotter. Charting has a built-in professional chart printing service that make it very easy to visualize what your wall chart will look like when it is printed and how much it will cost to order it from us.

To start the professional layout process, click **Order Chart** on the **Publish** tab. When you do, the *Order Option* panel is displayed along the right side of the Charting window. You will also notice that the chart area changes to the paper size currently shown in the Order Option panel. Plotter paper only comes in three widths, 24", 36", and 42" wide. You can print your chart on one of these paper widths. The length of the chart can be up to 12 feet long. If your chart is wider than 42", you can have it printed in two or more strips.

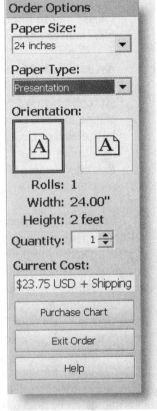

**Orientation of the Paper**

**Portrait** – When you have portrait mode selected, the paper roll on the screen goes from the top down. As you increase the height of your chart, the roll will extend in one-foot increments. If your chart extends off to the right of the current paper roll, another strip is added. If you have selected 24" paper, another 24" strip is added. If your chart only needs 36" or 42" in width, you should change to that width of paper, thus using only one strip instead of two or more.

**Landscape** – When you have landscape mode selected, the paper goes from left to right. As you increase the width of your chart, the roll will extend in one-foot increments. If your chart extends off the bottom of the current paper roll, another strip is added. Again, if you have selected 24" paper, another 24" strip is added. If your chart only needs 36" or 42" in height, you should change to the appropriate width of paper so that you minimize the use of additional strips.

The charting service offers four different types of paper upon which you can have your chart printed. These include:

**20lb Bond Paper** – Bond paper is about as heavy as typing paper. It is not archival but is perfect for research charts that are going to be written on and added to. It is not heavy enough for good picture quality however. Cost: $15 plus $1, $2 or $3 per linear foot (for 24", 36", and 42" respectively).

**24lb Presentation Paper** – This is a quality presentation paper that is about as heavy as typing paper. It is archival, bright white, UV coated, and is perfect for charts with decorative elements. Cost: $15 plus $2, $3 or $4 per linear foot.

**Glossy Photo Paper** – This is an archival 80lb heavy glossy photo paper. The gloss makes photos appear crisp and clear. Cost: $15 plus $6, $9 or $12 per linear foot.

**Artist Grade Matte Canvas** – This is a heavy matte archival artist's canvas. The canvas giclée printing process is the same archival quality as a fine art reproduction from an art gallery. It is a rich, beautiful medium for a classic looking genealogy chart. The light texture helps lower-quality antique pictures look cleaner. Cost: $15 plus $20, $28 or $35 per linear foot.

### Pricing
As you select the paper size and type, the printing cost for your chart is displayed.

### Purchasing a Chart
When you are ready to place an order for a printed chart, click the **Purchase Chart** button. Charting takes you through a 3-step review of your order to double-check the size, orientation, paper type, quantity, cost, and shipping information. Finally, you indicate your desire to place the order by clicking the **Order Chart** button on Step 3 and then you are taken through the payment and shipping steps, and find out what the shipping cost will be to your location from our Utah-based printer. (Other printers at other location may be added in the future.) Sales tax is also added for Arizona, Utah, and Washington State orders. At the end of this process you then do a final confirm of the order, upload your chart file and then sit back and wait for your beautiful charts to arrive at your doorstep. (You should allow up to two weeks for chart delivery. Rush delivery is available for an extra charge, cutting the normal delivery time in half.)

# The Help & Options Tab of the Ribbon

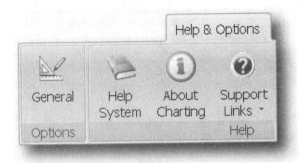

The **Help and Options** tab is part of the main Ribbon of Legacy Charting. (See The Ribbon for more information on how to use this main toolbar.)

### Options
#### General
Clicking on the **General** button displays the *Chart Options* window.

#### View Tab
##### Appearance
**Show page boundaries** – Shows the page boundaries with dashed red lines. This is determined by the current printer and page size selected in the Printer Setup.
**Use short locations** – Uses the short version of the location names. (Note: You must reapply the current theme when you change this option.)

##### Default Privacy Options when a chart is created
**Suppress private individuals** – If, by default, you don't want to include the private individuals from your charts, select this option.
**Suppress private information** – If, by default, you want to suppress information that is marked as [[private]], select this option.
**Suppress details for living people** – If, by default, you want to not include the detail information for individuals that are still alive, select this option.
**Use "Living" instead of their name** – If you would like to set as a default to use the word "Living" instead of displaying a living person's name, select this option.

##### Default Box Item Settings
**Font** – Select the default font for the text items in a box.
**Size** – Select the default font size for text items in a box.

### Measurements

Choose between inch or metric measurements to be shown in the program.

## User Information Tab

Enter your name and contact information here. You can include this information in the chart Legend if desired.

## Folder Locations Tab

**Chart File Folder** – Specify the default folder in which to store your chart file.
**Genealogy File Folder** – Specify the default folder to display when you are browsing for a genealogy family file to load for charting.
**Image Folder** – Specify the default folder to display when you are selecting an image to display on the chart.
**Export Folder** – Specify the default folder to display when you are choosing where to export a chart file.

## Date Options Tab

### Date Format

Select from six date display formats:

| | |
|---|---|
| mmm dd, yyyy | Nov 30, 1854 |
| dd mmm yyyy | 30 Nov 1854 |
| mm-dd-yyyy | 11-30-1854 |
| dd-mm-yyyy | 30-11-1854 |
| yyyy mmm dd | 1854 Nov 30 |
| yyyy-mm-dd | 1854-11-30 |

### Separators for numeric dates

If you are using either the dd-mm-yyyy or mm-dd-yyyy format, you can specify the separator character to place between the date parts. Click the option button for the appropriate symbol.

If you are using a date format that doesn't include separator characters, such as 21 Apr 1900, then Charting uses the selected date separator character between any year ranges. For example, 21 Apr 1953-1958 would appear as 21 Apr 1953/1958 if the slash was chosen as the separator character.

### Month Format

You can further alter the way dates are formatted by selecting abbreviated or full month names and initial or all uppercase month names. Click the option buttons corresponding to the desired format.

### Character format

You can display the months with Initial Caps, all uppercase, or all lowercase.

**Note**:  The date settings are only applied when a new theme or box item is added to the chart.

### Help System
#### Online Help
To open the help system for Legacy Charting, click the **Help System** option.  From the help system you can search by topic or use the **Contents** tab to answer your questions.

If you want context-sensitive help (help on what you are currently doing), press the **F1** function key on your keyboard.

#### About Charting
Legacy Charting is developed and distributed by Millennia Corporation, Surprise, Arizona.  Copyright 2008, Millennia Corporation.  All rights reserved.

#### Support Links
Get information concerning customer support, reporting a bug, suggesting new features, or going to the Charting web site, you will find it here.

## The Tips & Updates Tab of the Ribbon

#### Updates
The current version number of Legacy Charting that you have installed is displayed on this tab.  If you are connected to the Internet, Legacy Charting checks to see if you have the latest update.  If not, a link is provided to download the most current update.

### Messages

If you have Internet access, the ***Message Center*** is the place to go to get the latest tips and tricks concerning your charting experience. Check here often for helpful articles and announcements.

## The Picture Settings Tab of the Ribbon

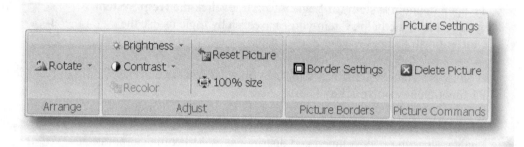

### Picture Settings Tab

The **Picture Settings** tab is part of the main Ribbon of Legacy Charting. It only appears when you have a picture selected within your chart. (See The Ribbon for more information on how to use this main toolbar.)

#### Rotating

You can rotate a picture right or left in 90 degree increments. This may be necessary if a picture was taken by rotating the camera to fit a person or scene better. You can also flip a picture top-to-bottom or left-to-right. Flipping a picture top-to-bottom is not the same as flipping the picture 180 degrees. When flipping top-to-bottom or left-to-right, the picture is actually reversed. If there is any writing on the picture or anything that would look "wrong," like a clock, or two people shaking right hands, the viewer will notice... so be careful.

#### Bring to Front & Send to Back

By default, text boxes are cover pictures. This means that if you drag a text box over a picture, the picture will appear behind the text box. To change this, click on the picture and choose **Bring to Front** in the **Arrange** section of the **Picture Settings** tab. (Or you can click on the text box and then click **Send to Back** in the **Text Appearance** section of the **Text Settings** tab.)

Pictures and text boxes cannot be brought in front of individual chart boxes. The chart boxes are always on the top layer.

### Image Adjustments

**Brightness** – You can adjust the image brightness from -40% (darker) to +40% (lighter) to make your pictures look better.

**Contrast** – You can change the contrast from -40% (blurrier) to +40% (sharper).

**Re-color** – Charting supports the displaying and printing of both color and black and white pictures. Color pictures can be converted to gray scale (black and white) by clicking **To Gray Scale**. This is often necessary if you are printing charts on a non-color printer or plotter. Color pictures sent to a black and white printer often come out looking muddy and washed out.

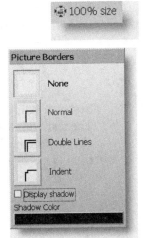

**Reset Picture** – To revert back to the original picture, abandoning any changes you have made to it, click **Reset Picture**. (When Charting places a picture on your chart, a copy is made of the original. As you make changes to the chart picture, you are working with the copy, not the original.)

**100% Size** – If you have stretched a picture smaller or larger, you can revert back to its original full size.

### Image Settings

**Aspect Ratio**

The aspect ratio of a picture is the original width to height ratio. If you stretch a picture wider or taller, the aspect ratio changes and the picture can look strange (although a small amount of tweaking can make a person look better in many cases…).

To restore a picture that has been stretched, to its original proportions, click **Reset Picture**.

To restore a picture to its full size, click **100% size**.

### Picture Borders

To place a border around your picture, click Border Settings  and then select the border style you would like. You can also have a drop shadow placed behind the picture.

### Deleting a Picture

To delete the current picture, click  .

# The Text Settings Tab of the Ribbon

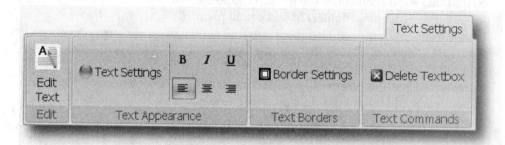

### Text Settings Tab

The **Text Settings** tab is part of the main Ribbon of Legacy Charting. It only appears when you have a text box selected on your chart. (See The Ribbon for more information on how to use this main toolbar.)

#### Edit

To add or edit the text in the text box, click **Edit Text**. When you have made the desired changes, click **OK**.

#### Text Settings

The font used for the text is selected from the **Text Font** option and the text size from the **Font Size** option. To change the color of the text, make the change from the **Font Color** option. You can change the background fill color of the text box by selecting a color from the **Background Color** option.

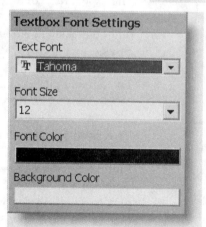

#### Styles & Alignment

The text within a text box can be bolded, italicized, and underlined by clicking on the desired style. The text alignment can also be set to left-, right-, or center-justified.

## Border Settings
### Displaying a Frame

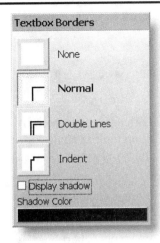

To display a lined frame around a text box, click on the **Border Settings** option. Choose the desired border style. You can also choose to have a drop shadow displayed behind the text box.

# The File Button

**The File Button**

The nice looking round button in the upper-left corner of the main screen is called the **File Button.** It lets you start a new chart, open an existing chart, save a chart, and change the name of a chart. You can also print your chart on your local printer from here, as well as change the settings on your printer. And last, but not least, you can close Legacy Charting.

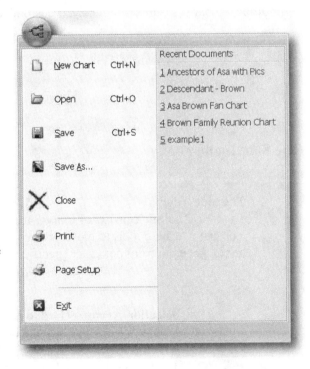

## The Quick Access Toolbar

### The Quick Access Toolbar

The small toolbar along the top side in the upper-left corner is called the Quick Access Toolbar. It is always visible and gives you some commonly needed options. These include starting a new chart , opening an existing chart , saving a chart , saving a chart under a new name , printing a chart , selecting a new starting individual , selecting a new chart type , and changing the number of generations for a chart 6 . Just to the right of the toolbar is a button that lets you customize it .

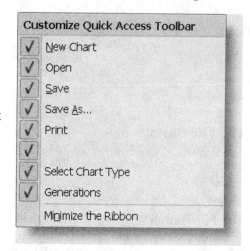

### The Side Toolbar

### The Side Toolbar

The **Side Toolbar** consists of tools that affect the layout and viewing of your chart. You can use these tools to move your chart around the page (or pages), move individual boxes, generations of boxes, or specific ancestor or descendant lines of boxes.

**The Selection Arrow** - Used to select one or more boxes and then move them around on the chart. When you select a box, the box's background turns black. To move a selected box, drag it with the mouse cursor. The number of boxes that actually move when you drag a selected box depends on the setting of the **Drag** button lower in the toolbar. You can select more than one box by holding down the **Shift** key while you click on additional boxes. You can also select multiple boxes by drawing a box that touches or encloses the desired boxes. (With your mouse, point to a place on the background that is above and to the left of the upper-left box you want to select and then press down and hold the left mouse button while you then drag a rectangular box around the boxes you want to select on the chart. When you release the mouse button, all the boxes enclosed or touched by the rectangle are selected.)

When you move any of the selected boxes, all the other selected boxes move with it (along with the other line or generation boxes specified by the current **Drag** button). If you drag a box off the right or bottom edge of your chart area, additional pages are automatically added to accommodate them. Likewise, if you drag all the boxes off of a page along the right or bottom side, the unused pages are removed for you.

**The Drag Hand** – When the chart is zoomed in to be larger than the main chart window, you can drag it around using the **Drag Hand** in order to view other parts of the chart. Just hold the left mouse button down while you drag the chart in any direction.

**Zooming In and Out** – You can zoom your chart in and out, from 3 percent to 200 percent - to get the big picture or to see fine detail. (You can also zoom in and out using the center wheel on your mouse, if you have one.)

**Center Chart** – Re-centers the chart within the least number of pages needed to hold it. Only the chart boxes and lines are repositioned. All pictures or text boxes that you have added are left alone.

**Zoom to Chart** – Sets the zoom level so that the chart fills the main chart window, if possible. (If the chart is very large, the zoom level is set to a minimum of 3 percent. You will then have to use the **Drag Hand** or the **Navigator Square** to move around the chart.)

**The Drag Buttons** – These determine which boxes are moved when you drag a selected box.

**Drag only one Individual** – Only the selected box (or boxes, if more than one has been highlighted) moves when dragged with the mouse.

**Drag Lines of Individuals** – The selected box and all connected ancestor boxes (for an ancestor chart), or descendant boxes (for a descendant chart) move when dragged with the mouse.

**Drag all Individuals of the same Generation** – All the boxes in the same generation as the selected box are moved.

**Drag All Individuals** – All the boxes on the chart are moved when the selected box is moved. This includes any text or picture boxes on the chart.

The **Reformat Chart** button – Resets the current chart to the default layout (after asking for permission to do so). If you have moved boxes around on an ancestor or descendant style chart, the boxes will be moved back to their default locations. So, if you have spent a long time rearranging your chart boxes, don't use this feature unless you want to start all over again.

**Note**: The **Reformat Chart** button doesn't have any effect on Fan charts.

## The Navigator Square

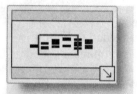

The **Navigator Square**, in the lower-right corner of the main chart window, gives you an overall view of your chart, no matter how big it is. If your chart is one page or 4000 pages, the entire chart is always shown. The red rectangle shows the current portion of the chart that is being shown on the screen. As you move around your chart, the red rectangle always shows where you are. This is especially nice when you have a very large chart. You can also drag the red rectangle in the Navigator Square to a new position on the small chart to change the portion showing on the main screen. This is often the best way to quickly zoom into a specific portion of a large chart. The Arrow in the lower-right ⌄ minimizes the navigation square. To restore the Navigation Square, click the arrow again ↖.

## The Status Bar

| Inds: 12 | Pages: 3 | Size: 25.50" x 11.00" | Zoom: 150% |
|----------|----------|------------------------|------------|

**The Status Bar**
The Status Bar, along the bottom of the main chart window, displays how many individuals are included on the chart, how many pages the chart would require to be printed on your local printer, the resulting overall size of the chart, and what the current zoom level is.

# The Ribbon

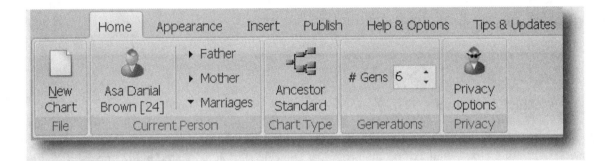

The Ribbon is designed to help you quickly find the commands that you need to complete a task. Commands are organized in logical groups, which are collected together under tabs. Each tab relates to a type of activity, such as chart appearance or publishing. To reduce clutter, some tabs are shown only when needed. For example, the **Picture Settings** tab is only displayed when you have a picture selected.

## How it Works
### Quick Overview
Clicking on a tab heading (Home, Appearance, Insert, Publish, or Help & Options) displays the *gallery* of options for that tab. To select an option, click on it. Most options then display a dialog box where you can choose what you want. For example, a color, a box item, the box sizes, the title of the chart, and many more.

### Always keep the Ribbon minimized
To minimize the Ribbon, right-click on any option on it and then choose **Minimize the Ribbon**.

The Ribbon will remain minimized with only the tabs showing. When you click on a tab, the Ribbon opens and shows the options associated with that tab. After selecting an option, the Ribbon closes again, only showing the tabs headings. Another way to quickly minimize the Ribbon is to double-click the name of any of the tabs.

### Restore the Ribbon

Click **Customize Quick Access Toolbar** and then click **Minimize the Ribbon** in the list. Or, double-click a tab again to restore the Ribbon.

## Other Toolbars and Buttons

### The File Button

The **File Button** provides access to all of the document and system-level functionality in the program. These include starting a new chart, opening an existing chart, saving and printing charts, and exiting the program. The File Button is located in the upper-left corner of the window.

### Quick Access Toolbar

The **Quick Access Toolbar**, located to the right of the **File Button**, is another place where you can access the options of the **File Button**. See **The Quick Access Toolbar** on page 214.

### Side Toolbar

The toolbar on the left side of the screen controls the mouse's actions on the chart. See **The Side Toolbar** on page 214.

### Status Bar

See **The Status Bar** on page 216.

# Chapter 8

# *Map My Family*

## How to Select Individuals and Families for Temple Submission

The *Map My Family* window plots all the locations associated with a person allowing you to see where he spent his life. This often shows a path or migration pattern for the individual and may offer additional clues as to where other events happened during his life. Along with the locations belonging to the individual, you can also include the locations associated with the birth and death of the spouse, children, and parents. Marriage locations can also be included.

To display the map, choose **Map of Places** from the **View** menu, or click the Mapping button if you have placed it on the toolbar. When the map is initially displayed, it is broad enough to encompass all the locations that have been selected to include.

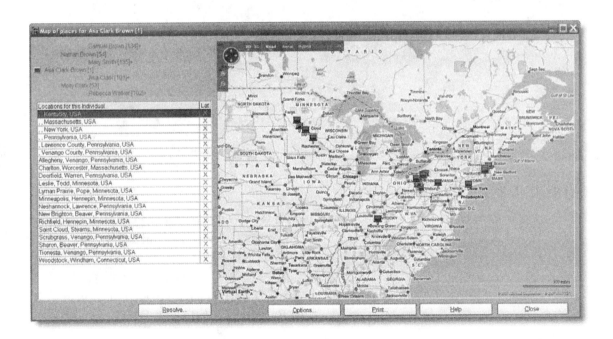

As you place the mouse pointer over each pin, a text balloon appears showing the name of the location and a list of the events that happened there.

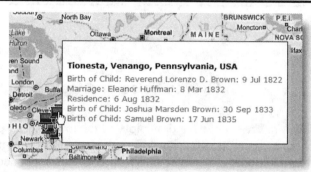

Initially, the pushpins might be stacked one atop another making them difficult to tell apart. To move the pins apart, use the **Zoom In** 🔍 button. As you enlarge the map area, the pushpins move apart and are easily differentiated.

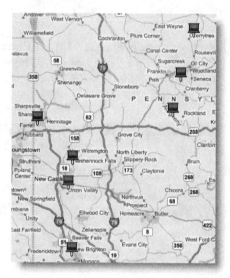

# Working With the Map

In the upper-left corner of the map is the *View Control*. The *View Control* lets you zoom in 🔍 and out 🔍, pan the map up and down and

sideways ✛, switch from **Road** (drawn map) to **Aerial** (satellite view) to **Hybrid** (a combination of **Road** and **Aerial**) and **Bird's eye** (an angled airplane view).

You can hide the *View Control* by clicking the ‹‹ button at the upper-right corner. To display the *View Control* again, click ››.

If you double-click anywhere on the map, the point where you clicked will move to the center of the map and the map will zoom in one setting. You can also drag the map in any direction with the mouse.

## Pedigree Navigator

A small, three-generation pedigree is shown in the upper-left corner of the window. The current individual is at the starting position in generation one. This is a live chart that you can use to move up to ancestors and down to descendant. To move to a parent, or a grandparent, simply click on their name. This moves that person into the starting position of the chart and redraws the map using location connected to him or her. To move down to a descendant (or to move to a spouse), click the small blue button to the left of the main person. This displays a popup list of the spouses and children where you can select the desired person to become the focus of the map.

## List of Locations

All the locations that are associated with the current person are displayed in the Location List. Each place name is only shown once, even if more than one event happened at that place. The **Lat** column at the right side of the Location List shows an **X** for each location that has been geo-coded and therefore has a latitude and longitude recorded for it. When the Location List is first filled with all the locations for a person, Legacy runs down the list to try to geo-code any places that have not been done. (This requires that you have an active Internet connection.) Any locations that can't be automatically geo-coded are shown with a **?** in the **Lat** column. If you want to manually try to resolve these locations using the tools from the *Master Location List*, you can highlight the location and click the **Resolve** button under the list.

## Options

Click the **Options** button under the map to access the following features:

### Items to Include on the Map
Select the event locations you would like to include on the map. These include locations for the main person's birth, christening, death, burial, and events. You can also choose marriage and marriage event locations along with the birth and death locations of any spouses. Birth and Death locations for parents and children can also be included.

### Zooming the List
You can choose the font size used in the Location List.

# Printing the Map

If you would like to print the map, click the **Print** button under the map.  If you would like to print the map in landscape mode, click **Preferences** from the *Print* dialog box and change the **Orientation** to **Landscape** and then click **OK**.  Click **Print** to send the map to your printer.

# How to Make a Graphic File From the Map

To capture the map on the screen and create a graphic file that can be attached to many events in Legacy, see **How to Make a Graphic File From the Map** on page 103.)

# Chapter 9

# *Research Guidance*

### Where to Look for More Information

The **Research Guidance** tab on the main screen of Legacy is your starting point for getting help finding more information about your ancestors. This fantastic resource points you to specific suggested sources from the tens of thousands contained in the research guidance system. And more are being added all the time.

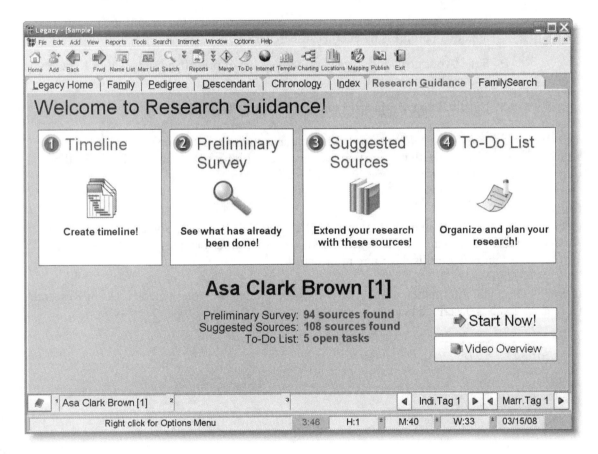

To start the Research Guidance process for someone, make that person the current individual on the Family, Pedigree, Descendant, or Index View and then click on the **Research Guidance** tab.

(You can also click on the **Research** icon on the personal toolbar of the Husband or Wife on the Family View ) The system then accesses the extensive source database and calculates and displays the number of Preliminary Survey sources and Suggested Sources for further research.

The number of Open to-do tasks is also shown.  To see the guidance results, click the **Start Now!** button to display the *Research Guidance Results* screen.

# Research Guidance Results

Legacy's *Research Guidance* helps you locate records that may contain information about your ancestors. It does this in four steps.

①　Legacy helps you review the ancestor's timeline, to be certain that you've already recorded everything you know about the ancestor.

②　Legacy suggests preliminary survey sources to help you learn if the research is already in progress by another researcher.

③　Select your goal, and Legacy provides a list of prioritized suggestions to help you accomplish your goal.

④　Finally, Legacy organizes the sources into a To-Do List.

The *Research Guidance Results* screen shows the current person at the top of the window along with his or her birth and death information.  If any piece of information has been estimated by Legacy, it is surrounded by angle brackets, and highlighted in red.

## Options
Clicking the **Options** button near the upper-right corner of the screen lets you print the current person's research suggestions, or change the font sizes of various portions of the screen so that you can see them better or display more information.

Below the personal information are four tabs corresponding to the four general areas of Research Guidance.  Each is described below:

# ① Review Timeline Tab

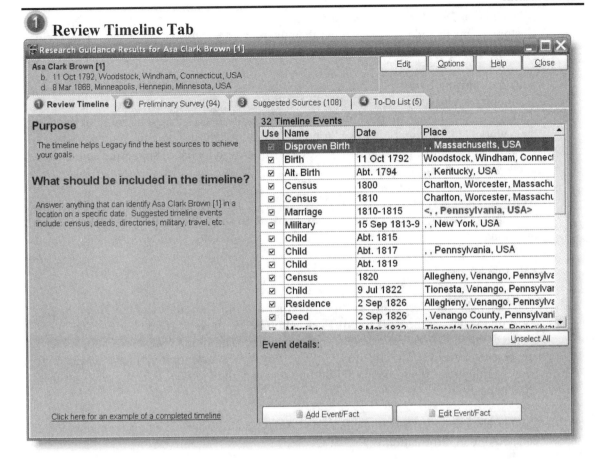

On the right is a list of the timeline events that make up the person's profile. This is the information used to display suggested sources that you should look at to find addition information for the individual. Some of these events are drawn from existing information and others are estimated by Legacy and shown in red with angle brackets around them. In general, the more timeline events that are known, the better Research Guidance can suggest helpful sources to research. If you know any addition information, even estimated information that would help, click the **Add Event/Fact** button, located below the *Timeline Events* list. Clicking the button displays a popup menu with the following choices:

### Add Vital Event
Vital events are birth, christening, death, and burial. This option displays the Individual Information screen for the current person where you can add additional dates and locations.

### Add Custom Event

Custom events include any facts other than the four vital information pieces. This option displays the Event window for the current person where you can add additional facts.

### Add Temporary Event

Temporary events are pieces of estimated or "guessed at" information that could help in the Research Guidance process. Perhaps family tradition says that your ancestor may have worked in the county jail in Maricopa County, Arizona. You could add a temporary event to indicate this. Legacy then makes adjustments in its list of suggested sources to allow for this possibility.

### Add Marriage Event

This option displays the *Add wife/husband* screen, to add a spouse to the current individual.

## Editing an Event

You can make changes to any event by highlighting the desired row in the *Timeline Events* and clicking the **Edit Event/Fact** button below the list. If you have a vital event selected, the *Individual Information* screen appears. The *Edit Event* screen appears for any non-vital events. The *Marriage Information* screen appears if you have a **Marriage** event highlighted. If you have a **Child** line selected, the *Individual Information* for that child appears.

Double-clicking any event in the list also displays the appropriate edit screen where you can add or edit information.

### What Information to Use

By default, all the timeline events in the list are used to generate research suggestions by Legacy. If you would like to turn off the inclusion of any particular event, click the checkbox in the **Use** column on the left to remove the checkmark. Subsequent clicking of the checkbox toggles the checkmark on and off.

## Preliminary Survey Tab

Before starting original research on an ancestor, you should learn if that ancestor has already been researched and documented by another fellow genealogist. In Step ② of Legacy's Research Guidance, Legacy suggests various sources and Internet sites where you can see if anything has already been published concerning your ancestor.

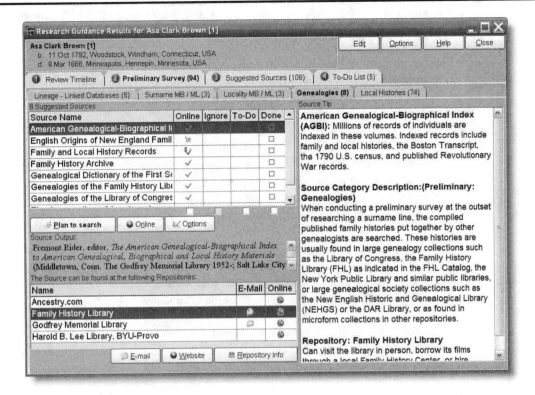

The Preliminary Survey tab contains five sub-tabs:
   **Lineage-Linked Databases**
   **Surname MB / ML**  (Message Boards and Mailing Lists)
   **Locality MB /ML**
   **Genealogies**
   **Local Histories**

Each tab indicates in its caption how many suggested sources are included.  The five tab areas are described below:

## Lineage-Linked Databases

A Lineage-Linked database is what is created as you enter information into your Legacy Family File. Many researchers choose to publish their linage-linked databases to the Internet. The sites listed here are major repositories for these electronic databases. Some can be searched freely, others require a nominal subscription fee.

The top portion of the tab area contains a list of the online databases containing lineage-linked pedigrees where you may find the current person.  The bottom of the area is a web browser. (To use the web browser, you must be connected to the Internet and have Internet Explorer installed on your computer.)

To search any of the lineage-linked preliminary survey databases, highlight the desired source in the upper list and then click the **Search** button below the list. The search page for the appropriate web site is loaded and displayed in the web browser.

### Surname MB / ML  (Message Boards and Mailing Lists)

Message Boards and Mailing Lists assist researchers in communication with each other. These should be searched before beginning original research to learn if others are already research your same family lines. These Message Boards and Mailing Lists are also places where you can submit queries about your research.

Like the Lineage-linked tab, the top portion of this tab area contains a list of the online message boards and mailing lists that match the current person.  For females, message boards are suggested that include each of their married names and their maiden name. The bottom of the area is a web browser.

To search any of the resources, highlight the desired message board or mailing list  and then click the **Search** button.  The search page for the appropriate web site is loaded and displayed in the web browser.

### Locality MB /ML

Like the Surname Message Boards and Mailing Lists, locality Message Boards and Mailing Lists are places where you can submit queries or search the archived queries relating to a certain locality.

This tab shows any locality message boards or mailing lists that might be useful in researching your ancestors.  It works the same way as the Surname MB/ML tab.

### Genealogies

Millions of books have been published over time. It is possible that one of those books contains genealogical information about your ancestor. The sources listed here assist you in locating a genealogy about your ancestor. Indexes and even some of the actual genealogies can be searched online.

If there is a suggested source in the list that you would like to search, you can either click on the **Plan to Search** button, to add that source to the To-Do List, or, if the source is marked as *online*, click on the **Online** button to search the source online.  If you want to ignore the suggested source, click on the **Ignore** button.

Below the suggested sources is a list of repositories. These are places where the suggested source can be researched.

The **Reason** section of the screen displays the reasons for which the source was suggested.

The **Source Tip** section may include additional helpful information about the suggested source.

## Local Histories

Learning about the history of the cities, towns, counties, and other regions helps you learn about your ancestors. The suggested sources in the **Local Histories** tab are sources that help you learn about this history. Many of these histories contain biographical information about the people who lived in the area. They may also provide information about where the people came from who settled the area. Finding your ancestor's name in print may not only help you solve your research problem, but it helps them *come alive!*

**Suggested Sources Tab**

Once steps ① and ② have been completed, the **Suggested Sources** tab, step ③, provides you with the best sources to learn about your ancestor.

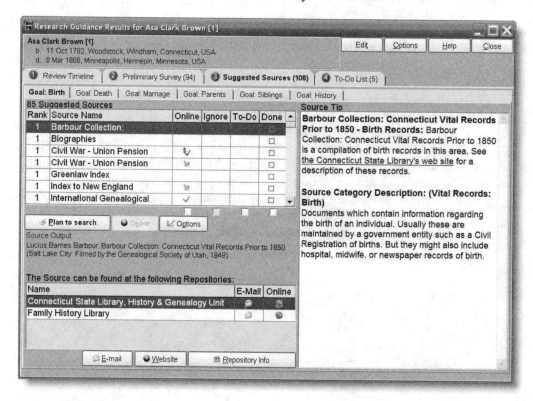

The **Suggested Sources** tab contains seven sub-tabs corresponding to the seven possible goals available in the Research Guidance system. These are:

- Birth
- Death
- Marriage
- Parents
- Siblings
- History
- Maiden Name

Each tab area has the same layout as described below:

### Suggested Sources

In the upper-left part of the tab area is the list of suggested sources for the current goal. This list is ranked in order of importance, which means that the researcher is more likely to find information relating to their goal in the sources that are ranked higher (1 is the highest). However, do not neglect the sources that are ranked closer to the bottom of the list, because one never knows all of the hidden information in various sources. If you would like to see more detail for a particular source, double-clicking it displays all the information.

The *Suggested Sources* list also indicates if the source is available online

### Source Output

Below the **Suggested Sources** list is a source citation for the highlighted source in the list. This can be used later, if you find information from this source, as the source documentation in Legacy.

### Source Repositories

The repository list shows one or more places where the source (highlighted in the Suggested Sources list) can be found. Each repository line also indicates if there is an e-mail link or a web site address available by showing icons in the **Email** and **Online** columns. To view complete address and contact information for any repository, click the **Repository Details** button below the list. (You can also double-click any repository for the details. To send an email to a repository (with an Email icon), click the **Email** button below the list. To launch your web browser and display the web site for the repository, click **Online**.

### Source Tip

As you highlight each source in the Suggested Sources window on the left, the reason for suggesting that source is displayed in the window to the right. For example, if the *Barbour Collection: Connecticut Birth Records...* source is suggested, the reason section explains that this source was suggested because the individual lived in Connecticut during the same time period that the source covers.

Along with the reason is more information about the source. In some cases, it lists the information that you might find in the source. It may suggest to you how to best utilize and/or analyze the information you might find.

## How to Use the Suggested Sources

If you would like to search the source, click on the **Plan to Search** button to add it to your **To-Do List**. This is an important step – adding the source to your To-Do List helps you keep a log, or a history, of the sources that you have searched.

Some of the sources listed in the list can be searched online. If this is true, an Internet icon appears in the **Online** column. Just click the **Online** button, and select the site that you wish to search.

If there is a source listed that you want to ignore, you can click on the **Ignore** button. This pops up a menu where you can selected to:

- **Hide/Show ignored sources**
- **Ignore the highlighted source for the current individual.**
- **Ignore the highlighted source for everyone**

## ④ To-Do List Tab

The final step in Research Guidance is to utilize the To-Do list that you have generated.

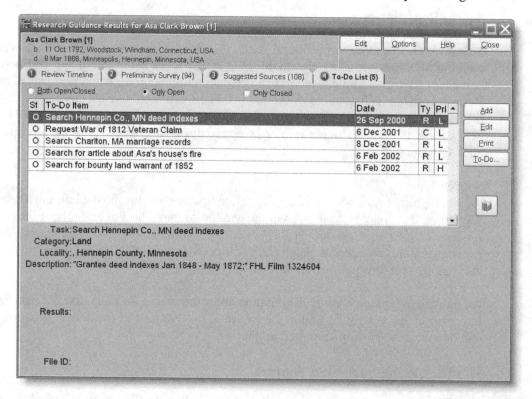

This list can be printed by clicking on the **Print** button on the right. As you search the sources, even the online sources, be sure to update the To-Do Item by clicking on the **Edit** button. Here you can record your results.

For example, if you searched the *International Genealogical Index,* and you did not find anything for your ancestor, be sure to record this. Record all variations of the name/surname that was searched, the time periods you searched, and any pertinent information so that you, or a fellow researcher, can understand exactly what you searched.

## Check Back Often

Legacy's Research Guidance system is updated often, so check back frequently for great new sources to search.

As you add new information to your Legacy Family File, the list of suggested sources may change. New sources may appear as you find more exact information.

There are a multitude of features in Legacy that are covered in great detail in the help system built into the program itself. Below, and on subsequent pages, is an alphabetized list of features and options with a summary of each one along with where to look in the Legacy Help file for more information.

## Focus Groups

A *Focus Group* is a subset of records and includes selected individuals, families, ancestors and/or descendants. The contents of a *Focus Group* determine who will be exported to a file or printed on a report.

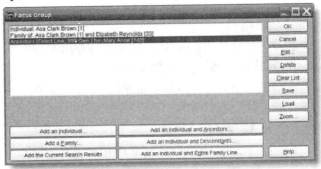

A *Focus Group* can contain as few as one individual, or as many as the entire contents of the family file. An individual and all his or her ancestors can be added to the group with a single selection.

For complete information about creating Focus Groups, see the Legacy Help system and search the index for: **Focus groups**

## Ancestor Coloring Options

Ancestor and Descendant type reports and many screens can now show colors associated with one of the four grandparents lines. There is also an option to color males and females differently on reports.

(Help index: **Ancestor colors**)

# Calculators

## Bearing and Distance Calculator

You can now use latitude and longitude values for something useful. This new calculator tells you the distance in miles (or kilometers) between any two points on earth. It also tells you which direction to travel from one point to the other. You can also convert decimal bearing values to needed degrees, minutes, and seconds. It even ties into the *Master Location List* where you can select any two cities (with latitude and longitude values) and quickly figure out how far apart they are and in which direction.

(Help index: ***Bearing calculator***)

## Date Calculator

The date calculator figures the time span between two dates, or calculates the beginning or ending date if you know one or the other along with an age.

(Help index: ***Date calculator***)

## Relationship Calculator

You can quickly figure out all the different ways that any two people in your family file are related.

(Help index: ***Relationship calculator***)

## Soundex Calculator

Soundex codes are used to group similar sounding last names together. These are often used when searching census records. Census takers often misspelled names when writing them on the census forms. Searching for surnames using the Soundex code finds all similar sounding names.

(Help index: ***Soundex calculator***)

# Customizing Legacy

## Customizable *Family View* Information Fields

There are up to five lines on both the *Husband* and *Wife* boxes of the *Family View* that can display information. Each of these information lines can be changed to other pieces of information you might want to view instead. To change the lines, click any of the descriptive labels to the left of the lines.

(Help index: *Customize - Family View information*)

## Customizable Toolbars

**Main Toolbar**  You can now choose which toolbar buttons to include at the top of Legacy. Select from nearly 40 options that are only a click away. Place your most-used options right on the toolbar, for the full width of your screen in any order you want!

(Help index: *Customize - main toolbar*)

**Family View and Pedigree View Toolbars**  The picture toolbars on the *Family View* and *Pedigree View* can be customized to show only the tools you want to use. You can also change their order.

(Help index: *Customize Family View toolbars* or *Customize Pedigree View toolbar*)

## Customizable Options

The *Options* menu in Legacy is provided to allow the user to customize the program to personal preferences. The *Customize* screen is reached by choosing **Customize** from the **Options** menu.

Following is a brief description of each tab and where to find complete information in the Legacy Help system.

## General Settings

Set certain parameters so Legacy shows you the information you require most.  For instance: How would you like the program to look when started? Should the main window be maximized? Which view would you like to see? Which family file should open? Who should be displayed? How would you like the surnames formatted? Do you want birth-death years added to names? How many columns of children should appear? What kind of pop-up help do you want to see?

(Help index: *Customize - general settings*)

## Data Entry/Edit

Control how you enter information and how it looks on the screen. This includes verification of new names and locations, jumping directly to notes after entering information, letter case formatting of names and locations, display of LDS information, and the behavior of the Enter key.

(Help index: *Customize – data entry/edit*)

## Dates

Legacy supports many different formats for both inputting and displaying dates in the program. You can enter dates in almost any conceivable format and they are reformatted to a consistent format per your selection. You can also include several prefix modifiers including Before, After, About, Between, Circa, B.C., and A.D. Legacy also recognizes several abbreviations of these modifiers.

(Help index: *Customize - dates*)

## Fonts

You can change the fonts used for screen forms and printed reports.

(Help index: *Customize - fonts*)

## File Locations

Set or change the default locations of your family files, multimedia files, and temporary files.

(Help index: *Customize - file locations*)

## Sources

Choose settings for AutoSource, Source Surety, and whether or not to print Master Source and Detail Source text and comments on reports.

(Help index: *Customize - sources*)

## Launch

Legacy offers to start your web browser, word processor, or text editor to view web pages or reports that you have generated. Normally, the default program for your computer is used. You can override these settings and use different programs to view the results by filling in one or more of the program fields.

(Help index: ***Customize - launch***)

## Other Settings

Miscellaneous settings concerning message boxes, report credits, RIN number warnings, automatic backup at program exit, at what age people should be presumed dead, toolbar location, custom ID # setting, and toolbar picture size.

(Help index: ***Customize - other settings***)

## View

Choose options for how things look on the screen. These include showing the birth-death range at the end of names; RINs, AFNs, or IDs at the end of names; using the desired term for christening; choosing how many columns of children to display; showing thumbnail pictures on the *Family View*; three-dimentional borders; choosing which headings to use on the *Family View*; and choosing how to show that children have spouses and children.

(Help index: ***Customize - view***)

## Colors

You can change the background color of some of the main input forms.

(Help index: **Customize - Customize colors**)

# Fixing Mistakes

## Removing an Individual

(Help index: ***Remove an individual***)

## Unlinking a Child From Parents

(Help index: ***Unlink child from parents***)

## Unlinking a Spouse

(Help index: ***Unlink spouse***)

## Attaching a Child to Parents

(Help index: ***Attach child to parents***)

## Attaching a Spouse

(Help index: ***Attach spouse***)

## Swapping Husband and Wife

(Help index: ***Swap husband and wife***)

## Married to the Same Spouse More Than Once

(Help Index: ***Married to the same spouse more than once***)

# Global Spell Checking

You can have Legacy run through your entire family file and check the spelling on any note-type field. You can even stop and resume at will.

(Help index: ***Global spell checking***)

# Master Lists

Legacy keeps several master lists of commonly used information in a family file. For example, the *Master Location List* contains all the location names that are being used in the current family file. Legacy only records one copy of each location and points any use of it to its entry in the list. This saves a lot of disk storage space by eliminating duplications.

Master lists have many great options that let you maintain the information in your file. See the following Help topics for more information:

**Master Address Lists**  contains the records used for addresses in the family file. (Includes mailing addresses, event addresses, and repository addresses.)

(Help index: ***Master address list***)

**Master Child Status List**  contains the child status names in the family file.

(Help index: *Master child status list*)

**Master Child-Parent Relationship List** contains the child-parent relationships in the family file.

(Help index: *Master child-parent relationship list*)

**Master Event Name Maintenance** contains the event names in the family file.

(Help index: *Master Event Name Maintenance*)

**Master Location List** contains the names of all the locations in the family file. Each location also has a **Short Location Name**, **Location Notes**, **Pictures**, **Latitude** and **Longitude** values, and a **Verified** tag.

(Help index: *Master locations list*)

**Master Marriage Status List** Contains the marriage status names in the family file.

(Help index: *Master marriage status list*)

**Master Picture Location List** Contains the drive and folder locations for all the picture, sound, and video files in the family file.

(Help index: *Master picture location list*)

**Master Source List** Contains the main source definitions that are cited from any piece of information in the family file.

(Help index: *Master source list*)

**Master Source Type List** Contains the names of all the source types (book, bible, newspaper, etc.) in the family file.

(Help index: *Master source type list*)

**Master Surname List** Contains all the surnames in the family file.

(Help index: *Master surname list*)

**Master Temple Name List**  Contains the names of all the LDS temples in the family file.

(Help index: *Master temple list*)

**Master To Do Category List**  Contains the names of all the categories used in the To-Do items in the family file.

(Help index: *Master To-Do category list*)

**Master To-Do Locality List**  Contains the names of all the localities used in the To-Do items in the family file.

(Help index: *Master To-Do Locality List*)

# Set Living Status

There are several Legacy reports, plus web pages, where the privacy of anyone whose **Living** status is set to **Yes** is protected by suppressing all personal details. When creating these reports, no information is included for ancestors born centuries ago if they are inadvertently left set as Living.

Normally, an individual's **Living** status is set at the time the record is manually entered. The process is automatic if that person's death or burial information is entered or that person's birth or christening date is more than 120 years ago. If no birth, christening, death, or burial information is entered, that person's status remains at the default **Yes**, unless manually changed to **No**.

It is an easy task to set the **Living** status of a few individuals manually, but the task can become formidable when adding hundreds or thousands of new names to your family file with a GEDCOM import. This is where the **Set Living** and **Advanced Set Living** utilities come in handy.

(Help index: *Set living*)

(Help index: *Advanced set living*)

# Chapter 11

# *Importing and Exporting Data*

### Transferring Information To and From Other Programs

## What Is a GEDCOM File

GEDCOM files are used to transfer genealogical information from one program to another. (See GEDCOM Files in the **Help** menu for more information.) Legacy imports and exports many different versions of GEDCOM files, recognizing nearly every variation from other programs.

**Tip**: The *Import Wizard* makes importing GEDCOM, Legacy, and PAF files a snap. Just choose **Import From / Use Import Wizard to Help With any Import** from the **File** menu. Legacy then searches all available drives for the file type you select and displays them in a list. Highlight the file you want to import and click **Next**. The rest is easy.

## Importing GEDCOM Files

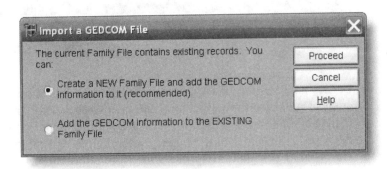

To import a GEDCOM file into Legacy, choose **Import From / GEDCOM File** from the **File** menu.

The *Import GEDCOM File* dialog box opens where you then select the GEDCOM file you want to import. After selecting the file, Legacy displays the *Import a GEDCOM File* window. If you want to create a new family file to contain the GEDCOM information, select the **Create a NEW Family File and add the GEDCOM information to it** (recommended) option. If you want to add the information from the GEDCOM file to your existing family file, select the **Add the GEDCOM information to the EXISTING Family File** option. Then click **Proceed**.

If you are adding to your existing family file, Legacy prompts you to make a backup copy of it before starting the import. This is a wise practice and is recommended. If you are creating a new family file, you are prompted for a new filename.

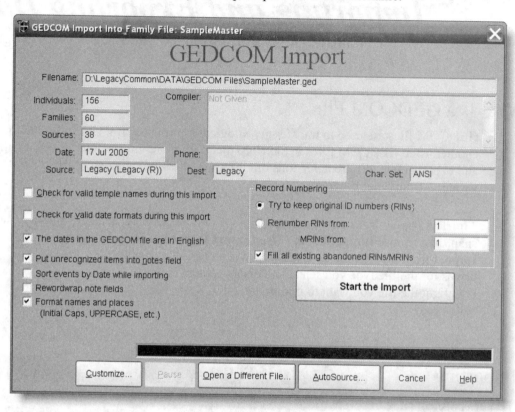

Legacy analyzes the GEDCOM file to make sure it is valid and recognizable. This analysis pass also shows you how many individuals and families are contained in the file. If Legacy finds information that it does not know what to do with, a message is displayed. You can then tell Legacy where to put the information. (See *Importing GEDCOM Files* in the **Help** menu for more information.) The submitter's name, address, and comments are also displayed along with the name of the program that created the file.

After the analysis pass, click **Start the Import**. Legacy reads the information from the GEDCOM file and places it in the appropriate family file. Anything that is not recognized is placed in an error file so you can see it later and decide what to do.

## Record Numbers

Most GEDCOM files are encoded with the record identification numbers (RINs) that were used in the exporting program that created them. Often users come to identify particular individuals within their files as much with their RINs, as with their names.

**Try to Keep Original Record ID Numbers (RINs)** lets you keep the same numbers if at all possible.

**Renumber RINs From** allows you to renumber the imported records from a specified starting number. The number can be entered for both RINs and MRINs. As an example, let's say you have 2,582 individuals in your current family file and are about to import a new batch. You might want to start numbering the new individuals at 3000, later making it easy to see which people were imported. (Of course, if you select a starting number that is already being used in the current file, Legacy will have to jump up to a number higher than the current batch.)

**Fill All Existing Abandoned RINs** tells Legacy to use any unused RINs as individuals and marriages are imported.

## Import Filters

**Check for Valid Temple Names During This Import** causes Legacy to check the validity of the incoming temple names against the *Master Temple Name List*. Any unrecognized names are displayed so you can correct them. Legacy also recognizes the older two-letter abbreviations and converts them to the latest style.

**Check for Valid Date Formats During This Import** Legacy uses consistent, logical formatting rules when it comes to dates. (See *Enter > Dates in date fields* in Legacy Help.) Other programs allow free-form dates that can include unrelated text, making the dates unusable for sorting and date arithmetic. During the import process, Legacy checks each date for a proper format and presents any unrecognized dates for you to correct or accept. If you would like to accept all dates, regardless of their format, clear this option. (Using the search engine in Legacy, you can produce a list showing the names and record numbers of all individuals who have unrecognized dates. Use this list later to quickly jump to each individual and make corrections.)

**Put Unrecognized Items Into Notes Field** puts any unrecognized information into the Notes field of the individual being read at the time. For example, a line such as OCCUP Bricklayer would be put into the Notes field because OCCUP is not a standard GEDCOM tag. (You can also remap unrecognized tags to standard tags before you start the import.)

**Rewordwrap Notes Fields** reformats notes into continuous lines. If the notes you are importing have hard carriage returns at the end of each line, such as notes from PAF 2.31 (or PAF 3.0 notes imported from PAF 2.31). Paragraph breaks formed by two consecutive carriage returns are left alone.

**Format Names and Places**   reformats all incoming names and places to the format currently set in the Preferences section. These formatting options include putting initial capital letters on given names, putting initial capitals or all capital letters on surnames, and formatting location names so there is a space after each comma.

## Open a Different File

This button lets you select a different GEDCOM file to replace the one you started with.

## AutoSource

The *AutoSource™* feature of Legacy lets you automatically assign a master source to each incoming individual when you are doing an import. This is often very useful as documentation of where you received the information, and is much easier to do and use than making an entry in the Notes field.

When you are about to import a Legacy file, GEDCOM file, or PAF file, you can select a master source to cite for each person by clicking **AutoSource** on the *Import* window.

## AutoSource Reminder

If you forget to set *AutoSource* when importing a file, Legacy asks if you would like to do so. (This can be turned off.) When the *AutoSource Reminder* window opens:

Click **Select a Master Source** to display the *Master Source List* where you can select a source to cite (or you can **Add** a new source and then cite it), or click **Don't Assign a Source** to tell Legacy to skip the source assignment during this import.

## Customize

You can suppress certain information while importing a GEDCOM file. For example, if you are not interested in address information, you can simply choose to omit it. To customize the import information, click **Customize**.

The *Items to Import* window appears showing a list of the valid GEDCOM tags that have been found in the file you are going to import. It also shows a list of any unrecognized tags that were found.

From this window, you can remove tags from the *Import these Items* box so they will be skipped during the actual import. You can also map unrecognized tags into standard Legacy fields.

**Items to be Imported** During the analysis pass, Legacy gathers all the recognizable GEDCOM tags and places them in the *Import These Items* box.

**Items Not to Import** If you find a tag you don't want to have imported, highlight the tag and click **Remove**, or just drag the tag from the *Import These Items* box to the *Items not to be Imported* box. You can move all but the first eleven, basic fields. If you want to import only the eleven fields (Name, Place, Sex, Birth, Christening, Death, Burial, Date, Husband, Wife, and Marriage), click **Basic**. All the other tags will be moved to the *Items not to be Imported* box. (You can move any tag back by highlighting it and clicking **Include**, or by dragging it back to the *Import These Items* box.)

**Unrecognized Items** Any tags that are not recognized by Legacy during the analysis pass are placed in the *Unrecognized Items* box. These are usually odd, nonstandard pieces of information that another program supports. If you can recognize the tag, you can map it to a standard field tag in Legacy. Or, you can always have the information placed in the Notes field so you don't lose it.

**Defining an Unrecognized Item** The *Unrecognized Items* list contains nonstandard GEDCOM tags that were found in the file you want to import. Often, these tags are slight variations invented by another program that are easily recognizable and can be mapped to a standard tag supported by Legacy. To start the definition process, highlight the tag you want to remap, and click **Map to a Recognized Tag** and then choose the GEDCOM tag you want to map it to.

**Creating Events From Unrecognized Tags** Some GEDCOM tags are obviously names for events, such as GRAD for Graduation. To convert these tags to events and have them placed in the event list for the individual involved, highlight the tag and click **Create an Event for this Tag**. Legacy then prompts you for an event name (up to 30 characters). During the import, all occurrences of this tag will be changed to the defined event name.

**Saving Your Settings** If you would like to save a particular import tag list, click **Save List** after you have selected the tags you want to import. Legacy prompts for a filename and then saves the list to disk.

**Loading Your Saved Settings** You can load a previously saved import tag list by clicking **Load List** and then selecting the desired list to be loaded.

When you are finished with any customization, click **OK** to return to the *GEDCOM Import* screen.

## Starting the Import

When you are ready to import, click **Start the Import**. Legacy imports the GEDCOM file while displaying a progress bar.

# Importing Legacy Files

You can import one Legacy family file into another or into a new, empty file. When importing a Legacy family file, incoming records can be filtered, limiting them to focus group entries or tagged records only.

▶ **To import a Legacy file:**
1. From the **File** menu, choose **Import From > Legacy File**.
2. Select the name of the Legacy file you want to import.
3. Click **OK**.
4. Decide if you want to import the Legacy file into the current family file or into a new family file, and click the appropriate button. If creating a new family file, Legacy prompts you for a filename before proceeding. Importing into a new file also allows Legacy to use the same ID numbers that were assigned to the individuals and marriages. If you import the records into an existing family file with existing individuals, Legacy may not be able to retain the incoming ID numbers because they might already be in use.
5. Set or change any of the options. Each is described below.
6. When you are ready to import, click **Start the Import**. Legacy imports the file while displaying a progress bar.
7. When the import is complete, Legacy asks if you would like to go through the *Merge* process. This procedure compares all the individuals in the combined family file to see if any of them are really the same person. This can easily happen when you import additional names into your family file.

## Importing Options

There are several options to consider when importing.

### Records to Import

When importing records from another Legacy family file, you can select which individuals to bring in.

**All Records in the Entire Family File**   includes every individual and family in the incoming family file.

**Selected Records Contained in the Focus Group**   imports specific individuals, families, and entire family lines that have been placed in a Focus Group.

(See *Focus Groups* on page 235 for more information.) Clicking **View / Set Focus Group** opens the current focus group of the incoming family file.

**All Records With an Individual Tag of**   imports individuals who have been tagged in the incoming family file. Be sure to set the tag number you want by using the **Up** and **Down** ▲▼ arrows.

**All Records With a Marriage Tag of**   imports those individuals who are part of the tagged marriages in the incoming file. Be sure to set the tag number you want by using the **Up** and **Down** ▲▼ arrows.

## Record Numbers

**Try to Keep Original ID Numbers**   tells Legacy to look for and try to retain the original record numbers whenever possible. (The only reason they can't be used is if they are already being used by other records.)

**Renumber RINs from**   causes the incoming records to be renumbered, starting at a given number.

**Fill All Existing Abandoned RINs**   uses any available unused record numbers while importing.

## Import Filters

**Check for Valid Temple Names During This Import**   causes Legacy to check the validity of the incoming temple names against the *Master Temple Name List*. Any unrecognized names are displayed so you can correct them. Legacy also recognizes the older two-letter abbreviations and converts them to the latest style.

**Format Names and Places**   formats all incoming names and places to the current format settings. This includes options to use uppercasing, initial capital letters, or leaving alone surnames, and initial capital letters on given names, and initial capital letters on locations.

**Import [[Private]] Notes**   imports records that have been marked as private in the incoming family file. If you are including these notes and would like them to remain marked as private, select **Keep [[ ]]s**.

**Import Private Events**   imports records from the incoming family file that have been marked as private.

**Import General To-Do Items**   imports general to-do items from the incoming family file.

**Exclude LDS Information**   excludes LDS information in the incoming family file.

# Importing PAF Files

Personal Ancestral File (PAF) is a popular genealogy program published by The Church of Jesus Christ of Latter-day Saints. Legacy directly imports PAF 2.31, 3.0, and 4.0 files. PAF 5.x file must be imported by using the GEDCOM format.

To import a PAF file into Legacy, select the **File** menu, choose **Import From**, and then select the type of PAF file you would like to read. The File dialog box opens where you then select the PAF file you want to import; specify the drive and path of the PAF file. PAF 2.31 only stores one family file in any particular folder. You will be looking for **INDIV2.DAT**. PAF 3.0 and 4.0 store their information in files ending with a **.paf** extension.

If you are importing into an existing family file that contains records, and you want to add the information from the PAF file to your existing file, select **Add the PAF Information to the EXISTING Family File**. If you want to create a new family file to contain the PAF information, select **Create a NEW Family File and add the PAF information to it**. If you are adding to your existing family file, Legacy prompts you to make a backup copy before the import is started. This is a wise practice and is highly recommended. If you are creating a new family file, you are prompted for a new file name.

Click **Start the Import**. Legacy reads the information from the PAF file and places it in the appropriate family file.

The import options are very similar to those available when importing a GEDCOM file. (See page 243 for more information.)

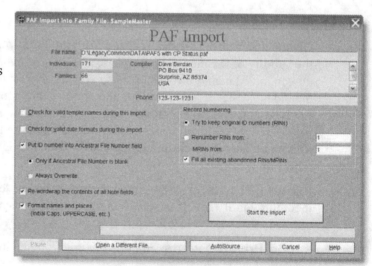

# Import Wizard

**Use the Import Wizard to help with any import.**
1.  Select **Import from > Import Wizard** from the **File** pulldown menu.

2.  From the *Import Wizard* dialog box indicate the type of file to import from the following items:
    a.  PAF 2.31 or Ancestral Quest 2.x file
    b.  PAF 3, 4, 5 or Ancestral Quest 3.x file
    c.  Any GEDCOM file.
    d.  Another Legacy family file
3.  Click the **Next** button
4.  Legacy automatically searches your drives for all files of the selected type and return a list.
5.  Click once on the file you want to highlight it and then click the **Next** button.
6.  You are then prompted to either create a new file and add the information to it or add the information to an existing Legacy file.

# Merging Event Definitions

The *Merge Event Definition* window appears when you are:

*   Importing the Master Event Definition List from another family file
*   Importing a GEDCOM file with event definition records
*   Combining duplicate location in the Master Event Definition List.

And the information items are not all identical.

This screen allows you to select or combine the differing information into each merged event definition record.

### To merge an event definition:
1.  Choose the desired fields to show. (Choose from Description, Date and Place.)
2.  Edit the event sentence definitions. If you want to copy the right definitions to the left, replacing them, click the ⬚< button.
3.  If you want to copy all the fields from the right record to the left, click ⬚<<< .
4.  Click **Save** to save the merged event definition on the left.

### Automating the Merge
*   To always keep the existing definition information no matter what the other event shows, choose the **Always keep the existing event definition** option before saving the current record.
*   To always accept the incoming definition information, including its blank fields, if any, choose the **Always overwrite the existing event with the incoming event** option.

- To copy information from the incoming event that is missing from the current event, choose the **Always copy the incoming event items that are missing from the existing event** option.

Choosing one of these options effectively turns off the displaying of the *Merge Event Definition* window for the remainder of the current operation.

# Exporting GEDCOM Files

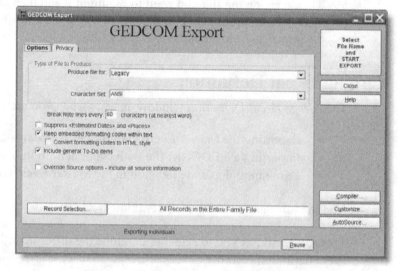

If you want to send part or all of the information in your family file to someone who is not using Legacy, you can do so by exporting a GEDCOM file. (If you are sending all your information to someone using Legacy, the easiest way is to just send them a backup copy of the family file. If you want to send just part of the file, such as a particular person and their ancestors, you can tag those people and export a GEDCOM from them.)

▶ **To export a GEDCOM file from Legacy:**
1. From the **File** menu, choose **Export To / GEDCOM File**. The *GEDCOM Export* window opens.
2. Select the type of GEDCOM file to produce.
3. Click **Record Selection** to change the records you want to include in the file.
4. Click **Compiler** to make sure the information about you - the submitter or creator of the GEDCOM file - is correct.
5. If you want to change the default list of field information to be included in the GEDCOM file, click **Customize**.
6. When you have made all the desired settings, choose **Select File Name and START EXPORT**.

7.  Select the folder where you want the file to be created and type a name into the *File Name* box in the upper-left corner of the window. Often, an appropriate surname or abbreviation makes a good file name.

## Producing a GEDCOM File

**For Legacy**  GEDCOM files destined for Legacy contain ALL the information that can be entered into a Legacy family file. This includes all individual field information; all notes; all sources; all events; LDS ordinance dates and temple names; pictures; sound; video; list ordering and tags; as well as preferred children; spouses; and parents. This GEDCOM file conforms to the GEDCOM 5.5 specification (with some extensions) and contains the most information. If you are exporting a GEDCOM file to be imported into Legacy or most other genealogy programs, with the exception of Personal Ancestral File (PAF), you should probably choose this option.

**For GEDCOM 5.5 Only**  Many other programs do not have a place to put all the information that Legacy handles, and an error file is generated. If you would like to limit the export fields to mostly those accepted by other programs, choose this option.

**For LDS TempleReady**  This format contains only the information needed when submitting names using the TempleReady program by The Church of Jesus Christ of Latter-day Saints. This type of GEDCOM files contains name, sex, birth, christened, death, buried, marriage, Ancestral File Number, sources, and all LDS ordinance information fields. The file is produced using the ANSEL character set.

**PAF 2.31 and PAF 3.0 / 4.0 / 5.0**  Since Personal Ancestral File is now used in four different versions, 2.x, 3.x, 4.x, and 5.x, and since they each handle notes, sources, and repositories in radically different ways, it is necessary for Legacy to produce four special GEDCOM formats to satisfy the special needs of these programs. Select the desired format.

**Pedigree Resource File**  This format is used when contributing your information for inclusion in the LDS Church's new Pedigree Resource File. This file is similar to the Ancestral File but the contributed files are left as received, and no attempt is made to link multiple files together. Submission can only be done through the Internet.

**Basic**  This GEDCOM file contains only the vital statistics. This type of GEDCOM file contains name, sex, birth, christened, death, buried, and marriage information.

**Generic**  This GEDCOM file contains name, sex, birth, christened, death, buried, marriage, user ID number, notes, sources, events, baptism, and marriage status.

**Clooz**  This file contains individuals to be exported to the Clooz program.

**Ancestry Online Family Tree**  This file contains individuals and marriages to be exported for uploading to Ancestry Online Family Tree.

**MyTrees.com** This file contains individuals to be exported for uploading to MyTrees.com.

## Character Set

Because there is a need to share genealogical information in different languages, Legacy offers three separate character sets when exporting a GEDCOM file:

**ANSI** This character set corresponds to the Windows character set on a one-for-one basis, including characters with diacritics.

**ANSEL** This character set represents certain characters with diacritics as two-character combinations.

Some genealogy programs, such as TempleReady, require the ANSEL character set. Most others will read both character sets but there are some that will not read the ANSEL set.

**UTF-8** This character set represents certain characters as two-character combinations.

## Length of the Note Lines

Note lines in Legacy Note fields are continuous until a carriage return is entered. If you increase or decrease the width of the note window, all the text is reformatted within the new width. Other programs, such as Personal Ancestral File 2.x, have fixed lengths for each line in the note field and each of these lines is exported to a separate line in the GEDCOM file. As Legacy is exporting a GEDCOM file it breaks the long continuous lines into smaller pieces. You can control how long these segments are by entering a number to indicate their length. (When a GEDCOM file is imported by Legacy, the line segments are recombined to their original state.)

## Records to Export

### Who Do You Want to Export

To change this click **Record Selection**.

**All Records in the Entire Family File** includes every individual and family in your family file. Selecting this option causes all subsequent options to be ignored.

**Selected Records Contained in the Focus Group** allows you to select specific individuals, families, and entire family lines to export by placing them in a focus group. (See Focus Groups on page 235 for more information.)

**All Individual Records With a Certain Tag Number** lets you include individuals who have been tagged. Be sure to set the tag number you want to use by using the Up and Down arrows.

**All Marriage Records with a Certain Tag Number** exports those individuals who are part of tagged marriages. Be sure to set the tag number you want to use by using the Up and Down ▲▼ arrows.

## Export [[Private ]] Information

Legacy has the ability to mark portions of your notes as private. When you are editing notes, you can add two opening brackets [[to start the marking of private notes that you do not want to be printed or exported. At the end of the private notes you add two closing brackets]] and everything following the closing brackets becomes public again. You can also use just the two opening brackets [[ and everything to the end of the note becomes private if there are no closing brackets. If you want to export the private portions of your note fields along with the rest, select **Export [[Private]] Notes**. If you want the square brackets to be included in the exported private notes, select **Keep [[ ]]s**. This will let you import the GEDCOM file later and retain the marking of the private notes intact.

## Changing the Compiler Information

If you want to change the name, address, phone number, and comment lines of previously entered information, or if you want to enter this information for the first time, click **Compiler**. The *Compiler Information* window appears, where you can add or edit the entries.

## Customizing the Export File

You can customize the GEDCOM file format in additional ways by clicking **Customize**.

## Starting the Export

When you have selected the individuals and families to include in the exported GEDCOM file, click **Select File Name and START EXPORT**. Legacy prompts for a file name. A .ged extension will be added. Legacy then creates the file and exports the specified information.

# Exporting to a Legacy File

You can export a Legacy family file to create another Legacy family file or to append to another, existing family file. When exporting a Legacy family file, you can filter the outgoing records, limiting them to focus group entries or tagged records only. Since you can tag an individual and all his/her ancestors or descendants, this is a good way to break a large family file into smaller, more manageable pieces.

▶ **To export a Legacy file:**
1. From the **File** menu, choose **Export To / Legacy File**.
2. Select a name for the Legacy file you want to create or the Legacy file you want to append to.
3. Click **OK**.
4. Set or change any of the options. (Each is described below.)
5. When you are ready to export, click **Start the Export**. Legacy exports the file while displaying a progress bar.

## Options

### Records to Export

**All Records in the Entire Family File** includes every individual and every family in the new family file. Selecting this option causes all subsequent options to be ignored.

**Selected Records Contained in the Focus Group** lets you select specific individuals, families, and entire family lines to export by placing them in a *focus group*. (See *Focus Groups* on page 235 for more information.)

**All Individual Records With a Certain Tag Level** exports only individuals who have been tagged. Be sure to set the tag number you want to use by using the **Up** and **Down** arrows.

**All Marriage Records With a Certain Tag Level** exports only those individuals who are part of tagged marriages. Be sure to set the tag number you want to use by using the **Up** and **Down** arrows.

### Export Filters

**Suppress Details for Living People** excludes personal information for individuals who are marked as Living in the family file. This includes birth and christening, as well as events, pictures, addresses, etc. If you select **Change name to "Living"**, then the individual's name is also excluded from the exported information. **Export Private Individuals** exports those individuals marked as **Private** on their Information screen.

### Record Numbers

**Try to Keep Original ID Numbers**  lets Legacy try to retain the original record numbers whenever possible. (The only reason they can't be used is if they are already being used by other records.) If this option is not selected, Legacy will still try to use the same ID numbers, but if it can't, it won't bother telling you about it.

**Renumber From**  renumbers the records in the new family file starting from the specified value.

**Format Names and Places**  formats all the names and places to the current format settings. These include uppercasing, initial capital letters, or leaving alone surnames; initial capital letters on given names; and initial capital letters on locations.

**Export [[Private]] Notes**  includes any part of any note that is marked as *private*. If you are exporting *private* notes, you can choose to include the markers [[ and ]], thus keeping the notes marked as private in the new file.

**Export Private Events**  includes events marked as private when exporting records. These include both individual and marriage events.

**Export General To-Do Items**  includes general to-do items in the new Legacy file.

**Exclude LDS Information**  removes LDS information from the new Legacy file.

**AutoSource**  allows you to assign a master source citation to each individual and marriage that is exported.

## Importing Master Lists From Other Legacy Family Files

You can copy various lists that you have built in other Legacy family files. These include lists for locations, surnames, event definitions, temple names, source types, marriage status, and child status, and picture/sound locations.

When you are entering information into one of these lists, if the entry is already in the list, the automatic type-ahead feature of Legacy fills in the remainder of the word(s) for you. Preloading a list with the entries you commonly use can greatly increase the speed of adding new information.

▶ **To import a master list from another family file:**

1. While viewing any master list, click **Options** and then choose **Import...**. The *Import Lists* window appears.

2. To choose the family file from which you want to import, click **Browse**. The *Select a Family File* dialog box appears.

3. Make sure the correct drive and subdirectory are selected and choose the family file you want to copy lists from. Then click **Open** (or just double-click the file name).

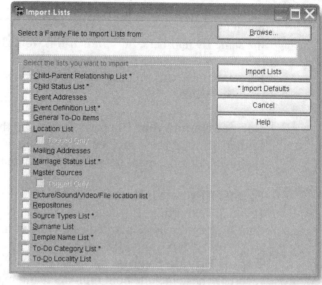

4. From the *Import Lists* window, select the lists you want to copy.

5. Click **Import Lists**.

## Resetting Lists to Their Default Settings

Some lists (Event Definitions, Temple Names, Source Types, Marriage Status, To-Do Category, and Child Status, start with a predefined set of entries. If you have removed some of these entries by deleting them from the various lists, and would like to restore them, click **Import Defaults**.

# Chapter 12

# *Merging Duplicates*

Combining Two or More People Who Are Really the Same Person

## Introduction to Merging

Legacy is unique from all other genealogy programs in the strength and flexibility of its merge program. Legacy offers the user complete control while combining records. We call it IntelliMerge™.

As your family file grows larger, either by entering new individuals and families, or by importing other family files and GEDCOM files, you may find that you have some people in your file more than once. You can either edit the two individuals manually, trying to also take into account any children, spouses, and parents, or you can use Legacy's powerful merge capabilities. In fact, it is suggested that you do not try to manually combine individuals who are linked to other relatives. It can be very frustrating and can lead to a jumbled mess.

The whole concept underlying the merge capability in Legacy is the process of integrating duplicate records as a result of importing records from another GEDCOM or PAF file with the existing records in the current family file. (Or from entering a person more than once.) This process is a very sensitive one because it ultimately means that the current family file, when the merge is complete, is changed to reflect the combination of the new information.

In many instances, one record will contain duplicate—and possibly enhanced—information on an individual or marriage in the current family file. Because of this, it is essential for the user to have the option to review both the current data and the imported data on a screen where both can be observed at the same time.

All of the above must be addressed, and decisions must be made and plans implemented in order to achieve a successful merge of data. By letting Legacy help you do these tasks, hundreds of hours can be saved over inputting the data manually.

Sound judgment suggests that the user make a backup of existing data before implementing any merge. This can be accomplished by using the **Backup** command on the **File** menu.

Legacy offers several methods to merge records in a family file. These include *Manual Merge*, where you initiate the process by selecting two individuals; *Find Duplicates*, where Legacy starts the process by comparing all the individuals in the entire family file and creating a list of possible duplicates; and *IntelliShare™*, which lets you share your family file with others and then integrate all the changes made by the various people back into the master file.

The merge process is exactly that—a PROCESS. Rarely do you just combine two people together. Most often it involves connections to other individuals such as children, spouses, siblings, and parents. It is important to properly handle the surrounding links, and the links surrounding the links, and so on…. Legacy is an expert at the merge process. When you tell the program to combine two people, Legacy looks around to see who else should be considered for a merge. It then automatically adds them into the process. This goes on until all the associated links have been handled. You may begin by thinking that you are going to merge only two individuals, but you end up merging an entire family line. *This is the only way to do it correctly.*

For example: Let's say you notice two men in your family file who you think are the same person, William Johnson and Will Johnson. You start a merge process by clicking **Merge**. Legacy compares the two individuals and shows you the differences, if any, between the information contained in the two records. After looking the information over, you decide that they are indeed the same person and click **Merge Right Individual Into Left Individual** to combine them. Legacy takes a look around and notices that William has two parents linked to him, named Daniel Johnson and Mary Anderson. Will Johnson has two parents, named D. Johnson and Mrs. Johnson. These two sets of names look like they could be the same parents, so Legacy adds them into the merge process. The next two people to be displayed are Daniel Johnson and D. Johnson, and then Mary Anderson and Mrs. Johnson. The process is continued until all possible duplicates in that line are presented. This goes also for ancestors, siblings, spouses, and children. The end result is a combination of names, information, and links for everyone in the line who is related.

## Manual Merge

If you have come to the *Merge Two Individuals* window by clicking the **Merge** button, the current individual is automatically loaded on the left side. You must now select the second individual by clicking the **Select Right** button and choosing the name from the *Name List*. After selecting the right individual, the merge procedure can progress as outlined in the *Merging Two Individuals* section on page 265.

## Finding Duplicates

Click **Merge** on the toolbar and then select **Find Duplicates**.

# Merge Options

## Normal Duplicate Search Tab

The illustration shows the *Normal Duplicate Search* tab. The upper **Match** section provides options for matching data. The lower **Take into Account** section provides options for conditions to be taken into account while looking for duplicates.

**Compare Surnames** Last names (surnames) can be compared either by exact spelling or by the way the names sound. When using the **Sounds Like** option, standard Soundex codes are used.

(Help index: ***Soundex***)

**Include Blank Surnames** causes individuals with blank surnames to match each other. This, combined with the given name comparison below, may find some duplicates that would otherwise be missed, but it will also find many pairs that are probably not duplicates.

**Check Given Names** specifies how many characters of the given name field are compared for duplication. For example, if the value is set to 5, Susan will match Susanna but Diane will not match Diana. If set to 3, Don will match Donald, and Dave will match David. But be warned, Mark will match Marsha, Marshall, and Marilee. When fewer characters are compared, more mismatches are shown.

**Check Dates**  specifies the allowable day range by increasing the value in each section. The larger the spread, the lower the accuracy.

**Include Blank Dates**  matches blank dates with other blank dates and any other date of that type, blank or not. This option, combined with matching last names and given names, can find some elusive matches, but be warned, many mismatches are usually found.

**Check Locations**  specifies how many characters to compare for matches. The lower the value, the more matches (and mismatches) will be found.

**Include Blank Locations**  matches blank locations with other blank locations and any other location of the specified type, blank or not.

## Other Criteria to Take Into Account

**Compatible Gender**  limits Legacy to compare individuals of the same gender.

**Ancestral File Numbers**  matches ancestral file numbers, no matter what other information doesn't match. Theoretically, any two people with the same AFN number are the same person. (These numbers are assigned only by The Church of Jesus Christ of Latter-day Saints to names submitted to the Ancestral File collection.)

**User ID #**  matches user reference numbers. Reference numbers can be assigned by anyone, so unless you are certain that they are unique, the value of this option is questionable.

**Compatible Parents**  matches parents. Insisting on compatible parents means that matches are found when the parents of the two individuals being considered are not *in*compatible. This means that they either *both* have parents who are named the same, or one has parents and the other doesn't, or one has one parent and the other has the other parent. For example, if one individual has parents named Bob and Mary and the other has parents named Roberto and Maria, no match is considered unless this option is turned off. When comparing the surnames of the parents, you can specify an exact letter-for-letter comparison or a sounds-like test. You can also specify how many letters to compare of the given names.

# Other Options

The following options apply to either of the two types of searches, *Normal* or *Special*. You should set these options before clicking **Continue**.

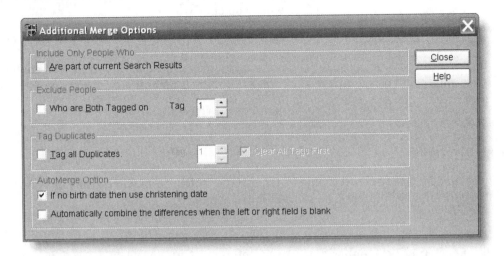

## Include Only People Who Are Part of the Current Search Results

Normally, Legacy looks through all the individuals in the entire family file when searching for duplicates. If you would like to narrow the search, you can limit it to only the individuals in the current search results. For example, if you have just done a search for all individuals with a last name of Jones, Legacy will look only at the entries in that subset when searching for duplicates. Here is another example: From the Name List, tag all the ancestors of a particular person with a tag #3. Click Options and then choose Show All Tagged/Tag #3 Individuals to include only those tagged ancestors in the list. You can now limit the duplicate search to just the entries in this list.

## Exclude People

If two individuals, who would otherwise be considered duplicates, are both tagged with the specified tag number, Legacy will not show them if this option is selected. This lets you manually exclude certain people from the merge process.

## Tag Duplicates

Select this option if you want the remaining individual of each merged pair tagged with a specified tag number. This would then let you later display a Search List of all the merged people by showing just the individuals tagged with that number.

## Tagging Duplicates

Select this option to put a tag on individuals when they are merged. This tags only the individual who remains after a pair is merged. You can select the tag number to mark. You can also choose to have any existing tags of that number cleared before the merge process begins (the tags are cleared when you click Continue).

## Automerge Option

If there is no birth date, use the Christening date when deciding if two records are the same and should be automerged. Normally, if there is no birth date then two otherwise identical records are not automerged.

# Special Searches

The *Special Searches* screen allows for specific matching on **Ancestral File Numbers, User Reference Numbers**, and **IntelliShare** numbers.

Three special-case searches are provided by Legacy. The first two processes only look at the **Ancestral File Number** or the **User Reference Number** when determining matching individuals. No other information is used. *If you are not using either of these number fields, these special searches won't be of any use.*

**Ancestral File Numbers** are assigned by The Church of Jesus Christ of Latter-day Saints (Mormon) to all records submitted to them. When this data is compiled it is provided on CD-ROM to the Family History Centers located throughout the world. Data acquired from these locations or from the Church Family History Center in Salt Lake City, Utah all contain an **Ancestral File Number**.

**User Reference Numbers** can be assigned by the individual within the program for accommodating special needs.

**IntelliShare Numbers** are unique numbers assigned to each individual in your family file as you enter and import records. When merging, any two records with the same IntelliShare numbers are considered the same person.

# Merging Two Individuals

From the *Merge Options* window, click **Continue**. The *Merging Two Individuals* window appears.

Use these buttons to copy the other information you want to keep to either *Notes*, *Alternate Names,* or *Events*.

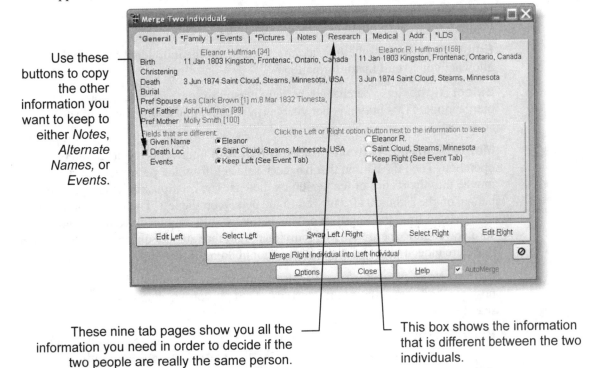

These nine tab pages show you all the information you need in order to decide if the two people are really the same person.

This box shows the information that is different between the two individuals.

## What Does This Window Show?

The *Merging Two Individuals* window shows two individuals side-by-side who could be the same person. There are nine tabs across the top, corresponding to the various pieces of information both individuals have. When a pair is first displayed, the *General* tab is selected automatically.

The record of the individual shown at the left of the screen is the one that will ultimately remain in the current family file. The individual on the right, if the two are merged, will be combined with the left.

Below the tab pages are several command buttons and a checkbox:

**Edit Left**   displays the *Information* window for the individual on the left, allowing you to edit his or her information.

**Select Left**  lets you change the left person to someone else if you are in manual merge mode. (This button is not visible if you are doing automatic duplicate searching.)

**Swap Left / Right**  trades the positions of the two individuals. The person on the right moves to the left side and the person on the left moves to the right. (The person on the left is always the individual who is retained. The information and links from the person on the right are merged into the left.)

**Edit Right**  displays the *Information* window for the individual on the right, allowing you to edit that information.

**Select Right**  lets you change the right person to someone else if you are in manual merge mode. (This button is not visible if you are doing automatic duplicate searching.)

**Merge Right Individual into Left Individual**  performs the actual merge operation. The information that has been selected from the person on the right is moved into the record of the person on the left. The relationship links from the person on the right are also moved to the person on the left. The person on the right is then deleted from the family file. This button should only be clicked after you are sure you want to merge the two individuals. If there are any questions as to whether these are indeed the same person, you should do more research before merging them.

**Skip to Next**  skips the current pair of individuals and moves to the next pair of possible duplicates. (This button is only visible if you are doing automatic duplicate searching.)

**Back**  displays the most recently skipped pair of individuals. Successive clicking of this button moves back through all the skipped pairs. (This button is only visible if you are doing automatic duplicate searching.)

**Not Duplicates**  ⌀  indicates that the two individuals are not the same person. They are added to the Not Duplicates list and are not shown in subsequent merge sessions.

## Options

**Print**: You can print a Family Group Record or Individual Report for the current pair of individuals. This may help you decide if they are the same person. (See Merge Information Report for more details.)

**Mark this pair as 'Not Duplicates:** There always seems to be some pairs of individuals in your family file that have similar names and vital information. When merging duplicates these pairs get displayed every time. You know they are different people and just wish they could be marked as such and left out of the merge process. This option lets you mark the currently displayed pair of individuals as not being duplicates. After doing so they will not be displayed in the future when you are merging duplicates. (You can remove pairs from the Not Duplicates list whenever you want.) Alt -X is also available as a shortcut key for this feature. (Deluxe Edition only.)

**Display the 'Not Duplicates' List...** shows the list of people currently marked as not being duplicates. (See Not Duplicates List for more information.) (Deluxe Edition only.)

**Zoom** lets you change the font size in the list windows.

**Close** stops the merge process and returns to the *Family/Pedigree* screen. Your location in the merge process is saved to disk so that you can resume the process at a later time. Remember, merging records is a process that must be completed from beginning to end in order for the operation to be successful. If you **Close** in the middle of a merge, Legacy asks if you would like to continue at a later time. Answering **Yes** causes Legacy to save the current location. Later, when you select **Merge / Find Duplicates** from the **Tools** menu again, Legacy shows the following message:

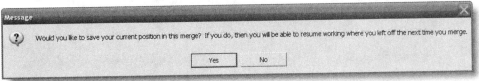

**Print** prints a Family Group Sheet or Individual Report for the current pair of individuals. This may help you decide if they are the same person.

**Help** displays the *Help* system, which shows information regarding the topic on the screen.

**AutoMerge** automatically merges when the information for two individuals is complete enough and matches exactly. If this option is checked, Legacy will ask you if you would like to use the AutoMerge option when the first pair that is eligible for auto-merging appears.

## General Tab

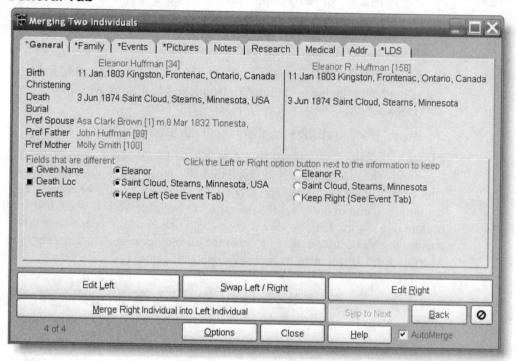

This tab shows two individuals from your file including names, and when they were born, christened, died, and buried. It also shows the *preferred* spouse's name and the *preferred* parents. Below this information is the *Fields that are different* box. This section shows a list of all the information that is different between the two individuals. Each piece of information has an option button to the left of it. The option button shows which piece will be kept. You can change the settings by clicking on the option button next to the information you want to keep. If the list is taller than the box, a scroll bar appears to the right, which can be used to display subsequent information.

## Preserving Information

When you are merging duplicate individuals, you will often want to save some of the information from the person you are deleting. Legacy allows you to copy this information to several different places, depending on what kind it is. This is done by clicking the small black button to the left of the desired field in the **Fields that are different** window. This opens a shortcut menu asking where you would like to copy the information.

**Names**   You can either create an entry in the *Alternate Names* list or copy the name to the General Notes field.

**Birth, Christening, Death, and Burial Information**   You can create an *Event* entry made up of the date and place, or you can copy the information to the General Notes field.

▶ **To copy a piece of information:**

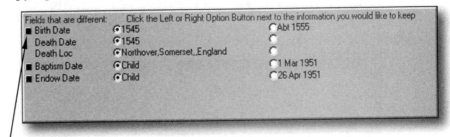

1. Click the small black buttons to the left of the information in the *Fields that are different* box. Only lines that can be copied will have the button.

   A shortcut menu appears with the appropriate choices.

   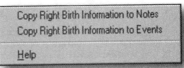

2. Select the destination field for the information. Only the allowable destination fields will appear on the shortcut menu. The information that is not marked to be kept (the empty option button) is then copied to the selected destination.

## Family Tab

This screen shows all the surrounding relationship connections to each person. It includes the parents, siblings, spouses, and children. This information is often very helpful when trying to determine if the two individuals are the same person. The birth, christened, death, and buried information for the currently highlighted person is displayed below the list.

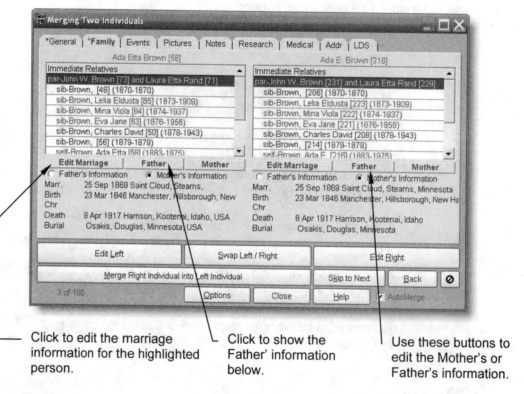

Click to edit the marriage information for the highlighted person.

Click to show the Father' information below.

Use these buttons to edit the Mother's or Father's information.

If the highlighted line is a marriage with two names on it, one of the option buttons below the list indicates whether the mom's or dad's information is shown. Click the other option button to switch to the other person. Other buttons let you edit the Marriage, Dad, Mom, Children, Siblings, or Self.

**Note:** Sometimes you will notice duplicate parents, spouses, or children in the Family List. Don't be alarmed; this is common while you are in the middle of a merge process. These duplicates will be reconciled later as you continue on.

## Events Tab

This screen shows a list of all additional events recorded in each person's record. As you click each event line, the details of that event are displayed below the list. Using the buttons at the bottom of the screen you can perform the following functions:

**Edit Left**  allows you to edit the left, highlighted event. (Any event can be highlighted by clicking it.)

**Delete Left**  deletes the highlighted event in the left window.

**Delete All Left**  deletes all the events in the left window.

**Copy**  copies the highlighted event from the right window to the left window, adding it to the end of the list.

**Copy All**  copies all the events from the right window to the left window, adding them to the end of the list.

**Edit Right**  allows you to edit the right, highlighted event.

### Event Sources

You can view, add, edit, or delete the source citations connected to the events on the left or right side by clicking the corresponding **Source** button.

## Pictures Tab

This screen shows any pictures that have been attached to each individual, along with their captions, dates, and descriptions. If a sound file is connected to a picture, it is shown also.

Using the buttons at the bottom of the tab you can:

**Edit Left**  allows you to edit the left, highlighted picture. (Any picture can be highlighted by clicking it.)

**Delete Left**  deletes the highlighted picture in the left window.

**Delete All Left**  deletes all the pictures in the left window.

**Copy**  copies the highlighted picture from the right window to the left window, adding it to the end of the list.

**Copy All**  copies all the pictures from the right window to the left window, adding them to the end of the list.

**Edit Right**  allows you to edit the right, highlighted picture.

## Notes Tab, Research Tab, Medical Tab

The Notes, Research, and Medical tabs display the various Note fields associated with each individual. Using the buttons at the bottom of the tabs you can:

**Delete Left**   deletes the contents of the Notes field on the left.

**Replace**   copies the note from the right window to the left window, replacing the contents of the left note.

**Append**   copies the note from the right window to the left window, adding it to the end of whatever is in the left window.

**The Research tab** has a **To-Do** button for each individual allowing you to add to-do items for further research.

**The Medical tab** also shows the **Cause of Death** field. There is a **Copy** button between the two individuals that allows you to copy the contents in the right field to the left field, replacing whatever is in the left field, if anything.

## Addr/Ref # Tab

The *Address / Reference* tab shows the Ancestral File Number, User Reference Number, and the address entry for each individual.

Using the buttons at the bottom of the tab you can perform the following functions:

**Edit Address**   allows you to edit the address entries above the button.

**Delete Left**   clears the contents of all the address and phone fields on the left.

**Copy Addr**   copies the contents of all the address and phone number fields from the right window to the left window, replacing the contents of the left address.

Between the individuals shown on this tab is a  <<  button that can be used to copy the contents of the corresponding right field to the left, replacing it with the contents of the right field, if anything.

## LDS Tab

This tab shows the LDS ordinance date and temple fields for each individual, if used.

Using the buttons at the bottom of the tab you can perform the following functions:

**Edit Left**   allows you to edit the LDS ordinance fields on the left.

**Delete Left**   clears the contents in the current, highlighted ordinance field on the left.

**Copy All**   copies all the ordinance information from the right window to the left window, replacing the contents of the left fields.

**Edit Right**   allows you to edit the LDS ordinance fields on the right.

# IntelliShare

Legacy has a great feature called IntelliShare. It is used when you want to share your family file with another person or group of people, and lets you quickly combine the changes made by anyone in the group without having to stare at endless duplicates on the screen as you merge.

### Here is how IntelliShare works:

One person in the group is designated as the "keeper of the records" (keeper, for short).

1. The keeper, sends a copy of the family file to all the other members of the group participating in the process.
2. Any or all members of the group can make changes to existing records and add new records to the family file.  The keeper can also make changes and additions to the master file.
3. At an agreed upon interval, all members of the group return their copies of the family file to the keeper, who will merge and reconcile.

### The keeper then follows this procedure:

▶ **To merge and reconcile:**
1. Import all copies of the family file into the master copy.
2. Click **Merge** and choose **Find Duplicates**.
3. From the *Merge Options* window, click the **Special Searches** tab and choose the **IntelliShare** option.
4. Click **Continue** in the upper-right corner of the *Merge Options* window. Legacy searches for all records with matching IntelliShare values and then automatically merges those that have exactly the same information. At the end of this process Legacy displays the records in which changes have been made by one or more persons.
5. Merge the records.  (See page 265.)
6. After the merge is complete, send the family file back to the other group members for future changes and additions.

# Undoing a Merge

There may be times when you want to start all over again. Either you merged two people who were not really the same person, or you want to go through it all again to make sure you saved the correct information in the correct places. Either way, if you stop in the middle of a merge and don't ever intend to complete it, you should restore from the automatic backup that was made when you started. This option is available by choosing **Undo Merge** from the **Edit** menu. Legacy asks you to confirm the restoration from backup and then returns the family file to its condition before the merge process started.

# Chapter 13

# *Pictures, Sounds, Videos & More*
## A Picture Is Worth a Thousand Words, Especially If It Can Talk

You can attach any number of pictures, sound files, video files, and other types of files to any individual, marriage, event, source, location, or address repository in your family file. Legacy reads all popular file formats. These can then be displayed at any time and the pictures can also be included in many printed reports.

When Legacy is installed, two folders are created within the Legacy folder. These folders are named **Pictures** and **Sounds**. It is strongly recommended that these two folders be used to store the pictures and sounds respectively. Video files can also be stored in the **Sounds** folder or you can create a **Video** folder.

It should be noted that Legacy does not create pictures. Pictures must be scanned in using a quality scanner, or supplied from another source such as a digital camera, or downloaded from a web site or sent to you by e-mail, etc.

It should also be noted that in order to add and edit sounds, the computer must be equipped with a sound card. A microphone must be plugged into the sound card in order to record sound files.

## Adding Pictures

You can add links to picture files for each individual or marriage, to events, sources, and addresses. There are two processes you can use to add pictures. The first is to use the *Picture Gallery*, the second is to use the *Picture Center*. The *Picture Gallery* method is done from a specific individual, marriage, or event and involves selecting pictures (or sounds and video) that you want to link to that particular person, marriage, or event. The second method, using the *Picture Center*, involves viewing a list of all the individuals and all the pictures, and indicating which pictures go where. The *Picture Center* lets you easily attach a lot of pictures to a lot of people, marriages, and events in a short amount of time.

## Picture Gallery

### Adding Pictures

▶ **To add a picture to an individual:**

1.  From the *Family View*, make sure the individual is in either the *Husband* or *Wife* box and then click the **Picture** 🔲 icon on their individual toolbar. (That is the button with the picture of two people.) The *Picture Gallery* appears.

    The *Picture Gallery* displays from one to twenty pictures at a time, although you can have an unlimited number of pictures attached to each individual.

2.  Click the Picture 🔲 icon. This opens the *Load Picture* window. Locate and select the name of the picture you want to add and then click **OK**. The picture is loaded and appears in the *Display Picture* window.

    The *Display Picture* window lets you view an enlarged picture and allows you to add a caption, date, and description. You can also attach sound files, change the picture attributes, and convert the picture file to a different format.

3.  Click **Close** to return to the *Picture Gallery*.

You can continue adding new pictures by clicking the **Picture** icon on the *Picture Gallery*.

## Deleting Pictures

▶ **To remove a picture from the *Picture Gallery*:**
1.  Highlight the picture by clicking in the **Caption** area below the picture.
2.  Click **Remove**. Legacy prompts for confirmation and then unlinks the picture from the individual. The picture file itself is not deleted ... only the reference link is erased.

## Moving Pictures

You can move pictures from one position to another by dragging them with the mouse. With the cursor over a picture, hold down the left mouse button and drag it to a new location. Releasing the mouse button puts the dragged picture in its new location and moves the other pictures one place over to make room.

## Setting the Preferred Picture

When you first begin adding pictures, the picture in the first position is considered the *preferred* picture. This picture is displayed on the *Family View* and *Pedigree View* whenever the individual is current. The *preferred* picture is also printed on reports that include pictures. To mark a different picture as *preferred*, highlight it by clicking in the **Caption** area under the picture, then click the ✱ button near the top of the form. An asterisk appears in front of the picture number. (You can also right-click on a picture and choose **Set as Preferred**.)

## Displaying and Editing a Picture

To see an enlarged view of a picture, highlight it and click **Edit**. The picture is loaded into the *Display Picture* window. From there you can add a caption, date, and description to the picture. You can also change picture attributes such as brightness, sharpness, and contrast as well as rotate, zoom and crop the picture.

## Adding Sound to a Picture

Legacy supports sound files in two ways. First, a picture can have a sound file linked to it. Second, sound files can be added to an individual without tying them to pictures.

▶  **To add a stand-alone sound file to an individual:**

1.  Click the Sound 🔊 icon,
2.  Specify the location of the sound file.

▶  **To link a sound file to a particular picture:**
1.  Highlight the picture.
2.  Click **Edit**. (See *Adding and Recording Sounds* on page 282 for more information.)

If you have a sound file attached to a picture, you can play it by clicking **Play**.

## Adding Video to an Individual

▶  **To add a video file to an individual:**

1.  Click the Video 📹 icon.
2.  Specify the location of the file.

To play a video file once it has been added, highlight it and click **Play**.

## Adding Other Documents to an Individual

▶  **To add a document or other type of file to an individual:**

3.  Click the Document 📄 icon.
4.  Specify the location of the file.

Note that documents and other types of files that are attached in this manner will not be included on report or web sites. They are simply for documentation purposes.

## Zooming In and Out

To take a closer look at a picture, highlight it and click **Zoom**.

## Showing More Pictures

The *Picture Gallery* can display from 1 to 20 pictures at a time. Use the **+** and **-** keys to display more or fewer pictures.

## Creating a Slider Show

To start a sliding picture show that contains all the pictures in the *Gallery*, click **Slider Show**.

(Help index: *Picture: Scrapbook options*)

## Creating a Slide Show

To view a sequential slide show of all the pictures in the *Picture Gallery*, along with their sound files, click **Slide Show**. (See *Slide Shows* on page 284 for more information.)

(Help index: *Picture: Scrapbook options*)

## Printing a Photo Album

To print all the pictures in the *Picture Gallery*, click **Print Pictures**. The *Photo Album Options* window appears, where you can select the type of photo album layout you want to print. (See *Photo Album* on page 284 for more information.)

(Help index: *Picture: Scrapbook options*)

## Tagging Pictures

The checkbox above the upper-right corner of each picture is used to tag or untag the picture. Tagging is useful when you want to select specific pictures to be printed on reports or displayed in screen shows or slide shows.

## Resizing the Window

You can stretch the *Picture Gallery* window by dragging its edges and corners. The picture boxes automatically resize when you do this. Legacy remembers the size and location of the window from session to session.

# The Display Picture Window

Adding a new picture or editing an existing picture is done from the *Display Picture* screen.

## Loading a Picture

▶ **To load a picture into the main window:**

1. Click **Load New**. The *Load Picture* dialog box appears where you can specify the picture file you want to view. As you scroll through the available picture files, they are displayed in the window to the right so you can make sure you are selecting the correct one.
2. Click **OK** when you have found the desired picture.

## Color Versus Black and White

Legacy supports the displaying and printing of both color and black and white pictures. Color pictures can be converted to gray scale (black and white) by clicking **To Gray Scale**. This is often necessary if you are printing reports with pictures on a non-color printer. Color pictures sent to a black and white printer often come out looking muddy and washed out.

## Supported Formats

Legacy supports the loading, displaying, and converting of the following common picture file formats, as well as about 30 others:

- Bitmap (.bmp)
- PCX (.pcx)
- Tiff (.tif)
- PICT (.pct)
- JPEG (.jpg)

## Zooming In and Out

Use the **Zoom In** and **Zoom Out** buttons to vary the magnification of the picture. To adjust the size to exactly fit in the window, click **Fit in Window**. To view the picture at 100% of its actual size, click **100%**. To zoom in to a particular area of a picture, click **Zoom Area** and then drag the mouse cursor over the area you want to magnify. When you release the button, the area within the drag rectangle is enlarged to fit the window.

## Printing the Picture

Click **Print** to print the picture on your printer. A *Print Size* dialog box appears, where you can select the size you want to print the picture. This can be from full page to 1/8th page. When printing a picture, be patient. Some high resolution pictures can take a few minutes to print.

## Converting to a Different Format

After loading a picture, you can save it again in a different format. Click **Save As**. The *Save Picture* dialog box appears. Click the **Down** arrow on the *Save File as Type* combo box. Select the file format you want to convert to and then enter a file name. Click **OK** to complete the conversion.

## Editing a Picture

There are several attributes of a picture that can be permanently changed. These include brightness, sharpness, contrast, rotation, and color.

### Brightness, Sharpness, and Contrast

Pictures that look blurry, dull, or washed out can be touched up to improve their appearance. Click **Picture Attributes** to see the *Adjust Display Attributes* window. Adjust the brightness, sharpness, and contrast controls and click **Apply** to see the effect on the picture. When you are happy with the changes, click **OK**. For the changes to be permanent, you must resave the picture by clicking **Save As**.

### Rotating, Flipping, and Flopping

You can rotate a picture in 90-degree increments by clicking **Rotate 90 Deg**. This may be necessary if a picture was scanned sideways or upside down.

Click **Flip** to reverse a picture from left to right. Click **Flop** to reverse from top to bottom. For the changes to be permanent, you must resave the picture by clicking **Save As**.

## Changing a Picture to Black and White

To convert a color picture to grayscale (shades of black and white), click **To Grayscale**. To retain the grayscaling, you must save the picture.

## Reloading a Picture

Sometimes the changes you make to a picture make it look worse rather than better. If you make changes that you don't want to keep, click **Reload Original** to reload the original picture from disk.

## Adding Sound Files

You can add a sound file to the current picture by clicking **Sound**. (See *Adding and Recording Sounds* on page 282.) After a sound file is attached to a picture, you can play it by clicking **Play**.

## Scanning Pictures

You can scan pictures from your scanner directly into Legacy. To begin the process, click **Scan Picture**. Legacy looks for any scanning software on your computer and displays a list of those found. Select the program you want to use and click **Select**. When your scanner software starts, proceed with the steps you would usually take to scan a picture. This usually involves a preview pass, a selection pass where you choose which part of a picture you want to keep, and a final scanning pass. When the picture has been scanned, Legacy displays a *Save* dialog box prompting you for a name and location for saving the file. After it is saved, the picture is shown in the *Display Picture* window.

## Cropping Pictures

If you want to select a portion of a picture and then crop it to show only that area, click **Crop**. The mouse cursor changes to a crosshair. Select the desired portion of the picture by dragging the cursor over it. As soon as you release the mouse button, the rest of the picture outside the rectangle disappears, leaving only the selected portion of the picture. If you want to change the position or size of the selection, click **Fit** to restore the original picture and try again. When you are satisfied that the selected portion is the only part you want to keep, click **Trim**. The picture then grows to fill the screen. It has been cropped and trimmed but it has not yet been saved. If you want to start over again, click **Reload Original**. If you want to keep the cropped picture you must save it; click **Save As** and choose a name and location. Don't save it over the original picture unless you don't want the original anymore.

### Saving the Changes

When you have made changes that you want to keep, you must save the picture to disk. Click **Save As** and save the picture to whatever format you desire. This can be to the same format and filename as the original, or to either a different name, or format, or both.

### Saving a Picture to a New Format

You can convert any picture into another format by selecting the format from the **Save as type** drop-down box on the **Save File** dialog box. The list includes Bitmap (.bmp), PCX (.pcx), Tiff (.tif) and JPEG (.jpg). After selecting the format type, click **Save**.

When you are through making changes to the picture, click **Close** to return to the *Picture Gallery*.

## Adding and Recording Sounds

Sounds are added from the *Display Picture* screen. This screen is accessed by clicking **Edit** when in the *Picture Gallery* window.

Click **Sound** on the right side of the *Display Picture* screen to open the *Sound Center* window.

This window functions similar to a tape recorder. Click **Record** to begin recording.

▶ **To record a new sound file:**
1. Make sure you have a microphone connected to your computer, then click **Record**.
2. Speak up to two minutes into the microphone to record something. A time meter shows how much time has elapsed.
3. When you are finished recording, click **Stop**.
4. To listen to the recording, click **Play**.
5. To save the recording, click **Save**. The *Save Sound File* dialog box appears.
6. Specify the location and name for the recording and click **OK**. The recording is saved and you are returned to the *Display Picture* window.

▶ **To load an existing sound file:**

1. Click **Load**.
2. From the *Load Sound File* dialog box, locate and select the sound file you want to load. The *Load Sound File* box then disappears.
3. To listen to the sound, click **Play**.
4. To return to the *Display Picture* window, click **Close**.

## Slider Shows

A Slider Show takes all of the pictures linked to the current individual and displays them in a dynamic show where each picture slides across the screen in random directions and random sizes. (There is no sound in a Screen Show.) This is a great way to display your pictures at a family reunion.

▶ **To start a Slider Show:**

1. From the **View** menu, choose **Scrapbook**.
2. Set the desired options on the *Picture Scrapbook Options* window.
3. Click **Display Slider Show**.

While the show is running you can:

1. Right-click on the background to toggle the color and gradient of the background through six different styles.
2. Click on any picture to bring it to the front and center and display the picture caption, date, and description. The other pictures continue to scroll across the screen in the background.

Click on the background to close the show.

# Slide Shows

## What Is a Slide Show?

The slide show feature is an automated sequential display of a group of pictures along with playing any sound files that are connected to them. This can give you a narrated display of an individual's pictures.

To reach the *Slide Show* window, click **Slide Show** from the *Picture Gallery*. When the window appears, the first picture is displayed.

## Starting the Show

To start the slide show, click **Start**. The pictures will begin displaying with a three second delay between them. If a sound file is connected to the picture, it is played through completely before the next picture is displayed, even if it lasts longer than three seconds.

## Stopping the Show

To stop a slide show in action, click the **Stop** button. This can give you a longer look at a particular picture. To continue the show, click **Continue**.

## Moving Manually

Whenever the slide show is not running, you can manually move forward and backward through the pictures by clicking **Next** and **Previous**.

## Sound

You can turn the sound on and off by checking or clearing the **Play Sound** check box.

## Changing the Display Time

To change the time delay between pictures, click the **Right** or **Left** arrows on the **Time Delay** bar, or drag the scroll bar handle to the right or left. This can be done at any time, even during a running slide show.

# Photo Album

You can print a *Photo Album* containing all the pictures you have collected for an individual. These pictures can be printed in different sizes and can include the caption, date, and description associated with each one.

The *Photo Album Options* window is reached by clicking the **Print Pictures** button from the *Picture Gallery* screen. This displays the *Photo Album Options*.

From here you can set many options pertaining to the layout of the printed photo album.

## Pictures Per Page

The size of the pictures varies according to the size of the page and the number of pictures printed on each page. You can select 1, 2, 4, 6, 9, 12, 16, 20, 25, or 30 pictures per page.

## Picture Spacing

The pictures can also be printed with different spacing between them. Pictures printed with Tight spacing are larger than those printed with Loose spacing.

## What to Include

Each picture can include its caption, printed above it, and the description and date printed below. You can specify that the description be left-justified or centered. A drop shadow is also available to give the pages a three-dimensional effect.

When you have set all the options for the photo album printout, click either **Preview** to see an on-screen view of the album before actually printing, or **Print** to have the photo album sent directly to the printer.

# Picture Center

The **Picture Center** in Legacy is a very easy way to link many pictures to many individuals from one place. You will often come upon pictures in groups that you want to link to the people in your family file. For example, you might have a box or picture album of many pictures that you then scan into your computer. The pictures are associated with several different individuals. The **Picture Center** lets you link each picture to as many people in your file as your picture relates to—from one convenient place within the program.

To reach the **Picture Center**, choose **Picture Center** from the *Tools* menu.

In its simplest form, there are three main sections to the **Picture Center** screen. On the left is a list of all the individuals in your family file. In the middle is a list of the pictures on your computer. On the right is a preview window showing the highlighted picture.

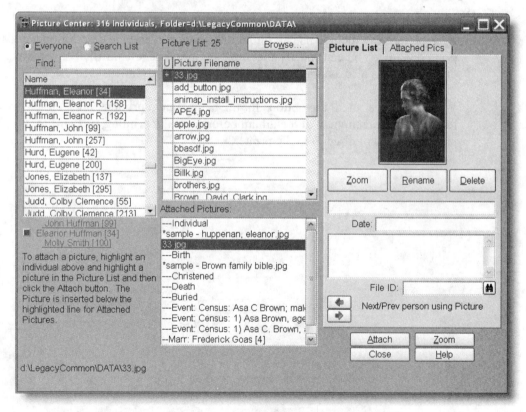

▶ **To assign a particular picture to a specific individual:**
   1. In the left window, highlight the individual.

2. In the upper-center window, find and highlight the desired picture.
3. Click **Attach** near the lower-right corner. This adds the picture to the individual's picture list.

There are many options associated with this process. These are described below:

## The Name List

By default, the **Name** list shows **everyone** in your family file. You can choose to show just the names that are in the current **Search List** by selecting the **Search List** option above the list.

The **Find** box above the list lets you quickly jump to anyone in the list by typing part or all of their name. Enter the name with the surname first, followed by a comma and then the given name(s). The highlight line jumps to the nearest match as you are typing.

## Active Pedigree Chart

Below the **Name** list is a two-generation pedigree chart showing the currently highlighted person and his or her parents. You can jump to either parent by clicking their names. There is also a button to the left of the main person. If the button is blue then it means that person has children and clicking the button takes you to the preferred child.

## The Picture List

The **Picture Filename** list shows all the supported picture, sound, and video file formats supported by Legacy. The current folder name is shown in the title bar of the window. You can change to a different folder by clicking **Browse** above the list. To choose a particular picture, sound, or video, highlight the name by clicking on it. If it is a picture file, the picture will display in the preview window to the right (if you have the **Picture List** tab selected).

The **U** column to the left of the picture filenames indicates whether or not each picture has been assigned to someone in your family file already. The **+** means that picture in that folder has been assigned to someone. The **−** means that file name has been assigned to someone but from a different picture folder. For example, you may be looking at **grandpa.bmp** in the **Legacy\Pictures** folder but another file called **grandpa.bmp** in the **Legacy\Reunion\Pictures** folder is currently being used somewhere in your file. (You should be careful not to have different picture files with the same name located in different folders. It will surely confuse you at some point…

## Assigned Pictures

Below the **Picture Filename** list is the **Assigned Pictures** list. It shows a list of all the events for the currently highlighted person and any pictures that have been assigned to those events. You can view the pictures from this list by first clicking the **Assigned** tab in the upper-right corner of the window, and then clicking on the desired picture name in the list. The complete filename for the highlighted picture, including the folder where it is stored, is displayed along the bottom of the window.

## Previewing the Pictures

### The Picture List Tab

When the **Picture List** tab is selected, you can preview the pictures that are highlighted in the **Picture Filename** list to the left. When a picture is displayed, there are several option available:

**Zoom**   opens a *QuickLook* window showing a larger view of the current picture. This window can be stretched to the full size of your monitor if desired. Click the **X** in the upper-right corner to close the *QuickLook* window.

**Rename**   allows you to change the name of the currently highlighted file in the *Picture Filename* list. The file is then renamed on disk. If the file has a + in the U column, any links to this picture within your family file are also renamed to match the change you made.

**Delete**   erases the currently highlighted picture file in the *Picture Filename* list. After confirmation, Legacy erases the file from the current folder. If any links to this file exist in your family file, they are removed. (If the picture is linked to anyone in a different family file, deleting the file will cause a "picture file not found" error when trying to access it from there.)

**Caption, Date, Description, User File Number**   displays a window where you can enter caption, date, and description information before assigning a picture to an individual. There is also a field for a User File # if you are assigning these numbers to your pictures. These entries are remembered by Legacy for future use even if the picture has not yet been assigned to anyone.

### The Assigned Tab

Clicking on the **Assigned** tab lets you view pictures that have already been linked to the current individual.

**Zoom**   (Same as **Zoom** on the **Picture List** tab.)

**Rename**   (Same as **Rename** on the **Picture List** tab.)

**Remove**   unlinks the currently highlighted picture in the *Assigned Pictures* list from the current event in the list. It does not delete the file from the disk.

**Caption, Date, Description, User File Number** allows you to view and edit the caption, date, description, and user file number entries for the current picture.

**Set Preferred** lets you change the preferred picture setting for any event that has more than one picture assigned to it. (The preferred picture is the one that prints on reports.)

**Changing the Order** lets you change the picture order by using the up and down Order arrow buttons. Highlight the filename you want to move and click the appropriate arrow to change its position up or down. You can also move a picture from one event to another using these buttons. If a filename is at the bottom of the event section, clicking the **down** arrow moves the picture down to the first position in the next event. The **up** arrow moves a picture to previous events in the same manner.

## Attach

Clicking **Attach** links the highlighted current picture in the **Picture Filename** list to the highlighted current individual in the **Name** list under the event that is highlighted in the **Assigned Pictures** list. The caption, date, description, and user file number from the **Picture List** tab go along with the assignment.

▶ **To assign a picture to more than one individual, for example to each person in a family reunion photo:**
1. Highlight the desired picture in the **Picture Filename** list.
2. In the Picture List tab, fill in the caption, date, description, and user file number as desired.
3. In the **Assigned Pictures** list, highlight the event where you want to place the picture.
4. Click **Assign**.
5. Highlight the next person.
6. Click **Assign** again.
7. Repeat steps 5 and 6 until the picture has been assigned to the desired group. (You can change the caption, date, and description fields between each attachment if needed, for instance, to say "Martha is the first person on the left" in Martha's description and "Ted is the second person from the left" in Ted's description, and so on.)

## Zoom

The **Zoom** button to the right of the **Attach** button is used to select the font size used in the various lists of the screen.

## Close

To close the *Picture Center*, click **Close**. All captions, date, descriptions, and user file numbers that you filled in while in the center are remembered and will appear the next time you open the center.

# Chapter 14

# *Searching for Individuals*
## How to Locate Individuals and Families

## Overview of Searching

Legacy includes powerful search capabilities. You can find anyone in the family file using any type of information. This includes names, dates, locations, and notes, as well as information in many other fields. You can look for field contents that *begin* with certain text or field contents that contain a word or phrase anywhere in that field. You can also create groups of information through the search option, such as a list of all people who were born in London, England, or a list of all people who died of cancer. Once a search group is found, you can quickly move from person to person, viewing or editing. Search groups are even remembered between sessions.

The search feature can be reached by either choosing **Find** from the **Search** menu, or by clicking the **Search** icon on the toolbar. The *Search* window contains three tabs, Query by Example, Detailed Search, and Miscellaneous Searches.

## Query by Example Tab

Query by Example is an easy fill-in-the-blanks type of search.

► **To query for information:**
1. Fill in one or more fields with the information you want to find.
2. Select **Male**, **Female**, or **Either**.
3. Select one of the **How to Find** options. **Exact** looks for only what you typed (searching for a last name of Roberts will find only Roberts, not Robertson). **Starts With** finds records where the information *starts* with what you typed (searching for a given name of "B" will find all names that begin with B). **Anywhere in field** looks for what you typed at any position within the field (searching for "abe" would find Abe, Abel, Mabel, Faber, etc).
4. Click **Find First** to look for the first matching record, or **Create List** to generate a *Name List* of all the records that match the search criteria.

If you clicked **Find First**, the record is immediately shown in the *Family View* or *Pedigree View*. If you clicked **Create List**, you can display any of the resulting records by highlighting a name and clicking **Select**, or by double-clicking a name. With the record displayed, you can display the next record by clicking **F3**, or the previous record by clicking **Shift-F3**.

### More Detail

If you click **More Detail**, the *How to Find* box disappears and a set of option buttons appears next to each field on the search screen. These are labeled *Equal, Starts,* and *In.* This lets you specify the type of search you want to perform for each field, instead of all the fields as a whole. For example, you could search for records with a last name equal to "Jones" and given names starting with "A."

# Detailed Search Tab

The *Detailed Search* tab allows you to search for individuals using much stricter criteria. You can use AND and OR modifiers to look for specific types of individuals in specific places.

### Who to Look For

Select the type of person you want to find. You can search for a male, a female, an individual (who can either be a male or female), or a marriage.

### Where to Look

Select the field you want to look in.
What you are allowed to enter into the **What to Look For** field is controlled by the field selected in the **Where to Look** field to the left. Depending on what you selected, the **What to Look For** field may be empty, in which case you will have to type in the needed criteria, or the field will contain preset options to choose from.

### How to Look

You can search by using Equal To, Not Equal To, Before, After, Contains, Starts With, Sounds Like, and Wildcard. (Some types of searches do not include all these search methods.) None of the searches are case sensitive; uppercase and lowercase letters always match.

**Equal To**   finds whatever you enter, matched letter-for-letter.

**Not Equal To**   matches will be found for everything except what you enter.

**Before and After**   is used for finding dates.

**Greater Than or Equal to**   matches anything from a given number and higher.

**Less Than or Equal to**   matches anything from a given number and lower.

**Contains** looks through the entire field contents to see if what you typed is found anywhere within it.

**Starts With** matches field contents that begin with what you entered.

**Sounds Like** finds surnames that sound like the name you entered. Everything is converted to standard Soundex codes before comparing.

(Help index: *Soundex*)

**Wildcard** provides pattern matching, like **Dav\*** (Dave, Davis, Davidson, Davenport, etc.) or **Berd?n** (Berdan, Berden, Berdin, Berdon, Berdun).

(Help index: *Wildcard search*)

## What to Look For

Type in the information you want to find, or select the item from the drop-down list box.

## Adding Search Criteria

You can specify up to three different conditions to search for. To enable the next condition, select **Second Condition** then **Third Condition**, choose **AND** or **OR**, and fill in the search fields.

## Using AND and OR

If you select the AND option for a search condition, both of the search comparisons must be true in order for the individual to be selected. For example:

**Male, Last Name, Equal To, Johnson**
**AND**
**Male, Age, Greater Than, 50**

displays all individuals who are male, with a last name of Johnson, and were born more than 50 years ago.

When you select the OR option, only one or the other (or both) of the search comparisons need be true to select the individual. For example:

**Individual, Title, Equal To, Duke**
**OR**
**Individual, Title, Equal To, Duchess**

will display all individuals, either male or female, who have either a title of Duke or Duchess.

If you use three search conditions, the search conditions are done in two stages. First, conditions one and two are combined using AND or OR, then, if this first comparison is true, the third condition is combined using its AND or OR. If the final result is true, the individual is displayed.

Here are some examples of single and combined search conditions:

| | |
|---|---|
| True | Displayed |
| False | Not Displayed |
| True AND True | Displayed |
| True AND False | Not Displayed |
| True OR True | Displayed |
| True OR False | Displayed |
| False OR True | Displayed |
| False OR False | Not Displayed |
| True AND True AND True | Displayed |
| True AND True AND False | Not Displayed |
| True AND True OR False | Displayed |
| False OR True AND True | Displayed |
| False OR True AND False | Not Displayed |
| False OR False OR True | Displayed |

## Starting the Search

After specifying a search criteria using one of the three search methods, you can either display the individuals found one at a time or in a list format.

## One at a Time

To display the records one at a time, click **Find First**. Legacy finds the first person matching the search criteria and displays that individual on the screen in the current *Family View* or *Pedigree View*. You can then press **F3** to move to the next person matching the search criteria. **Shift+F3** moves backward through the group.

## Creating a Search List

To create a list containing all the individuals who match the search criteria, click **Create List**. If you are creating a list, you can either begin a new list, add to an existing list, or search a previously created search result group.

**Clear List before this search**   clears any existing search list before doing the current search. The resulting search list will contain only the people from the current search.

**Add results to existing Search List** retains any previous search list and adds the current search results to it. This way you can combine two or more subsets of people into one list.

**Only search the Search List** causes Legacy to restrict its search to the existing search list. For example, if the previous search list contains all the people born in Boston and you are now searching for all people who died of cancer, the result will be all the people who were born in Boston and died of cancer.

# Search List Window

The *Search List* window is the same window that appears from the *Name List* command. Through this window any person in the Legacy family file can be quickly and easily found. When the *Search List* has been created through a search command, it can be

closed and called up again later by clicking on the **Results** ▼ icon (Deluxe Edition only) on the toolbar or by choosing **View Search List** under the *Search* menu.

Notice that the details for each individual in the name list are shown on the right side of the screen. This data changes as each individual is selected. The field name titles such as Born, Chr., Death, etc., can be changed by clicking on a line label and selecting from the list of available options.

Once a *Search List* has been created, additional individuals can be found and added to the list by selecting the **Add results to existing List** option on the *Search* window, before clicking **Create List**. The search results remain active and available until they are replaced by another search. You can even quit Legacy, come back later, and use the old search list. It is automatically saved.

# Miscellaneous Searches Tab

The following searches are also available:

## Searches Dealing With the Current Individual

**Focus Group**  finds all the members of the current focus group. (See *Focus Groups* on page 235 for more information on setting up these groups.)

**Oldest Direct-Line Generation**  finds all the individuals who are in the oldest ancestor generation. This could be one person or many. For example, if the ancestors go back 10 generations and there are five individuals in that 10th generation, those five will be found. If it goes back 11 generations and there is only one person, that individual will be the only person found.

**Youngest Direct-Line Generation**  finds all the individuals who are in the youngest descendant generation.

**Direct-Line Ancestors With no Parents**  finds all the ancestors of the current individual who have no mother and father linked to them. In other words, the ends of all the ancestor lines.

**Direct-Line Descendants With no Children**  finds all the descendants of the current individual who do not have any children. In other words, the ends of all the descendant lines.

## Searches Dealing with the Entire Family File

**Linked Individuals With no Children**  finds all individuals who are linked to either a spouse or a parent, but have no children linked to them.

**Linked Individuals With no Parents**  finds all individuals who are linked to either a spouse or a child, but have no parent linked to them.

**Unlinked Individuals**  finds all individuals who are not linked to anyone.

**All Records With an Individual Tag # of x**  finds all the records that have been tagged with the specified tag number.

**All Records With Bad Dates**  finds all individuals who have an unrecognized date anywhere in their information. (This can happen because of ignored warnings when editing and importing.)

**Individuals who are Married**  finds all the people who have one or more spouses linked to them.

**Individuals With an Unknown Spouse**  finds all the people with some marriage information but no actual spouse linked to them.

**Individuals With Multiple Spouses** finds all the people who have two or more spouses linked to them.

**Individuals With Multiple Parents** finds all the people who have two or more parents linked to them.

# Missing Sources Search

You can search for individuals who are missing a source citation on various pieces of information that has been entered. This will give you a list that you can use to go back and figure out where the information came from.

Select the checkboxes for the items to search on. You can select as many as you want to. In the **How to combine the selected fields** box in the lower-right corner you can indicate how to handle multiple selections. Either **ALL of the selected fields must be missing information for a match** or **Only ONE or more of the selected fields must be missing information for a match**.

When you have selected the desired field and set the combine option, select one of the options below to begin the search:

# Missing Information Search

You can search for individuals who are missing various pieces of information. This will give you a list that you can use to go back and try to fill in the blanks.

Select the checkboxes for the items to search on. You can select as many as you want to. In the **How to combine the selected fields** box in the lower-right corner you can indicate how to handle multiple selections. Either **ALL of the selected fields must be missing information for a match** or **Only ONE or more of the selected fields must be missing information for a match**.

When you have selected the desired field and set the combine option, select one of the options below to begin the search:

# Search the Internet

The Internet is a great place to search for your family members. Billions of people are documented in thousand and thousands of genealogical sites across the World Wide Web. From Legacy you can search the Internet for information about people in your family file. This is often a good way to extend your family lines and find other living relatives working on the same things.

To start a search on the Internet, choose **Search Internet for Current Person** from the **Internet** menu.

There are many, many places on the Internet where you can search for information about your ancestors. Legacy comes preloaded with eight sites to begin your searching. Any number of additional sites can be added at any time.

The *Search the Internet* screen, has several fields that are preloaded with information concerning the current individual. Below the fields is a list of up to eight Internet search sites where you can look for addition information and about this person and their surrounding family. Each Internet site requires some or all of the information shown in the top half of the screen. The fields that are not needed for the currently selected site are disabled (grayed out). The remaining "live" fields can be changed before initiating the search. As you select different search sites, the appropriate fields are made available.

▶ **To start an Internet search:**
1. Click on the desired search site.
2. Make sure the information in the fields reflects the person you are looking for.
3. Click **Search**.

If you would like the *Search the Internet* window to remain displayed after you search for a person, make sure the **Close this window after each search** option is cleared. Selecting this option will cause the window to close when a search is done.

To customize the list of eight Internet search sites, click **Customize Searches**. (This is a *Deluxe Edition* only feature.) The *Customize Internet Searches* window appears with the eight currently selected sites showing. You can then change any of the sites to something different.

When you are done searching, click **Close**.

## Customize Internet Searches

The *Customize Internet Searches* window is reached by clicking **Customize Searches** on the *Search the Internet* window.

To add or change one of the eight Internet search sites, click **Select** to the left of the site you want to change. The *Select an Internet Search* screen appears where you can choose a site to search, or add a new one. (See *Select an Internet Search* below for more information.)

To reset the current list of eight site to the defaults that came with Legacy, click **Defaults**.

When you have a group of searches set up the way you like them, you can save them for future use. Any number of search sets can be saved and reloaded at any time. To save a search set, click **Save** and then specify the name and location where you would like them saved. To reload a set, click **Load** and specify the set you would like to pull in.

# Select an Internet Search

The *Select an Internet Search* screen is reached by clicking one of the **Select** buttons on the *Customize Internet Searches* screen.

Legacy comes with several Internet search sites ready for you to use. The Available Internet Searches list includes these and any others you have defined. As you highlight each line, the search string is displayed below the list. The character sequence that is used to replace a space in the search string is also displayed. (Internet search strings do not have any blank spaces in them. So, to pass information that contains a space, like a givenname-middlename combination (John Francis), the space is replaced by one or more other characters. These are usually a plus sign (+) or the hexadecimal version of the character like **%20**.)

To select a site from the list, highlight the desired line and then click **Select**.

To make changes to an entry in the list, highlight the entry and then click **Edit**. The *Create Custom Internet Search* screen appears where you can make any needed changes.

To add a new Internet search to the list, click **Add**. The *Create Custom Internet Search* screen appears where you can enter the search string to be used.

You can also delete any search entries you no longer want to keep in the list. To do this, highlight the line you want to remove and then click **Delete**.

# Creating Custom Internet Searches

The *Create Custom Internet Search* screen is reached by clicking **Add** or **Edit** on the *Select an Internet Search* screen.

This screen is used to add a new Internet search string or to edit an existing string.

(Help index: ***Define:Internet Search***)

# Search and Replace

Search and Replace helps you globally search through your entire family file to make changes. You can search for and replace the contents of Given Names, Surnames, Titles, Alternate Names, Notes, Dates, Lists, Sources, Multimedia, Addresses, Events, Repositories, To-Do items, and more. Over 100 fields can be changed.

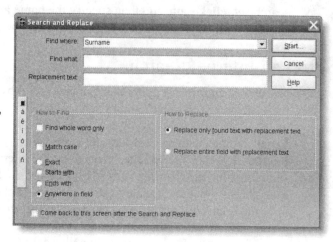

▶ **To use Search and Replace:**

1. From the **Search** menu, choose **Search and Replace**.
2. From the **Find Where** list, select the field in which you want to perform the search and replace.
3. In the **Find What** field, fill in the contents you want search for.
4. In the **Replacement Text** field, enter the text you want to change it to.
5. Under **How to Find** and **How to Replace**, set any desired options.
6. Click **Start**.

## Special Characters

When entering information, Legacy offers a feature to help you quickly enter international characters. You can choose up to eight characters to be displayed in a ribbon on all input screens. (This ribbon can be turned off if not needed. See *Customizing Legacy* on page 236.) Whenever you need one of these letters within a field, simply clicking on one automatically fills it in where you are typing. To select the characters that you want to display on the ribbon, click the small blue button at the top of the ribbon and then double-click on up to eight characters from the *Character Map*. You can also click **F6** whenever you are in a text input field to display the *Character Map*, where you can then select any character needed.

When Legacy finds the first matching search text, the *Replacement* screen is displayed. If you want to make the replacement, click **Replace**. Click **Skip** if you would like to move on to the next match. If you are confident that you want to automatically make the change on all the remaining matches, click **Replace All**.

# IGI Search

The IGI Search currently allows automated searching of the IGI (International Genealogical Index) on the FamilySearch.org web site. The IGI is a partial index to vital records from around the world. Searching the IGI also allows LDS users to search for completed ordinance information.

Because the entire FamilySearch.org site is being rebuilt during 2008, the IGI Search feature in Legacy will be changing soon to accommodate the new system. Rather than document a soon-to-be obsolete feature, you will find the instructions for the current implementation in the Legacy Help system.

(Help index: *FamilySearch*)

# Chapter 15

# *Web Page Creation*
How to Create Web Pages for the Internet

Publishing your genealogy on the Internet can be a highly effective way of sharing information with others. Legacy's comprehensive *Web Page Creation* utility generates five styles of Web pages including Ancestor Book, Descendant Book, Pedigree, Family Group, and Individual. All styles are easy to navigate and each includes a table of contents, name index, customizable content, and extensively cross-linked pages.

Legacy also allows custom HTML codes to be embedding by advanced users who want to add buttons and other features. Web pages can include links to other sites and downloadable GEDCOM files.

## Planning a Web Page

Before you begin creating your own web site, take some time to plan it. There are three basic things to determine before you can begin:

- Where and how will you upload your pages to the Internet? Contact your Internet service provider (ISP) for details.
- Decide on a Web page style that best presents your genealogical information on the Internet.
- Decide whom you want to include (and exclude) in the web pages.

## Creating a Web Page

▶ **To make a Web page:**
1. From the **Internet** menu, choose **Create Web Pages**. The *Web Page Creation* window appears.
2. Choose the style of Web pages you want to create by selecting a style from the **Web Page Style** box at the right of the window. You can choose from: **Ancestor**, **Descendant**, **Pedigree**, **Family Group,** or **Individual**.
3. Select the options you want to use from the ten tabs (described below).
4. Click **Create Web Pages**.

### Project Tab

**Project name**   Name the folder where your web pages will be saved. A file name can contain up to 255 characters, including spaces.

**Folder name for pictures**  Name the folder where your pictures are to be stored. This is useful if you plan to create more than one style of web site and share the pictures among them.

**Home page title**  Give your home page a customized title, if desired.  The default title on the home page changes according to the Web Page Style selected. The title appears at the top of the opening page when the web pages are generated.

**Include the main name from each page as the page's title**  Include the main person's name from each page as part of the title. Each subpage can have its own title. (This option is only available for pedigree style web pages.)

**Introduction to appear at the top of your home page**  Enter text here to welcome people to your site.

**Name and address to appear on home page so others can contact you** Enter your personal contact information.

**E-mail address that others can click to send you e-mail messages**  If you have an e-mail address, enter it here.

## Who to Include Tab

**Who to Include on an Ancestor or Descendant Style Site**  If you are producing an ancestor or descendant style web site, select the starting person.

**Who to Include on a Pedigree, Family Group, or Individual Style Site** Select the records you want to include on the web site. You can also choose to include or exclude single males and females if building a family group style site.

## What to Include Tab

Choose the items you want to include on your web site. Most of these options are the same as those included on reports. (See *Other Report Options* on page 134 for their descriptions.)

## Other Tab

### GENDEX genealogical index
Select this option to generate a special index (GENDEX.txt) to be uploaded with your Web pages.  This is an index file containing the names, dates, and places of the individuals on the resulting web site.  This file used to be used by several search sites like **GenealogyToday.com, tngnetwork.lythgoes.net**, and **FamilyTreeSeeker.com** to add the information to a large master index. Gendex.com was closed in early 2004 but the gendex.txt files are still used by some individuals for making master indexes of web site groups, therefore the option remains available for those who want to use it.

### Include source citations

Describes the locations of the information for the individual. Source citations can be grouped together on their own Web page, or appear on the Web page with the individual to whom they belong.

### Slashes around /Surnames/

Select this option to format surnames with surrounding slashes to make them stand out.

### Uppercase SURNAMES

Select this option to format surnames as all upper case to make them stand out.

### Remove quoted names for narratives

If you want to have a quoted name removed from the full name of an individual, check the box next to the **Remove Quoted Given Names** option. This way, the name Robert Alan "Al" Smith will be printed as Robert Alan Smith.

### Use quoted names for narratives

If there is a quoted name within the given name field for an individual, you can have that name used with the narrative portions of a Web page. For example, if a person had a name of Robert Alan Smith but was known as Al, you could enter his name as Robert Alan "Al" Smith and have that appear on Web pages.

### Suppress details for living people

Select this option to remove information on living persons. This will protect the privacy of living individuals who do not want personal information disclosed over the Internet. See Living Individualsfor more information.

### Change names to "Living"

Selecting this option will provide total anonymity by substituting Living for the names of living persons.

**GEDCOM file**   If you would like to include a GEDCOM file on your Web site for others to download, click **Select** and choose the file you would like to include. (You must create the GEDCOM file before selecting it here. See *Exporting GEDCOM Files* on page 252 for more information.) Click **Clear** if you don't want a GEDCOM file.

### Include pictures of individual

If you have linked one or more pictures to an individual, you can have the primary picture included with their information. These pictures can be printed in three different sizes (small, medium and large) to suit your tastes.

### Include child pictures

Select this option to include pictures of children on Descendant or Family Group style Web pages.

## Graphics Tab

**Background**   Select the pattern you want to appear as the background on all the pages of your web site. Legacy provides many different styles to choose from, or you can use your own.

**Bullets**   Select the style of graphic you would like to use for bullet points on your pages. These are used to set off the different sections of your site.

**Divider line**   Select the style of line you want to use to divide the different sections.

**Generation arrows for Pedigree style**   If you are producing a pedigree style web site, choose the style of arrow to be used when navigating to older generations.

## Formatting Tab

**Name formatting**   Choose the format you would like to use when displaying names on your site.

**Surname index**   Include an index, sorted by surname, on your web site with links to all names.

**Headers**   Choose left-justified or centered headers.

**Ancestor and Descendant page breaks**   When producing an ancestor or descendant style web site, have all the generations placed on one page or have each generation placed on separate pages. If there is a lot of information in each generation, it is often better to place them on separate pages so they will be smaller and thereby load quicker.

**Include main entries for**   If you are producing a descendant style web site, choose who gets a main entry in the report. This can be either **Individuals with Children**, or **Individuals with Children or Spouse(s)**.

**Name list style**   Choose the type of index style for the *Name List*. This is the index that people use to look up specific individuals on your site. On web sites that contain a large number of people, you can break large *Name Lists* into separate, smaller pages for quicker loading.

**What to include on the name list**  Choose additional information to include next to each name on the *Name List*. This often makes it easier to find a specific person among a group of people with the same name.

**Filenames format**  Choose the format for file names within your web site. Some web site service providers have computer servers that require that all file names be lowercase. Others allow mixed case.

**Maximum files in a folder**  Choose how many separate web page files to place in a folder before creating additional folders to hold more pages. An individual folder in Microsoft® Windows® cannot hold more than about 40,000 files. If you are generating a web site that has tens of thousands of pages, you can specify the maximum number for each folder. Reducing the number of web pages to 1,000 will result in more subfolders; however, the web pages of each subfolder will upload faster than if they were in one large folder.

## Title Page Tab

**Picture for title page**  Choose an image you would like to include on the title page of your web site. You can also enter a caption paragraph to be placed below the picture on the page. (The picture and caption are optional, of course.)

## Links Tab

**Home button**  If you are producing a web site that will end up as a subsite, place a **Home** button on the title page (or on the bottom of every page) that takes users back to your main home page.

**Custom HTML headers and footers**  (Advanced users) Customize the links in the headers and footers on the top and bottom of each page by adding your own HTML code.

(Help index: *Customized HTML headers and footers*)

## Misc. Tab

When you type a URL in your browser and don't include a specific file name, a default file is looked for and opened if found.  In the majority of cases this file is usually called "**Index.htm**." Some Internet Service Providers may use a different name, such as **default.htm**. Others, using Unix or Linux servers that use case-sensitive file names may use **index.htm**, **Index.htm**, or other variations including an extension of **.html**.

By default Legacy produces a starting page called **Index.htm**.  If your web hosting service requires a different name or extension, you can set the following two options:

**Default starting page root file name** Enter the name of the starting page without an extension. This will usually be Index but could also be index (lowercase), Default, default, or perhaps something else.

## Extension to use on all web pages

You can choose between **.htm** and **.html**. This will be used as the extension for all the pages generated for the web site. "**.htm**" is the default and is the most common but **.html** is sometimes required by certain service providers.

Many Internet Search Engines (e.g. Altavista.com) have "bots" or "spiders" that search out Web pages on the Internet and automatically add them to their indexes. To do this they look in Web page Meta tags for key words and descriptions. When Web surfers query an Internet Search Engine, they can find sites that match the keywords and phrases they are searching on.

**Include a description in the web site** Document and describe what your site is about. This is not displayed on any page but is included in the HTML header section as part of the DESCRIPTION meta tag.

**Include keywords in the web site** Add information that will help Internet search engines index your site. Many Internet search engines (e.g., AltaVista.com) have "bots" or "spiders" that search out web pages on the Internet and automatically add them to their indexes. To do this they look in web page *Meta* tags for key words and descriptions. When web surfers query an Internet search engine, they can find sites that match the keywords and phrases they are searching for. Adding information here is important if you want others to be able to find your web pages. In the keywords box you may want to list all of the surnames you are researching for (e.g., Alden, Allerton, Brewster, Mullins, Warren).

Now that you have selected who and what to include, as well as the style, formatting, and graphics, you can store these options by clicking **Save**. They can be reloaded later when updating your web pages.

## Wording Tab

You can specify phrases when creating the narrative paragraphs of the report. These include:

Individual Events
Marriage Events
General, Research, Medical, Marriage, Birth, Christening, Death, and Burial Notes

To generate your web pages, click **Create Web Pages**. After the pages have been created, Legacy offers to display them in your default browser.

For examples of the various web page styles produced by Legacy, visit our web site (www.LegacyFamilyTree.com).

# Chapter 16

# *LDS Temple Submissions*

How to Select Individuals and Families for Temple Submission

At the publishing of this manual, The Church of Jesus Christ of Latter-day Saints is in a transition period to a new temple ordinance submission process as part of the New FamilySearch program. Legacy is integrating this new process into its feature set, but because the submission process is still in a phased release, it is not possible to include the instruction on how to use it in this manual. So, you are hereby referred to the Legacy Help system for up-to-date instructions.

(Help index: **Temple Submission**)

# Chapter 17

# *Miscellaneous Tools and Utilities*

Handy Utilities to Make Life Easier

## File ID Number Assistant

Many users create a filing system for the documents they collect during their research. Filing numbers are part of this system and are used to organize the documents. File number fields are available on Master Source documents, source citation documents, To-Do items and Pictures. The File ID Number Assistant is used to help you figure out what the next available ID number is for any of the different categories. If you are using a system of filing numbers that contains letters and numbers and you need to be reminded of the next available increment of the number portion, the Assistant can help. The

Assistant is reached by clicking the 🔍 button to the right of any **File ID** field.

(Help index: ***File ID Number Assistant***)

## File Maintenance

File maintenance in Legacy consists of four options: Check/Repair Family File, Master Lists Cleanup, Compact Family File, and Set File Sorting Order. These options do some checking to make sure the integrity of your family file is correct.

### Check/Repair

The solution to many family file problems can be found by performing the **Check/Repair** option in **File Maintenance**. This option rebuilds indexes, performs over 100 integrity checks of all information, and repairs errors that it finds. Anything that appears to be wrong is reported to you.

(Help index: ***Check and Repair Family File***)

### Master Lists Cleanup

**Remove Abandoned Information**   You can have unused entries removed from any or all of the master lists maintained by Legacy. For example, abandoned entries can happen in the *Surname List* if you were to delete all the people with a certain surname from the family file. That surname would still remain in the master list as an unreferenced name. You can have Legacy run through the *Surname List* to remove any names that are not being pointed to. This is most often the case if you entered a misspelled name and then later corrected it. "Smiht" could end up in the list, taking up room, and never be referenced.

(Help index: ***Master Lists Cleanup***)

## Compact Family File

When individuals are deleted from the family file, all references to them are removed, but the record is still taking up space in the file. To remove the unused records, select this option. Legacy goes through the file and deletes all records that are not referenced, making your family file smaller.

## Set File Sorting Order

The sorting order of a family file determines the order that the various letters of the alphabet are displayed in lists and on reports. You can choose from the following sorting orders:

1. English, French, German, Portuguese, Italian, and Modern Spanish
2. Dutch
3. Norwegian and Danish
4. Spanish
5. Swedish and Finnish

When you change the sorting order of a family file, all the internal indexes must be rebuilt. (Since this is a change to the family file, it is a good idea to make a backup before proceeding.) Depending on the size of your family file and the speed of your computer, this operation may take a while.

(Help index: ***Set File Sorting Order***)

# Backing Up Your Family File

Making regular backup copies of your family file information is essential, yet is often taken for granted or ignored by many. Backups are a fundamental part of using a computer. If you don't make backups, there will come a day that you *will* be sorry.

(Help index: ***Backing Up a Family File***)

# Deleting a Family File

If you want to erase a family file, choose **Delete Family File** from the **File** menu. After confirming your intention, Legacy deletes the currently opened family file.

# Setting Direct-Line Preferences

As you move from younger generations to older ones in both the *Family View* and the *Pedigree View*, Legacy automatically chooses the *preferred* parents of the current individual. (You can change the *preferred* parents, if there is more than one set, by right-clicking on an individual and choosing **View / Parents List**.) As you move back down to younger generations, you will oftentimes get "lost" because you can't remember which child to select.

You can have Legacy automatically reset all the direct-line ancestors of a specified individual to *preferred*. This way, as you navigate up and down through the generations, you can find your way back down the same way as you went up.

(Help index: *Direct Line*)

# Testing Picture and Sound Locations

When you import information from a GEDCOM file that contains references to picture, sound, and other files, Legacy needs to know where they are located on the new computer. Most of the time, when you receive a GEDCOM file from another person, it is not accompanied by the multimedia files. To reconcile the file links, have Legacy search for them.

(Help index: *Checking Multimedia Locations*)

# Clearing Import Tags

Whenever you import records into your family file, Legacy marks them as "Imported." You can see if a record was imported by popping up the *Last Modified* window by clicking on the **Modified Date** box at the right end of the status bar at the bottom of the main window. If you want to clear all the "Imported" marks, choose **Clear Imported Tags** from the **Tools** menu.

# Trees in This Family File

## What Are Trees?

A tree is a group of individuals who are all linked together in some way. Ideally, there should be only one tree in a family file. But, in the process of deleting or unlinking individuals, unintentional trees of unlinked lines or individuals may result in a family file. Or, you may add unlinked individuals or groups, hoping to find where they fit into your family in the future. To find the various trees in a family file, use the **Tree** utility in Legacy.

(Help index: ***Counting Trees***)

# Chapter 18

# What's New in Version 7.0

### The Best Just Keeps Getting Better

## Wall Charts (Full capabilities in Deluxe Edition only)

You have spent many long hours collecting and entering your family history. A feat that few other people even attempt, let alone accomplish in their lifetimes. Now you can experience the enjoyment of showing off your family tree by producing stunning full-color wall charts. Use them for your next family reunion or for a deserving wall in your home. Wall charts make great gifts for any holiday, birthday, or anniversary. They also make your own continuing genealogy research easier by having a large, easily readable working chart nearby to refer to.

Wall charts tell a story that can be seen at a glance. They are a graphical representation of your family that can extend forward or backward for many generations. Large charts are often a gathering place for conversations that bond your family together. They become family heirlooms of great importance that will be passed on into the future. So, show off all your hard work – print some wall charts!

## Interview Reports (Deluxe Edition only)

The Interview Report contains over 1200 questions in thirteen different categories that can be used when you interview a family remember. They are great at jogging the memory of the person being interviewed and elicit more in-depth responses.

## Source Templates (Deluxe Edition only)

Version 7 of Legacy heralds the introduction of **SourceWriter**. *SourceWriter* is a template driven sourcing system that makes it easy for you to select the correct input screen so that you enter all the pieces needed to correctly cite any source of information in the thousands of formats that exist for them. The information you enter is correctly and precisely formatted to match the genealogy industry standards for source citations when printing footnotes, endnotes, and bibliographies. Multiple citations for an event can be combined into one paragraph, thus avoiding a long string of superscripted numbers within the report body.

Prior to version 7, Legacy's citation methods were rudimentary and straight forward but didn't offer the expert help needed in order to automatically produce correct citations. Actually, in version 7, you can use either of the citation methods, the new or the old. We will call the new system *SourceWriter* and the previous system the "Basic System."

# Map My Place

We've redesigned the Master Location List screen. If an Internet connection is present, Legacy plots the selected place on the map below the list. When a location is highlighted, it automatically displays a list of all individuals who use the location. These individuals can now be edited from this screen by clicking on the **Edit** button. (If you access the Master Location List from within the Individual's Information screen, you cannot edit a person from the list.)

# Map My Family (Deluxe Edition only)

With Legacy Mapping you can see an overall view of a family's territory spanning the entire earth if necessary. You can also zoom right into the street level of anywhere in any country in the world. When all the locations where a family lived and worked are plotted on a map together, you can easily see the overall area in which the family spent their lives. You can visualize how the family members migrated from place to place as they grew older. (Or you can see if they stayed in one place their entire lives.) New research opportunities come to light as you see the surrounding cities, counties, provinces, and countries.

# Guided Setup Wizard

The new wizard is available when starting Legacy 7.0 for the first time as well as when creating a new family file from **File > New Family File**. You can even use it when importing at **File > Import from > Use Import Wizard...** The wizard takes you by the hand and guides you through the process in an easy-to-understand way.

# New Relationship Calculator (part Deluxe Edition only)

You can now see how any two people are connected, not only through direct blood relationships but also by marriage. A person might be the "great-grandfather of the wife of your $2^{nd}$ great-grandniece. You can also specify how many of these non-blood relationships you want to see.

# Best Fit Child Columns

A new selection has been added. The Best Fit option expands or contracts the child list columns to fit the number of children for the current couple. No more trying to guess the optimum number of child columns. Legacy does it for you.

# More Powerful Searching

Many new searching options have been added to make it easier to find missing information within your family file. You can now search for individuals that are missing parts of names, birth or death information, marriage information and much more. You can also search for missing source citations as you document your family files.

## Standardization Tips

We have added many standardization tips that will pop-up if something questionable has been entered in the Individual's Information screen. These have also been added to the Potential Problems report. See **Tools > Potential Problems > Standardization**.

## Edit Records from the "Used By" Lists

All of the master lists in Legacy have an option to view the individuals who use the items in the list. You can now edit those individuals right from the list instead of having to exit the list and edit them separately.

## Easily Attach Documents to Individuals and Marriages

Along with attaching pictures, sounds, and video to individuals, events, locations, and sources, you can now also attach any other kind of document.

## Enhanced Welcome Tips

That little window that greets you when you start Legacy and gives you nice helpful tips and tricks just got better. There is now a Show Me How button that pops up a complete explanation of the tip – how to get where you can use it, all the nitty gritty.

## Potential Problems

Standardization and LDS event verification checks are now included. See **Tools > Potential Problems > Standardization** and **LDS** tabs.

## Enhanced Backups

Legacy can now backup your family file and multimedia files at the same time, making it easier to transfer everything to another computer.

## New Toolbar Icons

New **Home** and **Add** icons have been added to the main toolbar. Icons have also been added to access the new **Charting** and **Mapping** features.

## More Remembered Entries

Right-clicking on the label for a date or location pops up a list of the last 10 entries so that you can quickly select repeating items. This capability has now been expanded to include Given Names, Surnames, and Name Prefixes and Suffixes.

# Chapter 19

# *Tips and Tricks*

All the Cool Things that Makes Legacy So Good!

## The Fun Stuff

Legacy is a very full-featured program that has lots of little features and convenience options that may not be obvious when you first start using it. Some of these may even escape your detection completely although most are documented somewhere in the Legacy Help system. Although these features are not essential to the successful operation of the program, you will find that they greatly enhance your effectiveness and efficiency and make for a very enjoyable experience while you work.

(Help index: ***Tips and Tricks***)

You might want to reread this help section from time to time as you become more familiar with Legacy. Each time you do, you are likely to pick up and remember new capabilities that you never knew were there.

Another great resource is to go to the **Tips from the Experts** in the **Support** box of the **Legacy Home** tab.

# Chapter 20

# *Troubleshooting*

Finding Out What Went Wrong...

## Technical Support

If you are a registered user of the Deluxe Edition of Legacy, you can get free technical support and notification of product upgrades.

We offer support information in several ways. You can contact us online, or by e-mail, phone, fax, or letter. Because it is easier to solve software "problems" if you are sitting at your computer, technical support by phone is by far the most effective.

**You can contact our Technical Support department for help with:**

- Program installation.
- Questions about how the program works.
- Defective materials.

Often, the information you are seeking is available in the online User Guide. When you run into a problem, or have a question while using Legacy, click **Help** or press **F1**. The help system is context-sensitive and tries to answer questions about the current task. If you still have questions, please see **Before You Call for Help**, below, for more information.

Our technical support staff can answer questions only about Legacy. Questions about Microsoft Windows, family history programs made by other companies, or genealogical research in general cannot be answered. For help with Windows, please consult your Windows user guide. For help with genealogical research, contact your local library, genealogical society, or historical society.

## Before You Call for Help

When you have a question or problem regarding Legacy, please follow the steps below before contacting us. It may save you the cost of a phone call.

- Check the online User Guide for solutions. The help system contains many tutorials and instructions.
- Make sure you can repeat the problem. Often, trying to recreate a problem leads to a better understanding of the cause. (Sometimes the problem will never recur.)

- Try quitting the program and rebooting the computer. Sometimes Windows just needs a fresh start.
- Visit our online *Troubleshooting Guide* (http://www.LegacyFamilyTree.com/Help.asp).
- Check the **Support** box on the **Legacy Home** tab while running Legacy. It contains many helpful resources.

## Customer Support

If you need help with any of the following subjects, call our Customer Support department at 1-425-788-0932, fax your questions to us at 1-425-940-1610, or send an e-mail message to Support@MillenniaCorp.com. We will be happy to help you.

- Questions about purchasing Legacy.
- Defective CD-ROMs or diskettes.
- Questions about your order.

## Millennia's Web Site

Visit our World Wide Web home page for exciting information on Legacy and other related products. We also have many links to other sites that contain more information on compiling your family history.

Our home page address is **http://www.LegacyFamilyTree.com**.

# *Index*

RootsMagic
800-766-8762